A Pine Barrens Odyssey

A Pine Barrens Odyssey

A Naturalist's Year in the Pine Barrens of New Jersey

Howard P. Boyd

Illustrations by Gwendolyn A. Stiles
Photography by Doris and Howard Boyd

Plexus Publishing, Inc.
Medford, NJ

Published by:
Plexus Publishing, Inc.
143 Old Marlton Pike
Medford, NJ 08055

Library of Congress Cataloging-in-Publication Data

Boyd, Howard P.
    A Pine Barrens odyssey : a naturalist's year in the Pine Barrens of New Jersey / Howard P. Boyd ; illustrations by Gwendolyn A. Stiles ; photography by Doris and Howard Boyd.
        p.   cm.
    Includes bibliographical references and index.
    ISBN 0-937548-34-0 (softcover)
    1. Natural history—New Jersey—Pine Barrens. 2. Pine Barrens (N.J.) I. Title
QH105.N5B69 1997   97-22070
508.749—dc21   CIP

Printed in the United States of America.

ISBN 0-937548-34-0 (Softbound)

Price: $19.95

Illustrations: Gwendolyn A. Stiles
Photographs: Doris and Howard Boyd
Cover design: Erica Oehler

*To all those who dedicate part of their
lives to help protect and preserve the
Pine Barrens of New Jersey
in their wild and natural state*

Contents

May

June

July

August

Preface

My introduction to the Pine Barrens of New Jersey was in the form of field trips to collect insects in the Pinelands, traveling from Philadelphia over the then-new bridge, now the Benjamin Franklin. That was back in 1938. Since then I have maintained an intimate association with the Pine Barrens, and during the past twenty-five years it has been my good fortune to have lived on the very edge of the Pinelands.

During this time I have kept a record of the earliest dates on which I have observed many of the natural events that occur each year in the pines. Originally, I had intended to include this record of earliest dates as a part of my *A Field Guide to the Pine Barrens of New Jersey*, but when it became clear that to do so would make the field guide too large and cumbersome for field use, this record was removed from that book. Now, revived and updated with many more dates, and some additional observations by naturalist Annie Carter at Batsto in 1979, that record provides the basis of this new book.

During the preparation of this book, I have made a concerted effort to include a reasonable balance of subject matter, particularly between flora, insects, and other natural features. At times this has been difficult because of the great numbers of both flowering plants and insects. I would remind readers that the Pine Barrens of New Jersey are noted more for their botannical features than for any other natural resource except water reserves, and that insects far outnumber all other forms of animal life.

Throughout this book, I include scientific names for all forms of plant life, for all insects, and for most amphibians and reptiles, but omit scientific names for birds and mammals. The reason for these omissions is that when referring to birds and mammals, common names are well established while scientific names are rarely used in everyday conversation.

However, in the plant world and in lower forms of animal life, especially insects, common names are not well established. Some forms have no common name at all, and many others have a variety of common names, so scientific nomenclature is necessary for positive identification.

During the many hours I have spent writing this book, I frequently found myself referring back to my field guide to check descriptions and other facts. On those occasions it occurred to me that any reader of this new book should have a copy of that earlier work available for ready reference because, in general, both pertain to the same subject matter even though they differ in purpose. The purpose of the field guide is to present descriptions of Pine Barrens' flora and fauna as aids to their identification. The purpose of this new book is to call attention, chronologically, to the many natural features and subjects that appear in the Pine Barrens throughout a year and to relate interesting, and perhaps little known, facts about some of these events and subjects. In a word, this is a seasonal and ecological treatment of the natural Pine Barrens.

Many people have helped make this book possible. Accompanying me on many explorations have been some great traveling companions, including Donald (Don) Kirchhoffer, August (Augie) Sexauer, Ralph and Ellen Wilen, Lois Morris, Theodore (Ted) Gordon, Mark Robinson (deceased), and, most important of all, my wife, Doris. George Henkel helped me learn how to use a word processor as did Patricia Palatucci from Plexus Publishing. Other Plexus personnel who contributed to this effort were my editors, Jim Shelton and Diane Zelley; Heide Dengler, graphics department manager; and my good friend, Tom Hogan, president of Plexus Publishing, whose support and encouragement made possible the publication of this work.

Don Kirchhoffer and William (Bill) Walker read the complete text and made many valuable suggestions, as did Doris, who kept constantly pulling me up short about misplaced antecedents and long, run-on sentences! Doris also came up with many fine ideas, including the title of this work. The beautiful art work for the four seasonal plates was contributed by our daughter, Gwendolyn A. Stiles. Some of the photographs were taken and contributed by Doris who, over the past two to three years, has constantly encouraged me to continue on and complete this, my final effort to develop greater public awareness of the wonders of the Pine Barrens and the need to preserve them.

WINTER
SOLSTICE

Winter Solstice
and the
Annual Bird Count

ecember 21 or 22! The first day of winter—or the beginning of spring?—or even the beginning of an entirely new year? In any case this is when we start our journey through the seasons in the Pine Barrens of New Jersey. Instead of beginning on the first day of January in the Gregorian year just ahead, we're starting now because this is the time when, due to the tilt of our earth and its 365-day cycle around the sun, the North Pole is furthest from the sun in what is known as our WINTER SOLSTICE, the word solstice meaning, literally, the "sun stands still." This is the time in our Northern Hemisphere when the rays of the sun give us the least amount of heat and also when we have the fewest hours of sunlight.

December 21st or 22nd is usually considered to be the first day of our winter season, but there are many who put a different interpretation on this annual event and consider it to be the first day of spring. Certain it is that from now on the sun will be getting higher in the sky each day and the number of hours of sunlight will gradually increase. Because more hours of light and stronger rays of the sun will combine and begin to awaken the natural world, there may be some justification for calling the winter solstice the "first day of spring," even though the cold and snows of both January and February lie ahead.

Plants and animals will be the first to respond to these changing conditions. Gradually over the next few months, as the days become both longer and warmer, buds on trees and shrubs will begin to swell. Insects, amphibians and reptiles ("herps"), and certain mammals will all start to awaken from their winter dormancy or hibernation. Birds that migrate north in the spring will begin to feel the urge to start up from their southern homes, just as Edwin Way Teale did in 1951 when he started his famous *North with the Spring* journey from Florida's Everglades. Even some mammals will begin to bestir themselves, witness that annual February second event in Punxsutawney, Pennsylvania, known as Groundhog Day. For us, watching for signs of these reawakenings in the next few months will help us pass through the dead of winter.

No matter how we interpret the winter solstice, this is the point from which we are going to begin our journey through the seasons in the Pine Barrens of New Jersey. So, come along to observe and enjoy the sights and sounds and learn to appreciate some of the reasons why it is important to protect and preserve this natural treasure.

What better way to start the new year—or end the old—than to participate in the CHRISTMAS BIRD COUNT for the National Audubon Society. This annual event is conducted in local areas all over the nation by individuals involved in birding and nature organizations. Each count is organized into circular territories, each with a seven and one-half mile radius from a central point. The count itself is conducted by teams of interested birders who count and record all the different birds they see on the one day selected during the Christmas and New Year holidays period.

A number of these counts include portions of the Pine Barrens. These are the Assunpink count centered at Routes 537 and I-195, the Belleplain count centered at the junction of Routes 670, 651, and 550 (spur), and the Lakehurst count centered in Silverton. The Lakehurst count is co-sponsored by the Ocean Nature and Conservation Society, the Jersey Shore Audubon Society, and the Nature Club of Leisure Village. The one count that lies entirely within the Pine Barrens is the Pinelands count which, starting in 1968, was organized and conducted for many years by Jim and Betty Woodford, assisted by members of the Burlington County Natural Sciences Club and the Audubon Wildlife Society of Audubon, New Jersey. The center of this count is near the intersection of Routes 541 and 206 in Shamong Township, Burlington County. Over the years, the greatest number of birds recorded in the Pinelands count was 12,269 in 1981. The largest number of different species of birds seen, 85, was in 1987. A few of the more unusual birds seen only once or twice on these counts include horned grebe, red-breasted merganser, goshawk, Virginia rail, sora, varied thrush, water pipit, western tanager, dickcissel, European goldfinch, red crossbill, and white-winged crossbill.

Nationwide, these counts have been conducted since 1900. They provide valuable information on gradual changes in ranges such as the northward movement of cardinals, mockingbirds, tufted titmice, mourning doves, and, most recently, red-bellied woodpeckers. They also show population fluctuations such as increases in blackbirds, the decline of warblers, and irregular invasions of unusual birds such as snowy owls and gyrfalcons.

Bald Eagles
and Owls

F or the next several weeks we will be in the dead of winter. Even though winter arrived, officially, in December, the recent holidays have tended to draw our attention away from the cold and snows of this new season. Although the shortest days of the year came in December, our coldest days come in January, and often extend into February. This is the time when life out of doors appears to be moving at its slowest pace.

Even though our January landscape may appear stark, dreary, and lifeless, and the prevailing colors are in hues of browns and grays, much green can still be seen in winter's barrenness. The Pine Barrens, especially, is blessed with a canopy of green formed from its abundance of evergreen trees. Chief among these are the PITCH PINES, *Pinus rigida*, supplemented by smaller stands of Virginia or scrub pines and short-leaf pines. It is for these trees that the area has traditionally been known as the *pine* barrens of New Jersey, the largest such area in the northeastern United States. One other evergreen that contributes to this year-round blanket of green is the ATLANTIC WHITE CEDAR, *Chamaecyparis thyoides*, that is found in small, dense stands along water courses and in cedar bogs and swamps. All these provide a year-round continuity of green that we tend to associate with the natural out-of-doors world.

This dead of winter period is really only one of dormancy when most forms of plant life and many forms of animal life are resting until their great bursts of activity recommence with the warmth of spring. Most plants have either died or have withdrawn their "vital signs" down into their roots to remain dormant over winter. Most birds have migrated south. Many mammals and nearly all amphibians and reptiles are in hibernation and most insects are in a condition known as diapause. The most obvious and easily observable exceptions to this dormancy are a few nonhibernating mammals such as squirrels and white-tailed deer, and a few "winter" birds. In fact, winter is probably the very best time to observe one of the most spectacular birds in the Pine Barrens, the BALD EAGLE, the symbol of our nation.

There are few more magnificent sights than an adult bald eagle flying overhead, its nearly pure white head, neck, and tail contrasting sharply with its darker body plumage. Bald eagles do not attain their adult plumage until they are four or five years of age. Juvenile bald eagles are dark brown all over and may be confused with two other large, dark, soaring birds. One of these, the GOLDEN EAGLE, has a somewhat smaller head and shorter tail, with a faint golden wash over the back of its head and neck. Golden eagles are not as common in southern New Jersey. Both eagles can be distinguished from our other large, dark high-soaring bird, the TURKEY VULTURE, by the eagle's larger size and the fact that eagles fly with their wings straight out, horizontally, from their bodies. Turkey vultures fly with their wings raised up on a slight dihedral angle to form a shallow U or V, and they tend to rock a little from side to side as they soar, glide, and circle around high in the sky.

Eagles, along with all hawks and owls, are birds of prey, which means they feed almost exclusively on other forms of animal life. Bald eagles are, by nature, fish eaters, which they take either alive or dead, so they usually nest close to larger bodies of water that can provide them with an adequate supply of food. Eagles are apt to be somewhat lazy when it comes to catching their own food, so it is not unusual to see an eagle attack an osprey carrying a fish it has caught, forcing the osprey to drop the fish, which the eagle then swoops down and catches. Eagles are also known to attack waterfowl, but are seldom successful. Finally, eagles also will capture and feed on small, ground dwelling animals such as rabbits, squirrels, mice, and snakes.

The recent history of the bald eagle population in New Jersey has been like a roller coaster ride. Years ago, there were at least twenty-two bald eagle nests in New Jersey, primarily in the southern part of the state, and the bald eagle population remained quite stable. Then came the introduction of DDT and other chlorinated hydrocarbons as pesticides during and following World War II and their subsequent widespread use in agriculture and other industries. Because these pesticides, once ingested, pass from one organism to another up through the food chain, those at the top of this natural chain, such as eagles, ospreys, and peregrine falcons, became storage reservoirs for these dangerous nonbiodegradable chemicals. One of the resulting effects was that the shells of their eggs became so thin and fragile that they were crushed during normal incubation. The result is obvious. Populations of these birds crashed in the early 1960s and, although DDT was banned in 1972, the damage had already been done. By the early 1970s only one solitary bald eagle nest remained in the entire state, that one in Bear Swamp in southeastern Cumberland County. In 1982, when that pair of bald eagles had failed to produce young the six previous years, the New Jersey Division of Fish, Game, and Wildlife moved in and began a restoration program to revive the bald eagle population. The results have been spectacular. During the summer of 1994, for instance, nine pairs of bald eagles nested in New Jersey and six pairs successfully produced twelve young.

Since midwinter is one of the best times to spot bald eagles, a survey of the bald eagle population in New Jersey is conducted each January. During the January 1997 survey, observers spotted a record one hundred seventy-six bald eagles and five golden eagles in the state. Tying this more closely to the Pine Barrens, in the January 1995 midwinter survey, observers Ed Bruder, Len Little, and Augie Sexauer sighted eleven bald eagles (two adults and nine immatures) over the Pine Barrens, mainly in the vicinity of the many cranberry bogs south of Chatsworth and over to Lake Oswego.

So, take your binoculars and get out and see how many of these majestic birds you can spot for yourself in the Pinelands. As you do so, be sure to dress well against the cold winds and snows of winter.

Just as eagles are most easily observed in midwinter, so are owls, but whereas eagles fish and hunt for their food during daylight hours, most owls are shadowy creatures of the night that hunt for their food and call in variations of *whoo-who-who* during nighttime hours. The best time to hear owls call is in the few hours immediately after dark and just before dawn. These are the times one should try to get out into pine woodland areas to listen for these otherwise noiseless birds of the night.

One of the distinctive characteristics of all owls is the way their eyes are situated. Owls do not have the ability to look sideways. Instead, their eyes are directed forward so that both eyes look in the same direction. This means that, in order to look to either side, an owl must turn its entire head. Sometimes it seems that an owl can turn its head almost halfway around so that it appears to be looking in a backward direction.

Another distinctive characteristic of owls is their digestive systems. Owls hunt and feed mainly on small rodents and other small mammals as well as small birds, reptiles, and large insects. After an owl has caught and eaten its prey, it digests the relatively soft and fleshy parts, which then pass through its digestive system and are excreted. The undigested fur or feathers and bones are compacted into a small oval mass, brought back up into the throat, and ejected through the mouth as an owl pellet. As these pellets fall upon the ground they become a tell-tale sign of an overhead owl perch and, sometimes, if you scan the tree above where these pellets fell, you may be able to find the owl that coughed up the pellets.

There are six different owls that are either year-round or regular winter residents in the Pine Barrens. These are the SAW-WHET OWL, LONG-EARED OWL, BARN OWL, BARRED OWL, SCREECH OWL, and GREAT HORNED OWL. Owls nest early in the new year, the earliest nester being the great horned owl which may begin nesting as early as late December. A couple of these owls will nest in man-made nest boxes or other man-made facilities such as old barns.

One of the most interesting owls is an occasional winter resident and rare breeder in the Pine Barrens. This is the NORTHERN SAW-WHET OWL, the smallest owl in our area, only about eight inches from head to tip of tail. The primary range of the saw-whet owl is in Canada and the northern United States, but during winter periods when food becomes scarce in their home range, numbers of these little owls come south into our area to hunt for their favorite food of small rodents. As a result, saw-whet owls usually cast up a single pellet each day consisting chiefly of the fur and bones of white-footed mice. Because of their small size and their habit of sleeping during daylight hours on low roosts in secluded thickets, especially evergreen thickets, saw-whets are a favorite owl for birders to try and locate. Try it yourself for a real challenge!

In sharp contrast to the saw-whet is our largest resident owl, the GREAT HORNED OWL. When seen roosting high overhead in a large tree during the daytime, its great size, bulky shape, white throat, and large ear tufts readily identify this owl. Great horned owls are the most powerful and

10

Barn owl

formidable of all owls and they are highly skilled and deadly in the pursuit of game birds, song birds, rabbits, squirrels, and all small rodents. These owls usually nest in cavities in large, old trees throughout the winter months and it is during this period that the great horned owls become rather vocal with their loud *hoo-hoo, hoo, hoo-hoo* calls.

SCREECH OWLS may be the most common of the several owls to be found in the Pine Barrens, and if you should go out at night or in the early morning to listen for owls, that series of quavering whistles you hear will be the call of the screech owl. This small owl, which occurs in two phases, red and gray, is an owl that will frequently nest in man-made nest boxes. Augie Sexauer, a neighbor and frequent field companion, has three such boxes in his front and back yards. For a number of years, usually starting in early November and continuing off and on through March, these boxes have been used by screech owls for roosting, but none have yet used the boxes for nesting. One box is so positioned that its occupant can be seen through a spotting scope Augie sets up in a front room of his home. Both red and gray phases appear from time to time, but the red phase owls have been more frequent. Their habit has been to sit in the entrance hole, most often in the early morning, or around noon hour, or late in the day, look around for a while, and then drop back down into the box out of sight.

3

Snow Fleas

Whenever we think of winter, probably the first two characteristics that come to mind are cold and snow. Throughout this season, all forms of life have to withstand the severe conditions brought on by the cold and snows of winter. Snow, particularly, makes life difficult, especially for those forms of animal life that do not hibernate or otherwise pass the winter in a dormant state, but there are a few exceptions.

Even though the amount of snow that falls in the Pine Barrens varies greatly from year to year, the usually light snowfalls that do occur rarely build up to form huge snowbanks and seldom last long periods of time. Thus we may not be as likely to see SNOW FLEAS, *Achorutes nivicolus*, as in more northern climates, but when they are present they can occur in vast swarms. Snow fleas are the most common and widespread of all winter insects. They are dark blue-gray in color and, although only about an eighth of an inch in length, they are able to leap distances many times their own length. Although called fleas these creatures are not true fleas but SPRINGTAILS, members of a primitive order of insects. Their most striking feature is their furcula, or "spring tail," an organ under the body which is bent forward and held in place by a "catch." When the catch is released, the spring snaps down and strikes the ground with enough force to fling the insect as much as six inches through the air. While airborne, the spring is reset, ready to operate again as soon as the animal returns to the ground.

Springtails live in large colonies in the ground and in leaf litter on the ground, and feed on microscopic bits of organic matter. Sometimes individuals are so densely clustered together that their whole colony appears to be a wriggling mass of tiny maggots. On bright days throughout the winter, whenever the temperature rises above freezing, snow fleas move up through the loosely lying snow or up through clear spaces around the bases of grass stalks, brush stems, tree trunks, and other objects to soak up the bright sunshine. Upon careful and close observation, these masses will be seen to be hundreds, even thousands, of tiny, dark blue-gray specks that are constantly in motion, crawling and jumping all over the snow. On occasions, springtails may occur in such vast numbers that they may actually blacken small areas of snow. On level surfaces, they may be as numerous as five hundred to a square foot, and in hollows and depressions in the snow they may be so abundant that they can be ladled up with a spoon.

So, whenever you are walking around in snow-covered woodlands during warm winter days, be alert to see if you can spot any of these tiny, wriggling bits of locomotion.

4

Preparations for
Spring and Summer

S ince prehistoric times, periodic wildfires have been a major factor
in shaping the vegetation of the Pine Barrens and in maintaining an
ecological balance between the pines, the oaks, and other vegetation. Today, however, due to the encroachments of civilization, wildfires
have become a threat to humans and their possessions and every effort
is made to put out wildfires as quickly as possible. The New Jersey
Bureau of Forest Management, State Forestry Service, through its prescribed burning program and other practices, does all it can to prevent
wildfires from developing and spreading throughout the Pine Barrens.

In a program that began in 1928 and became official policy in 1947,
this service deliberately sets CONTROLLED or PRESCRIBED BURNS in
forest lands. Starting as early as mid-November and continuing until the
middle of March, state forest fire wardens conduct controlled, low-inten-
sity ground fires over hundreds, perhaps thousands, of acres of pine and
oak woodlands. The purpose of these controlled fires is to burn off the
ground cover of dead, dry leaves, pine needles, and fallen branches so
that when the real forest fire season starts later in the spring, wildfires will
not have this litter to serve as tinder to feed the flames. Controlled burning thus makes it easier to extinguish any wildfires that do occur later in
the year. Thus, prescribed burns are one of the important preparations to
protect against potential spring and summer forest fires in the Pine
Barrens; and they are undertaken during the winter months because there
is less danger at this time that these prescribed burns themselves could
get out of control and become wildfires.

15

Almost everything has both positive and negative values. Even though prescribed burning is a positive in helping to prevent wildfires from destroying human homes, possessions, and even lives, ecologically there are some negatives. First, the lack of high intensity wildfires and crown fires has an adverse effect on plant diversity and on maintaining the traditional, natural balance of vegetation in the Pinelands, principally between the pines and the oaks. Reasonably frequent wildfires favor the regeneration of pines. Lack of these periodic hot fires favors the oaks. Over a sufficient period of time without wildfires, the present Pine Barrens could conceivably become an oak barrens. Another negative is that repetitive controlled burning over the same segments of forest, as sometimes takes place, can be very detrimental to the richness and population dynamics of all the arthropod groups that live in the soil, and which are at the base of the food chain pyramid upon which larger forms of animal life are dependent.

During this same midwinter period, pineland cranberry and blueberry farmers are also preparing for the seasons to come. Farmers "sand" their CRANBERRY BOGS by spreading a thin layer of fresh sand over their bogs to renew the soil, and all winter long they keep their bogs flooded to depths of one to two feet. Since we seldom have more than ten to twelve inches of ice, flooding the bogs protects the shallow roots of the cranberry vines from freezing. Although cranberry is a native, North American plant that has grown in the wild and withstood the rigors of freezing weather for centuries, farmers have learned that flooding commercial bogs lessens the danger of winterkill. Thus, given this year-round protection and care, it is not surprising that cranberry vines in commercial bogs continue to grow and produce indefinitely. Some bogs are still producing cranberries after more than one hundred years of cultivation.

Blueberry farmers are also hard at work in their BLUEBERRY FIELDS pruning the bushes in preparation for the best possible production of blueberries in the coming summer season. The best blueberries are produced on new growth from the previous year, and the largest fruits are produced on the most vigorous bushes. So, blueberry farmers annually cut out old, nonproducing canes during the winter so that all the plant's energies next spring will go into fruit production and new growth. If properly pruned each year and otherwise adequately cared

16

for, blueberry bushes live and produce as long as cranberry vines do, up to a hundred years or more for, again, these are simply cultivated versions of a wild, native, North American plant.

While humans are performing all these duties, much of the natural world in the Pine Barrens is quietly waiting for spring to arrive. Almost all forms of plant life are still shut down for the winter, their above ground vascular systems closed off and their below ground root systems simply waiting, both poised to start up again just as soon as warmer weather arrives. Similarly, many forms of wildlife such as the amphibian frogs, toads, and salamanders, the reptilian snakes, turtles, and fence lizards, a few mammals, and even different stages in the life cycles of most insects are still hibernating, often underground, or in the mud under ponds and swamps, or in various hiding places above ground, all waiting for their biological clocks to awaken them and stimulate them into springtime activity.

5

February

Winter Wildlife

E arly in February, around the fourth, we reach the mid-point of winter when the slanting rays of the sun send very little warmth into the Pine Barrens, so our cold wintery days continue through much of this month.

Even though we are in the middle of winter, this is a good time to get out and take a hike along some Pinelands trail, especially one near a stream. Enjoy the wilderness with a hike along the Batona Trail, a fifty-mile hiking trail that runs north to south from Ong's Hat in Lebanon State Forest to Lake Absegami in Bass River State Forest. The stretch beside the Batsto River between Quaker Bridge and Batsto can be especially rewarding. As you hike along, listen for the calls of some resident winter birds, ones that stay with us all year. Be sure to have a pair of binoculars with you so you can look as well as listen. You can thus coordinate the calls of the birds with the sight of them, and fix both in your mind for future recall. Several of these resident winter birds often flock together. At the center of these groups may be numbers of CAROLINA CHICKADEES, each individual giving voice to its *chick-a-dee-dee* call from overhead among the pitch pines and the many species of oaks while searching for insect eggs and larvae. Others that frequently flock and travel with the chickadees are the mouse-gray TUFTED TITMOUSE that gives voice to a loud, clear, *peter, peter, peter* call, and the grayish-blue and white WHITE-BREASTED NUTHATCH that walks down, headfirst, as well as up and around tree trunks and branches, all the while calling its nasal *yank, yank, yank* as it searches for insects.

Nuthatches are particularly interesting birds. No other bird can compete with a nuthatch in its ability to run up and down and around tree trunks. A nuthatch is able to do this because it has short legs and strong feet which the bird places widely apart, one foot reaching forward under its breast, the other reaching backward under its tail. Thus, standing on a wide base and holding safely to the bark with the three foreclaws of its upper foot turned backwards, it hitches nimbly down a tree trunk head first.

Be on the lookout, also, for different woodpeckers that you may first notice by hearing a tapping or a rapid drumming in a nearby tree. These sounds could be made by either a small black and white DOWNY WOODPECKER or a larger look-alike, a HAIRY WOODPECKER. If the bird's beak seems long in comparison with its body, it probably is a hairy woodpecker; but if its beak seems about the proper size or even short, it likely is a downy woodpecker. In either case, a red patch on the back of its head indicates whether it is a male. A third, slightly larger woodpecker is the RED-BELLIED WOODPECKER, a relatively recent arrival in northern woodlands from further south. Its name is misleading because its red belly is quite faint and difficult to see. The male has a brilliant red head and nape (back of head) while the female has the same brilliant red nape, but not a red head. The red-bellied woodpecker is a rather noisy bird, often calling attention to itself long before one realizes it is around, by frequently uttering a distinctive, rolling *churr, churr, churr* note that can be heard for quite some distance.

Woodpeckers are particularly interesting birds with unique physical adaptations. Whereas most birds have feet with three forward and one backward pointing toes, most woodpeckers have strong feet with two forward and two backward pointing toes which enable these birds to grasp and hang onto the bark of a tree. In addition, woodpeckers use their stiff tail feathers as a prop against the tree to provide additional support. Finally, woodpeckers have stout, chisel-shaped beaks which they use to drill holes in wood in order to find insects and to excavate nest cavities, and they have extremely long, cylindrical, barbed tongues to reach out and capture their food.

A couple of other resident winter birds that may be both heard and seen along the trail are the bright red, male CARDINAL giving voice to its repeated loud and clear *cheer, cheer, cheer* from the top of an exposed perch, and a CAROLINA WREN whose very loud and wonderfully clear *tea-kettle, tea-kettle, tea-kettle-tea* call may sound very near to you whether it is or not. You may have difficulty spotting this bird in the bushes, for it usually remains low in the shrubbery and moves rapidly from one secluded place to another, rarely exposing itself to view. I still recall how absolutely startled I was many years ago when, as a twenty-three year old from New England who had never before seen or heard a Carolina wren, I was walking along one of the trails in Philadelphia's Wissahickon Park and a nearby Carolina wren let loose with its loud but beautiful song.

As you continue hiking along the Batona Trail, you might be startled by a sudden, thunderous whirring of wings as a large brown bird rises nearby, scattering fallen leaves like a whirlwind as it flies off into the shadowy recesses of the deep woods. You probably flushed a RUFFED GROUSE, a common but secretive inhabitant of Pine Barrens woodlands. This is a ground dwelling game bird much prized by hunters, but the bird's manner of rising with a great bluster and whirring of wings is its method of escaping quickly and confounding its enemies. Often, this swift bird escapes before any startled gunner can take aim.

In addition to the regular resident winter birds, another group of winter birds, migrants from the north, come and spend the winter here or further south, and then return north in the spring. Perhaps the first to arrive and the most common and conspicuous of these are the DARK-EYED or SLATE-COLORED JUNCOS that flock together in low shrubbery and fly rapidly away in a scattering flight showing their white outer tail feathers. Mixed in with the juncos may be some WHITE-THROATED SPARROWS whose three to five plaintive, whistling notes remind some people of more northern summer woodlands. Another winter migrant often seen in small flocks is the GOLDEN-CROWNED KINGLET, a tiny bird that is even smaller than warblers. These birds, with their small yellow (female) or orange (male) crown patches flit rapidly about in tree tops, like chickadees.

Other migrants that spend their winters here are the RED-BREASTED NUTHATCHES, smaller editions of the white-breasted but with light, rusty red-brown underparts, and the BROWN CREEPER, a small brown tree climber with a slender, decurved bill. This interesting, little bird always flies to the base of a tree and works its way up and around the trunk, often in a spiraling pattern, before flying back down to the base of another tree, all the while searching for insects and other small animal life hidden in crevices in the bark. Somewhere along the trail you might also come across a small flock of CEDAR WAXWINGS, or some of those infrequent winter migrants, the PINE SISKINS, or EVENING GROSBEAKS, or even some REDPOLLS. Good luck!

While out along the trail, don't forget to take a few good looks skyward for higher flying and larger birds such as CROWS (either COMMON or FISH CROWS), a RED-TAILED HAWK, an EAGLE or two, or some VULTURES.

21

Last month we talked about bald and golden eagles and briefly reviewed how to tell their flight from our other large, black, soaring birds, the TURKEY VULTURES, or buzzards. People often ask, "What is that large, black bird flying around up there high in the sky?" and follow up with "Is it an eagle?" The answer is no, not usually, and probably not once in many times for more often than not it is a turkey vulture.

Turkey vultures are most often seen flying around in circles high in the sky, or feeding on the carcass of a dead animal beside the road or out in a field, or roosted for the night on the limbs of a dead tree, often in company with other vultures. Vultures are masters of gliding and soaring flight as they circle round and round on six-foot wingspreads with an ease that is fascinating to watch. Often several vultures can be seen at the same time soaring together as they search the ground for food. Not until late in the day do they begin to drop down to roost for the night on some favorite dead tree perch.

After their overnight roost, vultures are slow to get started again the next morning. Shortly after they begin to feel the rays of the early morning sun, they open up their wings to absorb some of the sun's warmth while remaining on their overnight roost. Later in the morning, after the sun has warmed the ground enough to create rising air currents, called thermals, the vultures take flight and let the thermals help lift them up to their soaring altitudes. As noted earlier, vultures fly with their wings raised up in a slight dihedral angle to form a shallow U or V, and they tend to rock a little from side to side in their flight pattern.

Vultures are valuable scavengers that feed on the remains of almost any dead animal, preferably freshly killed but even well decomposed, that they are able to spot with their great eyesight from high above and then zero in on with their keen sense of smell. It also seems that soaring vultures may have some means of communication, possibly by sight, for just as soon as one bird drops down to feed on some newly discovered food, in almost no time at all other vultures fly in from miles around and drop down to join in the feast.

Close up, turkey vultures are far from being the world's most beautiful birds. In fact, many people would call them ugly, primarily because their large heads are completely devoid of feathers or hairs, and are a deep crimson to beefsteak red in color. Immature birds have dark gray to blackish heads. Vultures nest on the ground under brush piles, in hollow logs, or under abandoned buildings.

In increasing numbers, there also are a few BLACK VULTURES in southern New Jersey, but these may be a little difficult for the casual observer to identify accurately in the field. In flight, black vultures are

22

slightly smaller (five-foot wingspan compared to six-foot for turkey vultures), have a shorter, more square tail, and have a whitish patch toward each wing tip. Close up, black vultures are seen to have a dark grayish head instead of a reddish head.

Some of the more obvious signs of mammal activity during this season of the year are the result of browsing by WHITE-TAILED DEER on shrubs and lower tree branches. The Pinelands contain an abundance of deer and, during cold, very snowy winters, large numbers of deer often cause considerable damage by over-browsing. This is one of the problems that hinders the regeneration of Atlantic white cedar. As you hike in the pines during this time of year, keep an eye open for the possibility of finding a deer antler on the ground, for male deer shed their antlers from late December into early February. If you would like to collect a deer antler, now is the best time to find one while it is new and fresh, for if it lies on the ground for even a short while it will be attacked and eaten by numerous small mammals such as mice and voles and by several insects, notably scavenging carrion and dermestid beetles, because antlers and bones have high nutrient value.

I was surprised one morning to see some unexpected mammal activity for this time of year. On a cold, cloudy morning early in February, I spotted an EASTERN CHIPMUNK running around in the oak woods. I first noticed a stirring in the dry oak leaves on the ground. Then I saw an unmistakable chipmunk jumping around in and under the leaves. As I watched, it came out into the open and, tail up, it ran along a dead log on the ground, then back to the base of an oak. Here it spent a few minutes running around and sprinting up and down the base of the tree before disappearing from sight. If I were given to fantasy or inclined to be anthropomorphic, I might interpret the activity of this lone chipmunk as one of pure joy at being up and out in the open air. More likely, something had disturbed its semi-hibernation and it came up out of its burrow for a few moments to check conditions before returning to wait out the balance of the winter season.

6

Spring Ahead!

Toward the end of February and into March, plant life begins to reawaken. The swelling of the staminate (male) catkins of the COMMON ALDER, *Alnus serrulata*, is an early sign of reawakening spring in hardwood swamps and damp roadsides. Its soft, yellowish catkins hang from the otherwise seemingly dead twigs of its bushes. Unless you are out looking for these and other early spring signs, you may not realize these are already in bloom, but the nearby buzzing of honey bees and bumble bees should call your attention to the catkins, for bees are already visiting every flower they can find. It is an interesting evolutionary fact that approximately two hundred million years ago, in the Paleozoic and Mesozoic Eras, flower producing plants co-evolved with the insects: the flowers needing the insects for pollination and fertilization while the insects needed the flowers for nectar.

By mid-February and into early March we begin to hear and see the earliest arrivals in the coming parade of migratory song birds. Robins, one of the traditional signs of spring, and red-winged blackbirds are among the first to arrive. Most ROBINS spend their winter months in our Gulf States and then move north in the spring in small groups of twos or threes or perhaps tens or twenties, flying as much as one or two hundred miles a night, for most migratory birds fly at night. Although some robins and red-wings may overwinter here, most of the ones we see now have migrated north to spend their summer with us. On bright, warm, sunny mornings, the well known *cheer-ily, cheer-up, cheer-io* songs of the robins are a pleasant wake-up call. Some gather in large flocks and then it may be possible to see dozens of robins moving across lawns and golf courses looking and listening for food, picking or pulling up tidbits, hopping a few feet to a nearby spot and repeating the process. Annie Carter, in her *Bits of a Batsto Year*, in 1979, reported "at least 200 fat robins all talking at once" on March second; and again on March seventh "at least a hundred robins on lawn looking for worms."

Whereas robins usually move north in relatively small groups, the RED-WINGED BLACKBIRDS are more apt to travel in large flocks, sometimes numbering into the hundreds. Red-wings are often heard before they are seen as they return to sing their liquid *konk-la-rees* from along the margins of bogs, marshes, and swamps. Usually males, resplendent with their brilliant red shoulder patches bordered with yellow, are the first to return and establish territorial rights by singing their distinctive calls from perches high on a reed or a cattail. Their speckled females, which look more like large sparrows, arrive a few days to a week later. But if some late winter snow should then cover the ground and make it difficult for them to find food, large flocks of blackbirds, as well as COMMON GRACKLES, may descend upon backyard feeding stations and, in short order, clean up whatever food may be available.

7

M a r c h

Spring Peepers,
Butterflies, and Migration

A s we move into March, it becomes more and more evident that the sun is rising earlier each morning and setting later each evening. Also, the sun is getting higher in the sky at noon. These two facts mean more hours of sunshine and daylight each passing day and greater heat from the sun during each hour of sunshine on the open sands of the Pinelands. Thus March may bring a few really nice, warm days, up into the seventy plus degrees during the day and not much lower than the forties overnight, even staying in the fifties on an occasional overnight late in the month.

From early to mid-March, at dusk and during early evening hours, we begin to hear the high-pitched *pree-e-ep, pree-e-ep, pree-e-ep* mating calls of the smallest and one of the earliest treefrogs throughout our area, the northern SPRING PEEPER, *Hyla crucifer*. Last fall, these tiny creatures buried themselves in the mud of woodland swamps and small ponds to overwinter in a dormant state. Now, with warmer days and milder evenings, they crawl up out of the mud and adjust their body temperatures to those of the atmosphere, for these are "cold-blooded" creatures whose body temperatures must be close to their surroundings. Soon they climb up nearby reeds and shrubs and begin to raise their voices in mating calls as they start their annual search for mates. This chorusing of spring peeper males is a true herald of the coming spring. Roger Conant, in his *Field Guide to Reptiles and Amphibians*, says that "a large chorus of spring peepers heard from a distance sounds like sleigh bells." I would add that the massed chorusing of these tiny creatures, close up, can be almost deafening.

The spring peeper is a very small creature, barely an inch in length. Like all treefrogs, it has tiny suction pads on the tips of its fingers and toes which enable it to cling to any surface and to clamber about easily on low vegetation. If you would like to see one of these creatures, take a flashlight, quietly move toward where you hear the chorusing, turn on your flashlight and slowly try to zero in on an individual's voice. Watch it inflate its vocal sac under its chin when it calls. Note its very small size, its ash-gray to olive-brown color, and the two dusky lines on its back that touch to form a rough cross. Please do not try to pick one up in your hand for these are very delicate creatures that can easily be hurt even by the most well-intentioned person.

In some locations within the Pine Barrens, the calls of two other frogs may be heard at this same time, occasionally mixed in with but as often heard apart from the evening chorusing of the spring peepers. These are the chorus frogs and the wood frogs. Close listening will distinguish these different voices from the *pree-e-ep* calls of the spring peepers. CHORUS FROGS, like the spring peepers, are also treefrogs, but these produce a repetitious, rolling *cr-eek* or *prr-eek* which rises in pitch toward the end, like running a finger along the teeth of a pocket comb. WOOD FROGS, which are true frogs, not tree frogs, produce a rough, low-pitched *kraa-airrak-kraakk* sound, something like that of a creaking wheel in need of oil.

Early March hardly seems the time to look for butterflies, but on a few warm, sunshiny days in late winter don't be surprised to see either or both of two different butterflies flitting around in pine and oak woodlands after having just emerged from their winter's hibernation. One is the MOURNING CLOAK, *Nymphalis antiopa*, a two- to three-inch butterfly with a pair of beautiful deep maroon wings with straw-colored borders and a row of iridescent blue spots just inside the borders. One may first catch your eye by flying around rather erratically, or posed upside down on the trunk of a tree, or resting on a carpet of leaves on the forest floor, almost always in full sunlight. Often, it will return again and again to the same sunny spot. The mourning cloak is one of the few butterflies that pass the winter in its adult stage, having lain dormant over winter in some hiding place such as a hollow tree trunk or log, under bark, or under debris in a pile of trash. Its emergence and early flight on warm, sunny, late winter days is one of the very best indicators that "spring is just around the corner." As soon as they emerge, adult mourning cloaks mate and the females lay their eggs on a variety of host plants. Then both males and females continue to fly until May or June after which they die. The newly laid eggs of the next generation will quickly hatch into tiny larvae that feed on vegetation and grow to full size, transform into chrysalids, and finally become adults by May or June. However, these new adults will rarely be seen at that time because most of them will aestivate, and pass the summer and fall in a state of torpor. These will then overwinter in hiding places before emerging the following late winter or early spring to thrill us with their rich beauty.

Another winter hibernating butterfly in the Pine Barrens, with the same general life cycle as the mourning cloak, is the large, two- to three-inch

Question mark butterfly

QUESTION MARK or VIOLET TIP, *Polygonia interrogationis*. This is the largest, most common, and most beautiful of several "angle-wing" butterflies, all of which have highly irregular wing outlines. The forewings of the question mark are decidedly sickle-shaped. Both the forewings and hind wings of the overwintering and early spring adults are a velvety orange-brown with dark spots and blotches, with the edges of the wings, especially the hind ones, shading off to violet, and with a distinct violet tip at the near edge of each hind wing. The hind wings of the summer or new generation are considerably darker. The undersides of both wings of all forms are a mottled wood-brown, the outer halves somewhat lighter. The undersides of both hind wings also have a small, silvery half circle and a dot that, together, look something like an incomplete question mark, the diagnostic character for this beautiful butterfly. Like the mourning cloak, question mark butterflies are frequently seen in sunny spots on tree trunks or on dead leaves along wooded roads.

When most of us think about MIGRATION, we probably think first about bird migration because, to us living in these mid-Atlantic states, the northern and southern flights of birds are the most obvious signs of migration. There are several reasons why birds migrate. Among these is the availability of food, the number of hours of sunlight, and instinct. Practically all bird migration is north-south. Birds migrate north in the spring to breed, to nest, and to raise their young. A principal reason for this is the abundance of food that is available here at this time of year. Insects, which are the principal source of food to feed to fledglings, are most abundant at the same time that adult birds have to fill the mouths of their hungry offspring. Another reason is that the longer days provide more hours of daylight for birds to forage for this food. Then in the fall birds fly south, not just because it is warmer there, but because more food will be available for them there during the fall and winter months and there will be more hours of sunlight there to obtain that food. All of this has to be instinctive. Birds are not taught to migrate. In some species of birds, adults leave for their southern wintering grounds considerably before their own offspring do, so the juveniles have to find their own way and face their long journeys by themselves. Thus, they do this naturally, instinctively, with only their built-in biological clocks and compasses to guide them when and where.

Robins and red-winged blackbirds have already led the parade of spring migrants into our area, but by the middle of March the flyways become crowded with the traffic of more birds arriving from southern areas. The NORTHERN or YELLOW-SHAFTED FLICKER announces its arrival by loudly proclaiming its *wik, wik, wiks* and *wick-er, wick-er, wick-ers* from tree trunks and branches. When it is clinging to a tree, look for its brown, barred back and a black crescent bib in front. When it flies, look for its conspicuous white rump patch and golden yellow under its wings. Perhaps more than any other bird, the flicker brings spring vibrancy as it loudly proclaims its arrival. Thoreau recognized this long ago when he wrote: "But how that single sound enriches all the woods and fields . . . this note really quickens what was dead. It puts life into withered grass and leaves and bare twigs, and henceforth the days shall not be as they have been." In addition to being a typical woodpecker seeking food in and around trees, flickers are very fond of ants which, whenever found, form a large part of their diet. Thus this bird is often seen on the ground feeding on ants and investigating ant hills.

Another mid-March spring migrant that will remain here all summer is the EASTERN PHOEBE. This bird is quite common near Pinelands streams and small ponds, especially where low, wooden bridges cross over water. Phoebes should be easy to spot because several characteristics readily distinguish them. A phoebe will probably first be seen as a small, brownish-gray bird perched on the tip end of some bare tree branch, often just above a stream. As it sits perched on its branch, it has the habit of pumping its tail up and down. Typical of the flycatcher that it is, it also has the habit of flying off its perch to catch a passing mosquito, gnat, or other small flying insect and then return to the same or nearby perch. Most obvious is its call, for it frequently sounds its own name in a slow, raspy, *phoe-be, phoe-be* song. It usually builds its nest under a wooden bridge over a cedar stream or on some isolated projection from a barn or other building, or on a ledge under an open porch or pavilion roof.

31

8

Pine Barrens Flora and the Value of Plants

Plants may be the most basic form of life on this planet, for almost all other forms of life in the world are dependent upon them, either directly or indirectly. Just for a moment, think about some of the ways in which plants are so indispensable to our very existence.

First off, plants breathe, just like we do. Vegetative breathing is an exchange of gasses that is done through pores, called stomata, in leaves and other plant parts. One product of this process is oxygen. Oxygen, of course, is the essential element in the atmosphere we breathe. Not only do plants produce oxygen, but in an interesting exchange of gasses between plant and animal forms of life, plants take in the carbon dioxide that animals exhale. The value of plants in this exchange of gasses is obvious.

Plants also are the primary producers of food for all forms of animal life in our world. From the lowliest insect herbivore that chews away and feeds on vegetation, to the mighty king of beasts that captures a gazelle that had first grazed on a grassy plain, plants are the basic source of food. This is because plants are actually food factories. Through photosynthesis, leaves manufacture carbohydrates which plants need for growth and survival. Extremely important byproducts result when animals, from insects feeding on leaves to mammals feeding on grasses, convert these carbohydrates into proteins in the many foods of animal origin that we consume. So, in a broad sense, plant and animal life complement and even sustain each other in a remarkable manner.

These are some of the many reasons why preservation of this unique botanical wilderness known as the Pine Barrens of New Jersey is so important. Not counting algae or fungi which are no longer considered part of the plant kingdom, there are approximately fifteen hundred different species of plants in the Pine Barrens. Slightly more than one-half of these are flowering plants. A distinctive feature of Pinelands plants is the number of both northern and southern forms that co-exist here. When the glaciers of the Ice Age moved down from the Arctic, the weight from the tons of ice scoured the surface of the earth and so the glaciers brought with them rocks, gravel, and plant life. When the glaciers melted some twelve to ten thousand years ago, the melt from them ran down over the sandy coastal plain depositing some of the plants that had been scoured off more northern terrains by the glaciers. Then, after the glaciers melted, the climate here became warmer and this allowed plants of southern origin to begin to move north into this area. Thus the Pine Barrens is a meeting ground for both northern and southern species of plants. One hundred and nine of these, plants such as pyxie and turkey beard, are of southern origin; fourteen of these, headed by curly-grass fern and broom-crowberry, are of northern origin.

CONRAD'S BROOM-CROWBERRY, *Corema conradii,* is one of the very earliest of all Pine Barrens plants to bloom each spring, usually around the middle of March. This is a very low-growing, multiple-branching, shrubby, cushion-like plant. To call the reproductive organs of this plant "flowers" may stretch one's imagination, for the flowers which develop at the tip of each little twig are so tiny that one has to get down on one's hands and knees and use a hand lens to see various parts of the male and female flowers which develop on separate plants. At flowering time this is a very drab appearing plant that looks as if it has had a hard winter. Beginning in May, however, well after its flowering period, crowberry plants put forth their new, green foliage and become much more attractive sub-shrubs. The gnarled, woody stems with their needle-like leaves grow almost prostrate, often in rounded patches, on bare, sterile stretches of sand. This unusual plant is unique to the Pine Barrens, is found at several locations in pine plains areas, and is almost entirely restricted to these areas. Because this basically northern plant seems so out of place in the Pine Barrens, it probably has attracted more attention from botanists than any other Pine Barrens plant except the also northern curly-grass fern.

The Pine Barrens locality for this plant is what is known as a disjunct population, one that is widely separated from the nearest population of the same species. In this case, the main geographical area of broom-crowberry is in Labrador where this sub-shrub reaches its maximum growth and greatest abundance. The nearest locality to the Pine Barrens where this plant is known to exist is in the Shawangunk Mountains, Ulster County, New York, where there is a small disjunct population. In New Jersey, Conrad's broom-crowberry is classified as an endangered plant species.

Because Conrad's broom-crowberry is almost entirely restricted to pine plains areas and because these areas are themselves unique, a word about them seems appropriate. Of the more than one million acres of ecological Pine Barrens in New Jersey, some twelve thousand acres are known as the dwarf or pygmy forests or the PINE PLAINS. These are world renowned and botanists from all over come to study the plants that grow in this uncommon and harsh habitat. There are four areas of pine plains forests which generally straddle the Burlington and Ocean Counties boundary, north and south of Route 72 and east and west of Route 539. These four areas are known as the West Plains (approximately six thousand acres) of which Coyle Field (N.J. Forest Fire Service) on Route 72 may be considered representative; East Plains (also approximately six thousand acres) about a mile south of Warren Grove on Route 539; the Little Plains, less than a mile west of Warren Grove at the end of the black-topped Beaver Dam Road; and the South or Spring Hill Plains along the northern edge of Penn State Forest.

What makes these pine plains areas unique is that they support a growth of unusually short, scrubby, stunted, four- to ten-foot high forests of mature trees. The dominant trees are a closed cone (serotinous) race of pitch pine, *Pinus rigida*, whose cones open only after being subjected to very high temperatures, such as those created by wildfires. Based on research in the 1970s and subsequently, there is some evidence that over succeeding generations of evolutionary development, these pines may be developing a genetic variation from more normal pitch pines. These pitch pines, together with blackjack oaks, *Quercus marilandica*, and scrub oaks, *Quercus illicifolia*, the only oaks in the pine plains, form a type of forest relationship indicative of repeated fires. These trees seem to be more fire resistant than others of the same species elsewhere. Considerable and rapid regeneration of these dwarf trees and shrubs takes place after fires, with multiple sprouts arising from older root crowns and even from the sides of the main trunks and branches. Reproduction is mainly vegetative rather than seed dispersal and germination. Ground cover is provided by shrubs such as black huckleberry, low blueberry, and mountain-laurel in the heath family and by sub-shrubs such as pyxie, broom-crowberry, and Pine Barrens heather as well as several heaths such as bearberry, teaberry, and trailing arbutus.

Several theories have been advanced to explain these stunted forests, but the general consensus seems to be that these forests are the result of a combination of factors such as infertile soils, aridity, an impervious subsoil, exposure to constant and strong winds, and, perhaps most important, repeated fires that occur with greater frequency and severity in the pine plains than elsewhere.

9

Soothsayers
and
Plasterers

N ow that we may be getting outdoors more, start looking for the small, light brown egg masses of a praying mantis. These are most likely to be found on old, dried, stiff stalks of grass or weeds or on lower branches and twigs of shrubs where they were laid last fall and have overwintered. When the eggs were freshly laid, they were part of a soft, frothy mass which quickly hardened into the almost impenetrably hard, protective cluster you now see. In the Pine Barrens, there are two species of praying mantis and each produces a different and distinctly shaped egg mass. If the egg mass is about three quarters of an inch long, compact, sort of cylindrical, and rather conspicuous, somewhat like a small walnut, it probably contains the eggs of the CHINESE MANTIS, *Tenodera aridifolia*, our larger species. If the egg mass is rather narrow, somewhat oval-elongate, up to an inch in length, and laid lengthwise on a twig or stem, this probably contains the eggs of the smaller EUROPEAN MANTIS, *Mantis religiosa*. In both cases the young mantids will hatch out some spring day and one to two hundred or more tiny insects will start their new lives preying upon and feeding on other insects and small animal forms. It is even very possible a good many of them will feed on each other. It is also likely that as many young mantids will become victims of other predators as will develop into adult predators themselves.

All mantids are carnivorous, feeding primarily on other insects. They have a long neck (prothorax) and their heads are attached in such a way that the insects have the ability to turn their heads in almost any direction. This is the only insect that has this ability to "look over its own shoulder." The front legs are large and armed with spines, and these legs are often held in an upright position as the insect prepares to seize its prey. This posing with its front legs raised, like a pair of uplifted hands in prayer, has given rise to its popular names of "praying mantis" or "soothsayer." It is interesting to note that Linnaeus apparently was impressed with its pose when he named the European mantis *religiosa*. There are a couple of other misconceptions about praying mantids. One is that it is against the law to harm a praying mantis and there is a considerable fine if one does so. School children often say this. This belief may stem from being taught in school that praying mantids are beneficial insects that should not be harmed and teachers may use the threat of law to impress their students. If true, this is unfortunate for students should be taught to respect all life forms for what they are and not out of fear. The other misconception is that praying mantids are completely beneficial insects that prey only on harmful insect pests. The fact is praying mantids do not discriminate upon which prey they feed. They are just as likely to feed on beneficial insects such as lady beetles and their immature forms as they are to feed on what we consider to be insect pests.

Whenever you hike or just walk some less used Pine Barrens trail, do you ever wonder what creatures may have made all those small holes you see in the ground along the way, sometimes with and sometimes without little mounds of sand around them? These may have been made by any number of small creatures, possibly ants, for these are among the most numerous of all insects, but there are other good possibilities. If you see some bee-like insects flying close to the ground around these burrows, chances are good they were dug by one of several types of burrowing bees that look a little like, but are somewhat smaller than, common honey bees. These likely are solitary bees that do not live in social colonies as do honey bees and most bumble bees. Instead, after mating, each individual female solitary bee makes her own nest, with a number of brood cells, in a hole she burrows in the ground (usually) or, depending on the species, in a stem, a post, an old wooden structure, or a rotting tree. She builds her nest cell and provisions each cell with a mixture of pollen and nectar which she gathers, rolls into a tiny ball, carries to her burrow, and lays a single egg on it. She then seals off the cell before moving on to develop a new cell.

In a few weeks the egg hatches and the emerged grub, or larva, will feed on the ball of pollen and nectar for about a month until it transforms into a pupa by early summer. It then remains as a pupa down inside the burrow until the following spring. Beginning around the middle of March, these pupae transform into adult bees to emerge from their overwintering burrows, and the bees you see flying around near these burrows are males that were the first to emerge and are hanging around waiting to mate with the females as soon as they emerge.

There are many different kinds of solitary bees. In fact, approximately eighty-five percent of all North America's native bees are solitary. Among the ones that commonly burrow in the soft sands of the Pine Barrens are PLASTERER BEES, *Colletes* spp., so called because they line their burrows with a thin translucent substance to prevent the burrow walls from crumbling. Although basically solitary, these bees are primitively social, and large colonies of several hundred burrows may sometimes be seen in relatively small areas. One colony on a sandy slope in Lebanon State Forest contained over five hundred and fifty burrows in an area approximately twenty-five by forty-five feet.

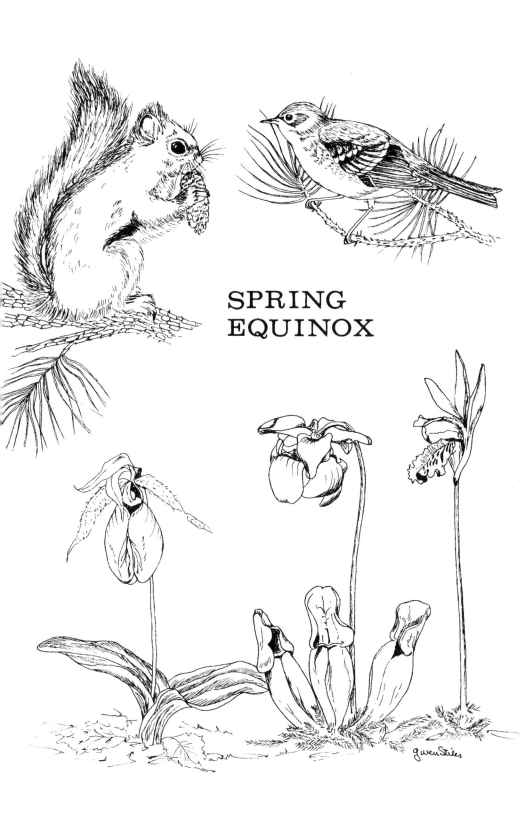

SPRING
EQUINOX

10

Spring Equinox, Swamp Maples, Tiger Beetles, and Spring Azures

The mid-point between the winter and summer solstices takes place in an instant of time around the 21st of March. This is known as the SPRING or VERNAL EQUINOX, the word *equinox* coming from the Latin words for equal and night. Right now, for a few days, the number of hours between sunrise and sunset is just about the same as the number of hours between the preceding sunset and sunrise. Day and night will be nearly equal in length, each just about twelve hours. From now on, each succeeding day will be getting longer than twelve hours and each succeeding night shorter until June 21-22 when these conditions will begin to reverse themselves and start going the other way—but more of that later. For now, let's rejoice in the sure knowledge that spring is finally here.

When I think of spring I think of rebirth, of reawakening, of renewal. In each word, the "re" refers to the fact it has happened before. It is not something that is really new. It is a repeat, a repetition of what took place at the same time last year, and the year before, and the years before that. How wonderful it is that spring does come back for us again, and again, and again.

Spring. The first blades of new grass. Early buds swelling on trees and shrubs. Alder catkins in bloom, the first of all shrubs to do so. Male red-winged blackbirds singing their *konk-la-rees* around a marshy pond.

Spring peepers calling from the lowland woods. Conrad's broom-crowberry in blossom out on the plains. The first mourning cloak butterfly flying about in the woods.

Clusters of SWAMP MAPLE trees, *Acer rubrum*, with the bright red colors of their spring blossoms and seeds, dress up many pond edges, stream banks, and damp roadsides. Maples often are the first trees to move into areas where white cedar stands have been clear-cut, and often crowd out regenerating cedars and convert former cedar bogs into hardwood swamps. Most maples in the Pine Barrens are rather distinctive in that their leaves are quite small and have only three lobes.

After more than fifty years of collecting and working with them, when I think of spring I think of TIGER BEETLES, my favorite family of insects. One of the earliest and most common species of tiger beetles in the Pine Barrens is a black and white form known scientifically as *Cicindela transquebarica*. My records over many years show that in some years adults of this species are up out of their winter burrows as early as the seventh of March. These continue being active through most of the spring or until around the end of May, after which, having completed their life cycle, they die. A second brood appears early in September and continues being active into early October. These beetles are particularly observable along dikes around cranberry bogs, where numbers of them may be seen running along the sandy dikes looking to feed on small forms of animal life such as ants. As you approach them, they will invariably take flight, fly a short distance ahead of you, and again land on the dike to continue their hunting activities.

Another wonderful sign of spring is the appearance, right around the time of the Equinox, of numbers of the beautiful, small, pale blue butterfly, the SPRING AZURE, *Celastrina argiolus*. These small butterflies, with a wing span of barely over an inch, are as welcome as the blue sky above. Males are a pale blue above, while the forewings of females are bordered with black. The undersides of the hind wings in both sexes are grayish-white with faint, small, black spots. After having spent the winter in its pupal stage, the spring azure is the very first butterfly to emerge and fly in substantial numbers in the Pine Barrens, and small clusters of them can often be seen flitting around in many Pine Barrens locations. Host plants of its larvae include dogwood, snakeroot, spirea, and blueberry. No wonder these are so common in the pines!

For many people, butterflies, with their bright attractive colors and their flitting from flower to flower, are among the most beautiful of all spring and summer creatures. Yet, these are among the most vulnerable of all forms of wildlife. In recent years, many species of butterflies have been noticeably declining, primarily due to the loss of host plants on which their larvae must feed, and this, in turn, is due to increasing losses of habitats. Because the potential loss of even a single species of butterfly would be an irreversible reduction in the world's biodiversity, there is a national organization known as the Xerces Society, named after an extinct butterfly, that was founded in 1971 for the purpose of monitoring butterfly and other invertebrate populations and calling public attention to their plight. There also are many active programs to encourage the planting of host plant shrubs and herbs for butterfly larvae, and flowering shrubs and herbs to attract adult butterflies. One such program in New Jersey is headed up at New Jersey Audubon's Cape May Observatory. Both the Xerces Society and the Cape May programs are well worth our support.

11

Ferns, Mosses,
and Pyxies

S igns of spring continue to appear everywhere. Another that is just as reliable as the swamp maples and the spring azures is the appearance of the first stout fiddleheads of the CINNAMON FERN, *Osmunda cinnamomea*, as they begin to break ground and push their way up into the daylight. Most other vegetative signs that have appeared so far have been produced by trees and shrubs, plants with woody stems that were already above ground and only had to leaf out and produce flowers. Ferns are among the very first of those plants that completely died down last fall and now are reappearing above ground for the new year, growing from underground rootstalks or rhizomes.

Ferns belong to a more primitive type of plant life than the flowering plants, so there are some major differences. For one, the leaves of all ferns, called fronds, come out of the ground tightly coiled up like a watch spring or the head of a fiddle. Because these are called "fiddleheads," people often want to know about and be shown a "fiddlehead fern," but no such plant exists. Fiddlehead is merely the term used to describe the very early, tightly coiled up stages in the above ground growth of almost all fern fronds. A second difference is that, instead of flowers and seeds, ferns produce spores in small capsules (sporangia) which, in the case of cinnamon ferns, are clustered on specialized fronds.

When the fiddleheads of cinnamon ferns first appear above ground, they are covered with a dense mat of silvery-white hairs which later turn to a rusty cinnamon-brown as the fronds develop.

Young fiddleheads of cinnamon ferns can be snapped off and eaten raw as they are supposed to be crisp and tender and have a nutty flavor. Young four- to six-inch stalks can be cut like asparagus, cooked, and eaten as a green vegetable.

As these new fiddleheads grow up out of the ground, they will gradually uncurl and increase in height to become graceful and conspicuous plants. The first fronds to develop will be those that will produce the reproductive spores. At first, these fronds will be dark green but as the spores ripen, the fronds will turn to a lustrous cinnamon-brown for which the plant is named. After the spores have been released, these fertile fronds will shrivel up and die. Meanwhile, the sterile fronds, or leaves, have been developing quite rapidly and, when fully grown to heights of three or more feet, will become the cluster of tall, sturdy, arching plumes we recognize as the familiar mature plant. Cinnamon ferns grow in partially shady, moist to damp locations such as wet woods and along the edges of swamps and ponds.

There is an interesting story that the generic name for this cinnamon fern, *Osmunda*, is supposed to have been suggested by the story of Osmund, the Water-man of Loch Tyne, who hid his wife and child in a thicket of these ferns when the Danes invaded Scotland.

In drier, more upland areas, there is another early fern that grows abundantly almost everywhere throughout the Pine Barrens. This is the BRAKE or BRACKEN FERN, *Pteridium aquilinum*. Bracken ferns grow up out of the ground in the same fiddlehead form as all other ferns, but they are not as stout or robust as the cinnamon fiddleheads. The mature fronds of bracken ferns grow to heights of two to two and one-half feet and usually are divided into three nearly equal sections of roughly triangular, dark green leaves that often flatten out into a nearly horizontal position. In some areas these are so common and grow so closely together that the fronds often interlock with each other and form such a dense tangle that it is difficult to walk through the matting.

The bracken fern is believed to be the "fearn" of the early Saxons and is one of the few ferns mentioned by name in the literature. In Scott's *Lady of the Lake* it is mentioned in the song of the heir of Armandave:

> The heath this night must be my bed,
> The Bracken curtain for my head.

Among the smaller plants of the Pinelands are the MOSSES that, literally, grow right at our feet. These are primitive but interesting forms of low plant life that remain green all year around provided they get an adequate supply of moisture. Even in the middle of winter, soft, bright green carpets of mosses line pineland trails and cushion our walks through pine and oak woodlands. While these may appear as carpets and clumps of green, actually, each cluster is made up of innumerable tiny, complex plants whose leaves contain chlorophyll. This allows these plants to manufacture food, through photosynthesis, throughout the year, even during the winter while other more advanced forms of vegetation such as trees, shrubs, and herbaceous plants remain dormant.

Mosses, even those that are entirely land based, need lots of water in order to manufacture their own food and to complete their reproductive cycle. Mosses are not able to store water in their leaves, stems, or roots, so during periods of drought their leaves fold up tightly against the stem or become twisted, curled, and brown and they stop manufacturing food. This cuts down on possible evaporation of water and protects the delicate grains of chlorophyll in the leaves. Then when it rains or other water becomes available, the leaves once again expand and resume manufacturing food.

In common with other forms of lower plant life, mosses do not produce flowers or seeds. Instead, they produce spores in tiny capsules that rise on wiry stems slightly above the leafy, green moss plants. When the spores become ripe, the capsules burst open to release the spores. Mosses reproduce by what is known as alternation of generations—when the spores land on a suitable habitat, the new plants that develop are different from the original plants that produced the spores. Then when these new plants mature, the resulting fertilizations produce new leafy plants of moss identical to the original moss plants— the ones we commonly see and know as mosses. Another way of saying this is that parents and children never look alike but grandparents and grandchildren always do.

There are hundreds of different mosses. No one really knows how many. Similarly, of the 274 species of mosses in New Jersey, as listed by Britten in 1889, no one knows how many there are in the Pine Barrens. In lowland areas where there is abundant moisture, there are at least twenty species of SPHAGNUM MOSSES that we will talk about next month. In lowland areas that are above water levels and in higher and drier areas there probably are another couple of dozen species. Of these, the largest and most conspicuous may be the HAIR-CAP MOSSES, some of which are sometimes called "pigeon-wheat" because their spore cases are near the size of and look a little like grains of wheat. Other common Pine Barrens mosses are BROOM MOSSES and the PIN-CUSHION MOSSES.

The Pine Barrens are of great interest to botanists because of the many plants that are unique to this area. One such is an attractive sub-shrub of the pine plains as well as through much of the Pine Barrens. This is PYXIE, *Pyxidanthera barbulata*, sometimes called pyxie "moss" because its leaves are so tiny and matted together that the plant appears to be a clump of moss. This is not a moss but a true flowering plant with a central root system, central stalk, stems that lie prostrate on the

Pyxie

ground, and leaves, flowers, and seeds. Its name comes from the Greek *pyxie*, meaning small box, and the Latin *anthera*, referring to the fact that the anthers of the male stamens appear like little boxes which open as if by a lid. These are so small that to see them one must get down on one's hands and knees and use a hand lens. When the leaves first begin to develop in mid-March, they often are brilliant red in color but they turn green by the time the plant blossoms late in March or early April. Clumps of pyxie sometimes form patches a foot or more in diameter. There are few rivals in the still brown woods to the beauty of these white, star-like blossoms that sparkle from their green moss-like setting, like little upside down stars looking up at you from below.

Another flowering sub-shrub is TRAILING ARBUTUS or MAYFLOWER, *Epigaea repens*, a member of the heath family. This small plant grows very close to the ground in a creeping, trailing manner and has leaves that are oval, leathery, hairy, and evergreen. In the dwarf or pygmy forests of the pine plains where trailing arbutus is fairly common, this beautiful little spring flower usually comes into bloom very late in March or early in April with white to pinkish-white, fragrant, terminal, tubular flowers tucked inconspicuously between the green leaves. The poet Whittier attributes the name of this plant to the fact that "the trailing arbutus or mayflower grows abundantly in the vicinity of Plymouth [Massachusetts] and was the first flower to greet the Pilgrims [who came over on the Mayflower] after their fearful winter."

Spring Courtship
in the
Pine Barrens

S pring migration continues apace throughout March and into April
and, while some early migrants such as robins and red-winged
blackbirds loudly proclaim themselves to the world by chorusing
their early arrivals, others come much more quietly and sort of sneak in
unseen and unheard. The bird that best fits this pattern is the AMERICAN
WOODCOCK, also known as the "timber-doodle." The woodcock is a
peculiar bird and almost everything about it is a curious mixture of con-
tradictions. Sometimes described as an upland shore bird, it has forsaken
its ancestral habitats of mudflats and salt marshes in preference to low,
wet, overgrown fields, thickets, and young, open woodlands near
streams. Ornithologically a member of the sandpiper family, it is most
closely related to the common snipe.

The woodcock is not a large bird, being only slightly larger than a
robin, but it is more round and chunky, so much so that it seems not to
have any neck at all, and it has very short legs. It is described as being
about the size of a large man's fist, with mottled brown, black, and gray
plumage that blends, in perfect camouflage, with dead leaves on the forest floor. Its head is about the size of a golf ball, with large, black eyes
set well back. Most conspicuous is a long, two and one-half to three-inch
bill that, when probed to the hilt in mud, can detect the movement of
earthworms, its main diet, and capture them. Woodcock also have the
habit of sometimes refusing to be flushed, especially when the hen is
brooding her eggs. In the July 23, 1960, issue of *The Saturday Evening
Post*, author George Heinold relates a story of a Maine game warden who

came across a hen woodcock on her nest. Wanting to get some good pictures of this phase of woodcock life, he dug a square of sod around the nest and, lifting nest, eggs, bird and all, he drove to a photographer's studio where several floodlighted pictures were made. Not once did the bird try to leave her nest even after she was driven back to her homesite and replanted, unharmed. Maine is noted for its tongue-in-cheek stories and its down east humor, so you can believe this one, or not, as you wish.

Soon after their arrival from the gulf states, male woodcock establish territories and begin to put on one of the most interesting courtship performances in the avian world. Toward evening, when it becomes so dark that the bird is barely visible in the field, a male woodcock will begin his courtship display and sky dance. First, he will start strutting around like a tiny drum major, with his bill pressed tightly against a ballooning chest, his blunt, white-bottomed tail elevated, and his wing tips dragging along the ground, all the while twittering, and every few seconds uttering a nasal, buzz-like *peent*. Then, as these movements and sounds speed up in tempo, suddenly the bird will spread its wings, take off, and whirl up in an erratic, spiraling, corkscrew-like flight, rising some two to three hundred feet, all the while, with wings fluttering, uttering varied whistles and cheeps. For a few seconds, when he reaches the climax of his spiraling ascent, all is quiet as he circles around and then comes a great burst of song as he plummets back to earth with a continuous, high-pitched cheeping. Just before crashing, he levels off and returns to nearly the same spot on the ground from which he took off, only to repeat the performance time and time again until well into the evening. Once it gets real dark, the calls and flights cease, to begin again an hour or so before dawn. Males will sometimes continue their courtship flights even after they have mated and the hen is sitting on her eggs. Sometimes, also, it is possible to see and hear three or four males performing in a common courtship area. If you would like to watch one of these performances, here are a few sites where male woodcock have established their courting grounds: 1) Medford Wildlife Management Area along Ark Road; 2) a low, open brushy field on the west side of Route 206, north of Atsion Road, almost opposite the Atsion Ranger Station in the Wharton State Forest; and 3) eastern edges of the village of Whitesbog, enroute out to the cranberry bogs. One's ability to see and hear these performances, however, is greatly dependent on whether there is still enough light to see the birds and whether one has sharp eyes and ears.

Cedar Swamps, Sphagnum Mosses, and Golden Club

As we move into the first full month of spring, we must stop a minute during the very first weekend to perform a small, spring ritual of our own, the moving ahead of our clocks one hour to DAYLIGHT SAVINGS TIME. This artificial device was originally introduced into our country in 1918 as a wartime experiment, but it is so commonplace today we tend to forget its origin as we prepare to enjoy the extra hour of daylight that is added to our summer evenings. This will remain with us until the last weekend in October.

Sometime this month, or no later than early in May, pineland CRANBERRY FARMERS will be draining off the waters that have been flooding their bogs over winter. The odor coming from the vegetation that has been under water for so long may be a little strong, sort of marshy, and there will be a scum that will settle over the vegetation. Both the odor and the scum will soon disappear as the cranberry vines, now exposed to full sunlight, will put out new growth, will spread further along the ground, and will send up new shoots, called uprights, that will produce the cranberry blossoms in June and the bright red fruits in September and October.

Next to pitch pine, the ATLANTIC WHITE CEDAR, *Chamaecyparis thyoides,* may be the most characteristic tree in the Pine Barrens, following

55

the courses of most streams and spreading out in low-lying areas to form dense cedar swamps. Under natural conditions, trees in a cedar swamp grow tall and straight, like flagpoles or masts on a ship. They grow so closely together that their tops form canopies that shut out much of the sunlight, leaving below cool, damp, dark cathedrals of tree trunks rising high above carpets of green sphagnum mosses in pools of very slowly moving cedar waters. White cedars are evergreen trees, but instead of growing needles like pines, the leaves of white cedars are very small, flat, and scale-like. Ordinarily, we may not think of white cedars as flowering trees because the minute flowers they produce are in such small catkins they are easily overlooked. These flowers open for a brief time around the first of April, followed by the setting of their cones. When first formed, these small cones are nearly round, or berry-like, somewhat fleshy, wrinkled, and bluish, but when these mature in late summer they open up to become small dark, woody, reddish-brown cones.

Over the years, the Atlantic white cedar probably has been the most valuable tree in the Pinelands, and the extensive virgin stands of these trees were greatly prized by the early settlers. White cedar is relatively decay resistant, nonresinous, lightweight, and straight-grained. For these reasons it was used extensively in house and other construction, cooperage, and fence posts and rails, but its primary use in the eighteenth century was for roofing shingles. In a very short while, virgin stands of white cedar were being cut at such a rate that, as early as 1749, Peter Kalm, a German botanist who was exploring and studying New World plants, complained about over-exploitation of this natural resource. Cedar trees are slow growing and stands of cedars take from sixty to one hundred years to develop to marketable size so, in time, after cedar stands had been cut over several times, the cedar marketing industry declined drastically. Some cedar cutting has continued ever since with the result that stands of cedars have been reduced to such an extent it is estimated cedar stands now total less than half of the original virgin forests. Today, there are almost no cedar trees of sufficient size worth lumbering for construction or shingles. Instead, today, private owners and state foresters both seem unwilling to allow cedars to develop to maximum maturity, preferring instead to cut remaining stands of small and medium-sized trees suitable only for fencing and small furniture construction.

There is another part of the cedar story that is both interesting and important. This has to do with Pine Barrens CEDAR WATER streams. A look at the map of southern New Jersey will show that no streams run into or through the Pine Barrens from outside the Pinelands. Yet there are at least a dozen streams that arise within the pines and are constantly carrying water from the Pinelands out into the Atlantic Ocean and the Delaware River. The main sources of all these streams are first, precipitation and second, waters from the Cohansey aquifer that lie in shallow depressions on the surface of the ground. Frequently these shallow waters become prime habitats for stands of white cedars in bogs and swamps, which then serve as reservoirs of slowly moving waters that become the headwaters of the many small streams and rivers that flow out from the pines. Because these waters stand in cedar bogs for long periods of time, they pick up

Cedar bog

tannin and other vegetative dyes from the roots of the cedar trees and other vegetation such as the sphagnum mosses. These dyes, plus the natural high iron content of the water, make these waters quite dark, sort of reddish-brown or tea-colored. This is unique to the Pine Barrens and the water is called "cedar water" for its point of origin. These waters also are quite acid; yet, in spite of these conditions, they are pure and unpolluted, especially in the upper reaches of these streams.

In the ecology of cedar swamps, SPHAGNUM MOSSES are an important component. In the Pine Barrens there are more than twenty species of mosses belonging to the genus *Sphagnum*. For most people, trying to determine the identity of individual species of sphagnum mosses is too technical and too difficult so all species of sphagnum mosses are often lumped together and simply referred to as "sphagnum." As a group, these mosses grow most abundantly and luxuriantly along the edges of, and in, cedar bogs and swamps, although occasionally a few may be found in other small, damp locations.

Individual sphagnum plants grow very closely together, often forming loose but dense green mats, so extensive that it is almost impossible to walk in cedar swamps and other boggy areas without sinking into soft, spongy, soaking wet carpets of sphagnum. It is the ability of sphagnum to absorb and hold water that is one of its most valuable assets. Some sources say that sphagnum plants can absorb water up to two hundred times their own weight. This may be an exaggeration, but it is certain that sphagnum plants do hold water like a sponge. To find out for yourself, pick up a handful of sphagnum from an area above water level, wring it out like a sponge, and watch the amount of water that will be squeezed out from the plants. This ability to hold large quantities of water on the surface of the soil is of great importance in water conservation, soil erosion, and even flood control. Further, this ability to hold water, thus providing a moist carpet over the roots of plants, provides Atlantic white cedars in bogs and swamps with a blanket of year-round moisture that the cedars need for their survival. And who knows how valuable these mosses are in helping to hold water in natural, upstream reservoirs of Cohansey origin and thus helping supply a continuous source of water for the many streams that originate in the Pine Barrens?

Over the years, sphagnum mosses have proven their value in many other ways. Sphagnum plants grow without roots. The upper stems of the plants continue to grow year after year while the lower and older stems die off, decompose, and, along with leaves and stems from other bog plants, become buried under the still growing plants and soil above them. Thus they become compressed into an organic mass that, in time, can be dug up as peat, cut into bricks, dried, and used as a fuel. For centuries, this has been a major and traditional source of fuel in countries of northern Europe, especially in Ireland and Scotland. Although limited quantities of peat have been dug in New Jersey from time to time, peat from New Jersey bogs is of an inferior grade and the digging of peat has never become a Pine Barrens industry.

Sphagnum is used a great deal by nurserymen as packing around the roots of plants to keep them moist while they are being shipped and transplanted. Gardeners also use sphagnum as peat moss to loosen and improve their soils and to help in the cultivation of plants that require a constant supply of water around their roots. Sphagnum mosses are reported to have antiseptic and curative powers, and researchers have found that they do indeed contain a bacterium that produces an effective antibiotic. In both World Wars, sphagnum mosses were gathered, processed, and used in army hospitals as an absorbent in surgical dressings. Sphagnum also has been valuable as a packing and insulation material and, in some cases, has even been used as filling for mattresses and pillows. Finally, it is said that the native American Indians used sphagnum to heal sores and that they gathered and dried sphagnum for use as diaper material for their babies.

For many of these reasons, therefore, the gathering of sphagnum or bog mosses was a major native industry for many years in the Pine Barrens. Generations of Pine Barrens residents have gathered these mosses out of the bogs, dried and baled them, and shipped them to florists, nurserymen, and others. Even today, a few old time residents still carry on a little of this activity as a supplemental source of income.

It is in the waters of cedar streams, bogs, and swamps that, quite early in April, one of the more interesting and characteristic Pine Barrens plants comes into bloom. This is GOLDEN CLUB, *Orontium aquaticum*, an aquatic herb that is closely related to skunk cabbage and jack-in-the-pulpit, but lacks the enclosing cowl of either of these. Its orange-yellow flowers are clustered at the tips of naked, club-like spikes that rise above the surface of the water, supported by white stalks that grow up from tuberous roots. Occasionally, these golden spikes poke up through wet, spongy clumps of sphagnum mosses.

In some places this plant is very prolific and becomes so abundant that, as one looks over a body of water, the surface is covered with thousands of yellow spikes sticking up above the surface of the water almost as far as the eye can see. One such place that comes to mind is Gaunt's Reservoir at Whitesbog. The leaves of golden club develop later than the flowers and usually lay on the surface of the water. These leaves have an unusual upper surface which is covered with a velvety film that repels water so that water rolls off its leaves as from the proverbial duck's back, giving this plant its colloquial name of "neverwet." Peter Kalm stated in his *Travels* that "the Indians called this plant 'Taw-Kee' and used its dried seeds as food."

14

Spring Shrubs, Sassafras, and Swamp Pink

W hite cedars head a small parade of trees, shrubs, and sub-shrubs that begin to bloom early in April. We've already seen and talked about several: alder, broom-crowberry, swamp maple, trailing arbutus, pyxie and white cedar. Next to bloom are leather-leaf, shadbush, sassafras, chokeberries, bearberry, sand-myrtle, beach plum, blueberries, and blackjack oaks—all woody plants that already have their vascular systems well above ground ready to go into action as soon as spring arrives. This readiness is fundamental to the fact that most early spring flowers are produced by plants of this type. In fact, of the first dozen and a half flowering plants in the Pine Barrens that blossom by mid-April, thirteen are trees, or shrubs, or sub-shrubs. The herbaceous plants, on the other hand, must first grow up out of the ground before they can develop their stems, leaves, and buds necessary to produce flowers. It follows, rather naturally, that, in general, trees and shrubs are among the first to end their blooming seasons, the last of these to come into bloom being buttonbush and sweet pepperbush around the 20th of July. Various herbaceous plants, on the other hand, continue to blossom well into the fall as, for example, the asters, goldenrods, blazing-star, and Pine Barrens gentian.

Very early in April, LEATHERLEAF or Cassandra, *Chamaedaphne caly-culata*, comes into bloom. This is a low, one and one-half to two-foot, pro-fusely branching shrub with small, leathery, almost evergreen leaves. It is a member of the heath family and produces white, bell-like flowers in one-sided rows of pendant flowers. Witmer Stone, an early southern New

Jersey botanist and ornithologist, and author of the 1910 classic *The Plants of Southern New Jersey*, wrote that its "one-sided racemes of white, cylindrical flowers . . . have gained for it the name of 'false teeth bush.'" Today, however, this term is at least equally and perhaps even more frequently applied to a later blooming close relative, fetterbush. Leatherleaf is an abundant shrub in peaty swales, wet bogs, spongs, and along the edges of ponds and swamps throughout the Pine Barrens. Around the edges of cranberry bogs it sometimes becomes an invasive pest that will, in time, if not contained, take over old cranberry bogs and turn them into spongs.

Another plant along moist edges is SHADBUSH, *Amelanchier canadensis*, which usually is a shrub but may sometimes become a small tree. This plant gets its name from the fact that it blossoms about the same time that shad run up rivers, like the Delaware, to spawn, usually early in April. The spikes of white flowers and downy, whitish leaf buds stand out in welcome contrast to the surrounding still bare and brownish tree trunks and dead leaves. Shadbush is fairly common in thickets and low, damp woods and may often be quite noticeable as it blossoms along roadside ditches. Shadbush has two other common names: Juneberry because its crimson fruits ripen so early in the year, and serviceberry because the Indians gathered these fruits in great quantities and, after much crushing and pounding, made them into a sort of cake. Shadbush is a member of the rose family, the same family that includes apples, peaches, pears, plums, and many other fruits, so it is understandable that the fruits of shadbush are a fine source of food for a great variety of wildlife.

In both upland and lowland woodlands, as well as along trails and roadsides throughout the barrens, there is a small tree that is quite characteristic of the pines. This is SASSAFRAS, *Sassafras albidum*. Right now, in early to mid-April, look for the small but conspicuous clusters of bright, greenish-yellow flowers that appear all over the greenish, terminal branches of this tree. Male and female flowers appear on separate trees. Sassafras, along with shadbush and the paired, winged seeds of the swamp maples, are the three brightest and most conspicuous of early flowering Pinelands trees and shrubs. Later, between the middle and end of July, the flowers of female sassafras trees develop into attractive blue fruits on long bright red stems.

Sassafras is of more than passing interest for several reasons. First, its leaves are quite distinctive in that these trees produce leaves in four different shapes or patterns: leaves with two lobes, or "mittens," one on each side; leaves with a lobe on the left side; leaves with a lobe on the right side; and leaves without any lobes at all. All four can be found on the same tree. Second, sassafras is a native, North American tree that was completely new to the early settlers and colonists. When these new arrivals "discovered" sassafras, they began to use it in a variety of ways. One was as a source of dye and, depending on the amount used, shades from pink to a warm brown were obtained. A second use was as a mildly stimulating beverage or tea made by boiling the roots, especially the bark of the roots, in hot water to make a deep red brew to which was added sugar and cream. During the Civil War, sassafras tea was in great demand in the South where tea from the Orient could not be obtained. Third, the bark of the sassafras root was distilled in large quantities for its aromatic oil to be used in flavoring medicines, scenting perfumes and soaps, and in making candies. Fourth was as a food. Young leaves and young pith are highly mucilaginous, so these leaves were dried, ground into powder, and used as a thickening or flavoring in soups, especially in Creole cookery. Even today, this is a basic ingredient for the gumbo soup so famous in New Orleans restaurants. Finally, and perhaps most importantly, sassafras was long considered to have great medicinal values and was often sold in drug stores. During colonial days, sassafras was in great demand in Europe where it was regarded as a cure-all for almost all kinds of ills, and it became such an important article of commerce that it was long sold in the stores of London. Today, sassafras is no longer of any great pharmacological value, but there still is a moderate demand in medicine for its extracted oil.

While trees and shrubs are generally the first Pine Barrens flora to bloom in the spring, there also are a few early herbaceous flowering plants. One we've already seen is golden club, an aquatic or semi-aquatic herb. The very first of our terrestrial herbs to blossom grows in wooded swamps and is aptly named SWAMP-PINK, *Helonias bullata.* This is one of the characteristic plants of southern New Jersey that is found in a number of scattered Pine Barrens locations, though it is often difficult to know where. Swamp-pink begins to bloom by mid-April while its flowering head is still very close to the ground, growing out of a center rosette of narrow, evergreen leaves. The flowering stalk rises rapidly and is a foot or more in height by the time the flowers are in full bloom. Its dense clusters of lilac-pink blossoms with their contrasting bright blue stamens are quite conspicuous against the background of otherwise still brown bogs and swamps. Swamp-pink is one of the most beautiful of all Pine Barrens flowering plants, but it is also one of our endangered plant species.

Although there are several places where swamp-pink is known to exist, there must be other spots that are unknown or have never been reported. Working on the New Jersey breeding bird census one nice, sunny mid-April day, Doris and I took what appeared to be an interesting but little-used side trail. We'd already had a pretty good day: twenty plus birds, including a pair of phoebes building their nest on a plate beam under an old pavilion and a pair of blue-gray gnatcatchers building their nest up in a budding oak; several spring azures and a mourning cloak butterfly flitting through the woods; leatherleaf in full blossom; sassafras just starting to bloom; and red-bellied turtles basking on stumps in a lake. As we moved along the trail, it became more closed in and much wetter underfoot until we came to a very muddy area where, sometime in the dim past, someone had put down a few boards and logs to make it easier to walk through that swampy area. These were all in pretty bad shape and the footing was getting treacherous. As we looked ahead, we wondered whether it would be worthwhile to try to navigate further along the trail when suddenly we discovered, in the middle of the muddy trail ahead, a whole stand of swamp-pink in several stages of bloom, from buds still just appearing to a few that were almost in full bloom. So, we carefully trod our way further along to observe these more closely and to photograph some of them. It was a beautiful and rewarding sight in a new and previously unreported location.

In drier, sandy, open woods and along roadsides, the BIRD'S-FOOT VIOLET, *Viola pedata*, is also a very early herbaceous flowering plant, opening its pale blue-violet or lilac flowers from mid-April through early May. The leaves of this plant are not at all like the usual heart-shaped leaves of common violets. Instead, these are cut into three to five segments, some of which are again cut and toothed so that some leaves may have as many as nine or more distinct points. This is the reason for its

Bird's-foot violet

common name, for the cut leaves of this violet seem to resemble a bird's foot. One of the best displays of bird's-foot violets can be seen along the east side of Route 563 between Chatsworth and Route 72, approximately opposite the Hedger House, but there are several other similar roadside displays throughout the Pine Barrens.

One should also be on the lookout for two other violets that bloom at this same time, but both of these will be found in much moister Pinelands locations. These are the LANCE-LEAVED VIOLET, *Viola lanceolata*, and the PRIMROSE-LEAVED VIOLET, *Viola primulifolia*. Both of these are lovely white violets with light purple veining at the bases of the petals. The major difference between the two is in the shape of their leaves as

65

one can easily tell from both their common and scientific names. The lance-leaved violet has smooth, lance-shaped to even narrowly lance-shaped leaves that gradually taper down to the stem. The primrose-leaved violets have leaves which are much broader, sort of egg-shaped or oblong, and which abruptly narrow down at the stem. Both are found in low, moist, sandy meadows, marshes, and damp roadsides but, of the two, the lance-leaved is by far the more common.

15

Carpenters
and
Snappers

A s early as some nice warm days in March, but more commonly by mid-April, most of the many cold-blooded denizens of the Pine Barrens become active and start to show themselves. These are our amphibians (salamanders, frogs, treefrogs, and toads) and reptiles (fence lizards, turtles and snakes) which, lumped together, are often called "herps." By cold-blooded, we mean that the blood temperature of these animals approximates that of their surroundings, either air, soil, or water, rather than their blood being a relatively stable, warm temperature as in warm-blooded birds and mammals. This means that when the temperature of the air, soil, or water becomes too cold, these animals gradually reduce and finally cease all activity and hide in protected places or bury themselves in the mud to hibernate throughout the winter until warmer weather returns the following spring. Generally, the critical temperature points are a low of 55°F and a high of 86°F. Translated, this means activity is restricted to a period roughly from warmer days in mid-March and early April through the end of October.

So, how do these animals "know" when to renew their active lives again in the spring? Probably the best answer lies in their built-in biological clocks. Some might call this instinct, but instinct is something different as we will see later when we talk about the higher insects. Biological clocks are the total of all the built-in receptors that all organisms have in response to a full range of stimuli from the environment. They react positively or negatively to light and the number of hours of daylight, to humidity and rainfall, to temperature changes, and to many other stimuli. It is the effect of the sum total of these stimuli which causes animal reawakening in the spring and cessation of activity and hibernation overwinter. Many years ago, the *New England Naturalist* published some dates when the first frog and toad calls were heard in the Boston area. Considering the difference in latitude between Boston and southern New Jersey, those dates would roughly translate to here as: spring peeper, February 24; leopard frog, February 28; wood frog, March 1; pickerel frog, March 3; green frog, March 7; Fowler's toad, March 15, Gray's treefrog, March 28; and bullfrog, April 20.

All frogs and toads, including treefrogs, are AMPHIBIANS, this word literally meaning "two lives." These are so named because most amphibians spend their early lives in fresh water and obtain their oxygen from the water by means of gills. As they develop, they transform into air breathing adults that may live only part of the time in water or they may live primarily on land. In almost all cases, these adults return to the water each spring to chorus their evening calls, to mate, and to lay their eggs in water in order to perpetuate their species.

Frogs and toads are primarily creatures of the night during the spring when males are calling in their various voices in efforts to attract females for mating. We've already heard the earliest and smallest treefrogs, the spring peepers, that began chorusing during evenings in March. At the same time we may also have heard two other evening choristers whose calls may have been mixed in with the spring peepers. These were the chorus frogs and the wood frogs that we mentioned earlier.

Although abundant in proper habitats in the pines, spring peepers are quite widespread in distribution throughout much of the northeast and so are not limited to the Pinelands. However, there are a couple of frogs that are distinctly characteristic of the Pine Barrens. One of these is the famous Pine Barrens treefrog which we'll hear and should see from early May into mid-June. The other is larger than most treefrogs, does not have any suction cups on its toes, and is what is known as a "true" frog. This is the CARPENTER or SPHAGNUM FROG, *Rana virgatipes*, which has a very limited range outside the New Jersey Pine Barrens. Here, acid cedar water bogs and swamps provide ideal habitats and breeding pools for these frogs, which also occur rather abundantly in ditches around cranberry bogs.

About two to two and a half inches long, the carpenter frog has four distinct yellowish stripes running down the back and sides of its body and these serve as positive identification of an otherwise drab looking frog. This is a difficult frog to locate and see because its coloring blends in so well with its background of dark cedar waters. About the best way to see one is to look for its head and two bulging eyes protruding above the surface of the water, but if you should approach too closely, its head will vanish downward only to reappear a few feet away just seconds later.

The carpenter frog has a very distinctive call—a hollow, thud-like sound, something like the striking blow of a carpenter's hammer—that has given this frog its name. Standing near where a colony is going full blast some warm evening, especially during the breeding season from April into August, their chorus of echoing "hammer-blows" sounds surprisingly like a gang of carpenters hard at work. Even during daylight hours, especially on dark, cloudy days, it is not unusual to hear carpenter frogs "pounding nails" out in the bogs!

There are two other "true" frogs that are common to abundant throughout the Pine Barrens, so one should be on the lookout for either or both of these around the edges of almost any body of water, from the sides of streams and along ditches around cranberry bogs to the shallow edges of small lakes, reservoirs, ponds, and even small pools of water, as well as in marshes, meadows, and low, damp grasslands. These are the green frog and the southern leopard frog. As its name implies, the GREEN FROG, *Rana clamitans melanota*, is green to greenish-brown, usually a brighter green on the head and shoulders shading to a dusky olive-brown on the back, with numerous greenish-brown blotches on the back and sides. This frog is apt to be found close to ponds and other bodies of water. The SOUTHERN LEOPARD FROG, *Rana utricularia*, however, is more apt to wander away from ponds into nearby meadows and marshes, so is sometimes called the meadow frog. It too is sort of greenish or bronzy-green, but it has two or three distinct rows down its back and sides of irregularly placed dark spots that are sort of rounded and are bordered with white. It also has a more pointed snout than other frogs. Both of these frogs are good jumpers, can leap great distances, and are real fast, so the best way to see one is not to try to catch it but to come up on it very slowly and quietly, yet keep some distance away while you observe it and marvel at its adaptations for survival.

In recent years, naturalists and scientists the world over have become increasingly concerned about a drastic decline in the populations of some species of amphibians, especially frogs. No one knows why this is happening. Atmospheric pollution in the form of acid precipitation or increased ultraviolet radiation due to breaks in the ozone layer have been suggested, but up to this point no one has the answer. Amphibians have particularly thin skins and it has been suggested that this may make these animals more susceptible to pollutants than other animal forms but, again, no one knows for sure. Finally, a number of individuals believe this decline in apparently more susceptible amphibian populations may be another warning, like the ill-fated canary in the mine, of impending problems for all of us and our descendants.

The other group of "herps" is the reptiles. In the popular sense, reptiles differ from amphibians in that their skins are covered with scales or plates and the toes of those that bear legs have claws. Also, the eggs of reptiles are always laid on land so the young that hatch from them are air breathers from the start. There are three types of reptiles in the Pinelands: one, and only one, small lizard which we'll encounter in warmer weather; a number of different and interesting snakes that we'll also see later; and turtles. Reptiles are not as cold-hardy as amphibians, so they emerge from hibernation only when the warmth of the sun raises their body temperatures enough for them to resume normal activities. Very likely, the turtles we may first see in the spring will be those that climb up on to logs and stumps in ponds, sometimes in great numbers, to bask in the warmth of the bright sunshine. These are the SPOTTED TURTLES, *Clemmys guttata*, the PAINTED TURTLES, *Chrysemys picta*, and the RED-BELLIED TURTLES, *Chrysemys rubriventris*. Superficial differences between these are that spotted turtles, as their name implies, have small, round, yellow spots on their upper shells, while painted turtles have a row of red and black markings around the edges of their upper shells. Both are rather small, from four to six inches in length. Red-bellied turtles look like big brother editions of painted turtles because these grow up to be ten to twelve inches in length. Also, their undershells are often quite reddish.

The most common of these three turtles are the painted turtles, which are most often seen sunning themselves or basking on floating logs and on tree stumps in almost every Pine Barrens pond or open swamp. Sometimes several painted turtles will line up quite sociably on the same floating log to sun themselves, and at times and in places these could number in the dozens. However, if you should approach too closely to them, they will all quietly slide back into the water.

Turtles are one of the very few animals that carry their "homes" around with them. The characteristic shell consists of a more or less arched upper part (carapace) and a flatter, lower part (plastron), the two firmly joined together on the sides by means of a bridge. Thus the shell is an integral part of the turtle and it is impossible to remove a specimen from its shell without resorting to butchery. Turtles do not have any teeth. Instead, the edges of their sharp, horny, beak-like jaws are sufficiently chisel-like to enable them to seize and cut up both fleshy and vegetative foods. All turtles are egg layers, and lay their eggs in holes they dig in the sand or soil with their hind legs and then cover them up with dirt or sand.

Two other turtles that are quite apt to be seen in the Pinelands are the box turtle and the snapping turtle. The BOX TURTLE, *Terrapene carolina*, is a strictly land animal, and is most often seen walking along the forest floor. It also is a wandering turtle that is constantly on the move. Small in size, up to six inches in length, its upper shell is highly arched and covered with irregular, elongate, yellow markings on a dark background. Its under shell is unusual in that the front and rear sections are hinged so they may be closed up tightly against the upper shell, thus creating a protective box. This is the only turtle that has this ability.

All of the turtles mentioned so far are relatively mild creatures that will either slide back into the water when approached or, if on land, will draw their heads and legs back within their shells and wait until the coast is clear before proceeding. Not so the SNAPPING TURTLE, *Chelydra serpentina*, for this is a creature that will snap, and even lunge, at anything that threatens it. This is our largest and heaviest turtle, weighing up to twenty-five to forty pounds, and is much sought after in the Pinelands for sale to restaurants for snapper soups.

Snappers are readily identified by their large size, by notches on the rear edge of their upper shells, by saw-toothed ridges on their tails, by their thick, heavy necks and heads, and by their feisty dispositions. They spend much of their time on the bottom of ponds, swamps, and marshes waiting for any opportunity to seize food such as fish, frogs, young muskrats, and waterfowl. Thus the likelihood of seeing a snapping turtle is limited to a chance encounter with one that is moving across land from one body of water to another.

Over the years, several encounters with snappers stand out in my mind, among them these three: years ago, on the 5th of May, a large, mean, heavy old brute covered with mud, lying in the marshes along the Delaware River near Hancock's Bridge; a young, clean looking one on the 18th of April near the old horse barn at Batsto; and another large, old specimen crossing over Route 563 between two of Haines' cranberry bogs. A relatively recent encounter was with a large, old snapper that was crossing over Park Road, off Route 206, heading into Miller's cranberry bogs, south of Dutchtown, Atlantic County. I was alone when I came upon this one at the edge of the gravel road one mid-July day and I wanted to photograph it, but it had other ideas. As I half-kneeled down to get close enough to photo it, the turtle demonstrated its very interesting but quite characteristic defense pattern. As long as I was in front of it and looked at it face to face, the turtle watched me very carefully with its head extended. But as soon as I started to get around to take a side view, it turned in whichever direction I went so that it was always facing me, and if I got too close it both snapped and lunged at me. The same thing happened when I tried to get a tail and rear-end view: it turned completely around so that it continued always to face me. Purposely, I repeated my efforts several times but with the exact same results. I never was able to get any decent side or rear view shots. Thinking I might do better trying to get a couple of underside pictures, I flipped it over with my boot but it almost instantly righted itself by using its head and long, thick neck as a prop. Clearly this animal, as are all snapping turtles, was well prepared to defend itself and after I ceased interfering, it moved across the verge and on into the swampy woods.

16

Spring Migration

Almost from the beginning of April we should start to look and listen for the very first of our spring and summer warblers, the PINE WARBLER, common wherever pines grow. Unlike many other warblers that pass through here during the spring to nest further north, pine warblers will remain with us all summer. A bright yellow breast and whitish wing bars will help identify this warbler by sight while its one-pitched musical trill, somewhat like a chipping sparrow's but looser, more musical, and slower, will alert you to its presence by sound. As its name implies, the pine warbler prefers to feed and sing in the tallest pine trees and it builds its nest only in pines. It usually is found on a pine limb, occasionally lifting its head to sing, or quietly stealing along a limb like a creeper, or hopping from twig to twig like any other warbler searching for its insect prey. Like all warblers, pine warblers are small, active birds that are constantly searching for and feeding on insects they find on tree trunks and branches and around little leaf buds that are just beginning to open in the pine woodlands.

By mid-April, we should begin to listen for what may be the most common and characteristic nesting bird in the upland forests of the pines. This is the RUFOUS-SIDED TOWHEE, or "chewink," a beautiful but noisy bird, almost the size of a robin. Males have black upper parts of their head, back, and tail, chestnut-colored sides, and white underparts. Flashy white wing and tail patches are conspicuous in flight. Females are brownish above with more muted chestnut sides and white underparts. In spite of the beauty of these birds, they are much more often heard than seen, for towhees are ground dwelling birds that prefer dense undergrowths and thickets. So, listen for the call of the towhee which is a fairly loud *che-wink* or *tow-hee*, while its song sounds something like *drink-your-teee* with an accent on the final syllable. Towhees feed on insects and seeds they find on the forest floor as they noisily scratch among the dead leaves. They have an interesting way of scratching for their food. Instead of standing on one foot and scratching with the other, as a chicken does, it jumps up from the ground and strikes the leaves with both feet, kicking away the leaves. Towhees make their nests on the ground or in low bushes, and are very clever in hiding them for their nests are seldom found.

Among the next to arrive is the BROWN THRASHER, another common Pinelands nesting summer resident. This is a large, attractive, reddish-brown, heavily streaked bird with a long tail and a long bill. It is said the term thrasher is due to the bird's twitching of its long tail when it is singing or when it appears to be nervous. It frequents woodland edges and brushy thickets and often perches on a topmost branch to pour out a medley of couplets that constitutes its song, one of the most musical and pleasant of all bird songs. Along with the catbird and the mockingbird, the brown thrasher is one of the so-called mimic thrushes. All three are notable songsters, unequaled for the rich variety and volume of their songs. Some mimic the songs of other birds. Others sing a melodious mixture of original and imitative phrases, each repeated several times.

The CATBIRD gets its name from its call note which sounds a little like the mew of a cat, but its song is a veritable mixture of melodious notes along with a medley of other bird calls and songs. As a mimic, the catbird exceeds the thrasher, but it is not as good as the mockingbird. As a songster, the catbird is the equal of the thrasher in sweetness, but not in the volume of its singing. It is amusing, at times, to listen to its melodious singing and then to hear it interrupt itself with a perfect imitation of a crested flycatcher or the spitting of a cat. This plain gray bird with a small black cap and a long tail may be the most common bird in low woodland thickets throughout the Pinelands, much as the towhee may be the most common upland woodlands bird.

Starting in April and continuing into early May, at almost the same time as the spring migration of birds arriving here from the south, many Pinelands birds that have been with us all winter will be leaving for their summer habitats further north. Among the earliest of these to depart will be the red-breasted nuthatches and tree sparrows, followed by the brown creepers, golden-crowned kinglets, evening grosbeaks, pine siskins, white-throated sparrows, purple finches, and the dark-eyed or slate colored juncos.

At the same time that these winter birds are leaving for the north, an interesting transformation is taking place with another of our winter birds, but this one stays with us throughout the entire year. This is the common AMERICAN GOLDFINCH, the state bird of New Jersey. Between winter and summer, the male goldfinch appears to be two different birds. Winter birds, both males and females, are rather subdued in color, sort of olive-greenish-yellowish above with black wings and conspicuous wing bars. But, toward the end of March and early in April, males begin to molt and change their plumage quite dramatically, and by mid-April these become bright, bouncing balls of brilliant golden yellow with black wings and tail and a small black cap and forehead patch, leading many persons to call this bird our "wild canary." Goldfinches are rather sociable birds and often travel in flocks. As the birds fly overhead, birders can identify them simply by their bouncing, undulating flight during which, with each dip, they sing a little *per-chik-o-ree* song.

From the middle of April on, the WHIP-POOR-WILL arrives from its wintering grounds down south. This is a night flying bird that hunts for insects and is much more often heard (at night) than seen (by day). During the day it is likely to roost on the ground or lengthwise along low branches, well camouflaged by its muted and mottled gray-brown plumage. Few birds are less frequently seen than the whip-poor-will, but its call is hard to miss. Three whistled notes, *whip-poor-will*, are repeated over and over for long periods of time after darkness settles over the pine and oak woodlands, loudly enough to be heard for a considerable distance. The whip-poor-will is a veritable, animated insect trap. Its wide mouth and long facial bristles enable this bird to capture large, nocturnal, flying insects that smaller day-flying birds can not capture, and it consumes quantities of them. Whip-poor-wills make their nests among dead leaves on the ground where their mottled plumage makes them very difficult to be seen.

Whip-poor-wills may not be as common today in the Pinelands as they once were. When we built our Tabernacle home over twenty-five years ago, there was only one house on one side of us, none on the other side, and nothing behind except ten acres of woodlands. Whip-poor-wills used to announce their arrival right on schedule every year. Now, with houses on both sides and a whole street full of houses behind, we haven't heard a whip-poor-will here in years. Similarly, whip-poor-wills were once numerous along Jackson Road in the area of the former Boy Scout camp in Medford. The camp has been replaced with a housing development and now whip-poor-wills are seldom heard there. Although there may not be any scientific study on this, it seems reasonable to assume this type of change has taken place over and over as housing developments have continued to encroach into and fragment natural areas throughout the Pine Barrens.

A closely related bird that arrives shortly after the whip-poor-will is the NIGHTHAWK. In spite of its name, this is not a hawk. Instead, like the whip-poor-will, it belongs to a group of birds known as nightjars or goatsuckers, all of which are nocturnal or crepuscular birds that feed on night flying insects. The interesting name of goatsucker comes from an old time superstition that these birds drank the milk of goats, undoubtedly due to seeing these birds flying near goats in the early evening hours searching for insects surrounding these animals. The nighthawk is more apt to be crepuscular than nocturnal and during late afternoons and early evenings, and sometimes during early morning hours, it flies around high in the sky, feeding on insects and giving voice to its short, nasal *peent* call. Like the whip-poor-will, it also has a large mouth with whiskers around it, which enables this bird to scoop up swarms of insects as it flies through the atmosphere. It can best be identified in flight by its long, pointed wings with a centered white wing patch, and by its repetitious *peent* calls.

In addition to the pine warblers that arrived early this month and will stay with us all summer, many warblers are spring migrants that merely pass through here on their way north. One of the earliest and most common of these is the YELLOW-RUMPED WARBLER, whose most conspicuous field mark is the bright yellow spot on its lower back just above the base of its tail. Like most warblers, these feed mainly on insects and are often seen flying out from branches to catch a flying insect before returning, almost flycatcher-like, to a nearby perch. The yellow-rumped is one of the few warblers that can also subsist for long periods of time upon seeds and berries, and one of the main parts of its diet during its migrations up and down our eastern coasts is bayberry. No doubt, those that migrate through the Pine Barrens make good use of Pinelands bayberries as well as the berries of red cedar, Virginia creeper, viburnums, poison ivy, and others. Almost every year, between April 20 and May 1, we have had four to six yellow-rumped warblers spend a few days in our back yard, using a dogwood tree and a couple of bathing pools as the center of their activities, alternately flying out after insects and bathing.

The BLACK AND WHITE WARBLER also searches for insects, but it does so by creeping up and down and around the sides of tree trunks and branches, sometimes even in an upside down position, somewhat like a nuthatch. This is one of our summer residents, and its black and white colors are in broken stripes that run from head to tail, so it is easy to identify. This warbler has little music in its songs—a rather plain repetition of two notes on the scale, the first higher than the second, repeated three or four times, as *zee-zee, zee-zee, zee-zee.*

Another warbler that is a summer resident in the Pine Barrens, but does not have the word warbler as a part of its name, is the very secretive OVENBIRD, which, like the towhee, is much more often heard than seen. Shortly after the arrival of the towhees and the brown thrashers, around the middle to the end of April, the ovenbird joins its noisy woodland neighbors with its loud, two-syllabled song that roughly translates into *tea-cher, tea-cher, tea-cher, tea-cher,* each repeat a little louder than the previous. The ovenbird, which looks like a small, olive-brown thrush, is quite unwarbler-like in its habits. This is a ground dwelling bird that much prefers dense undergrowths and thickets, and walks over leaves on the forest floor, bobbing its tail during frequent pauses, as it searches for insects and other food among the dead leaves. It gets its name from the shape of its nest, which it builds on the ground and covers with a little roof of dead grasses and leaves in the shape of a tiny mound, or a small oven, with a hole on one side for an entrance.

Finally, in late April, we should begin to listen for the PRAIRIE WARBLER to sing its wiry, ascending notes from the tops of taller scrub pines and oaks. Seldom has a bird been more incorrectly named, for instead of inhabiting grassy plains and prairies, the prairie warbler much prefers dry, sandy, burned-over lands overgrown with bushes, shrub oaks, and pitch pines. Even though the Pine Barrens is no "prairie," it is a favored habitat for this beautiful warbler with black stripes confined to the sides of its yellow breast, and a *zee, zee, zee* song that rises in pitch like going up a chromatic scale. The prairie and the pine warblers and the ovenbird are the most characteristic Pinelands warblers and all three will remain here all summer long.

This spring migration of birds will continue well into May, and among the birds whose arrivals are most eagerly anticipated by birders are the warblers. Of the approximately one dozen warblers to be found in various Pine Barrens habitats, we've already mentioned the pine, prairie, and black and white warblers, and the ovenbird. Others we will look for in May will be the yellow warbler and the yellowthroat, the prothonotary and the parula warblers, and the redstart, all of which should stay in Pine Barrens habitats throughout the summer. Because the Pine Barrens is not noted for the richness of its avifauna, the number of good birding areas is rather limited. Probably, in general, the best areas are in state forests and parks, mainly Lebanon, Wharton, Double Trouble, and Bass River, along with several state-owned and operated wildlife management areas. For more specific information on which birds to be found where and for directions, one should consult Boyle's *Guide to Bird Finding in New Jersey.*

17

Gypsies and Mosquito-Hawks

B ack in March, the mourning cloak, the question mark, and the spring azure butterflies proclaimed the arrival of spring. Now, in April, other insects, and arthropods like spiders, become increasingly active as our spring days become longer and warmer. In recent years, beginning around the middle of April, an insect scourge that has caused considerable damage to oak trees has blanketed various parts of the Pine Barrens. This is due to the spread of the GYPSY MOTH, *Lymantria dispar*, a native European species that escaped from a research laboratory in Medford, Massachusetts in 1868. Since then, gypsy moths have spread to vast areas of our northeastern forests. The tiny larvae (caterpillars) of the gypsy moths begin to emerge from their egg masses at about the same time the oaks come into leaf. These caterpillars, somewhat reddish with blue dots, feed on the leaves of a wide variety of broad-leaved trees, which means, in the Pine Barrens, mainly on oaks. They usually feed at night and then crawl down the trunks of the trees in the morning to hide in ground litter during the day. Their feeding can be extremely destructive to the foliage of the trees and sometimes many acres of oak forests are completely defoliated as a result of their voracious feeding, causing some weak and diseased trees to die.

By mid-June, through a series of growth stages known as instars, the caterpillars have grown to their full size of about two inches and each is capable of consuming several leaves a night. They then find hiding places on trunks and branches of trees and shrubs and any other protected places. Next, they proceed to transform into reddish-brown pupae, wrapped in very flimsy, dark brownish cocoons, attached to their hiding places with strands of a very coarse silk. Adult moths emerge about two weeks later, from late June into early July, and males immediately seek out females for mating. The small, brownish males fly during the daytime and, in areas of heavy infestation, the erratic flights of numbers of these are quite conspicuous. Females, which have creamy-white wings with wavy black bands, are larger and heavier, so heavy with eggs they are unable to fly. The best they can do is crawl up the base of a tree trunk or other object, release a scent (pheromone) and wait for a male to fly to her and mate with her. She doesn't have long to wait! Each female then proceeds to lay from four to six hundred eggs in a cluster which she covers with a pale, tan, felt-like material (hairs) she takes from her own body. The females then die and the eggs overwinter until they hatch next April.

Over the years there has been much controversy concerning the best methods to control this destructive insect. The basic problem stems from the fact that it was introduced from the Old World where it has existed for generations, but where enough natural controls such as predators, parasites, and viruses had developed to keep the numbers of gypsy moths at an acceptable level—the natural balance of nature! When it was accidentally introduced into the New World, none of those natural controls were here to keep it in check. The result was a population explosion of gypsy moths.

Early control efforts relied on the use of chemical pesticides. Back in the 1920s and '30s, arsenate of lead was used, but this gave way in the 1940s to DDT with what we now know to have been the devastating side effects so ably brought to the public's attention by Rachael Carson in her *Silent Spring*, much to the consternation of the chemical industry. Next came Sevin, but it had widespread lethal effects on beneficial insects such as bees, as did its replacement, Dimilin. The fact is none of those chemical pesticides were safe, so scientists began turning to more natural controls. One result was BT, a bacterium that infects and kills leaf-eating caterpillars, but BT kills *all* leaf-eating caterpillars, thus killing beneficial insects as well as harmful ones. This created a serious break in the natural food chain by depriving natural predators and others of much needed nutrients. Finally scientists, particularly entomologists, turned to introducing some of the long established, natural predator and parasitic controls from the Old World. This program, conducted by the Beneficial Insects Introduction and Research Service of the United States Department of Agriculture, is working and is ongoing, but the numbers of these beneficial introductions have not yet reached sufficient strength to completely control the gypsy moth.

What is now known, for sure, is that chemical pesticides, alone, are not the answer and, in fact, do more ecological harm than any success they may have in controlling the gypsy moth. Long range controls may have to be a combination of chemical and biological methods in programs known as integrated pest management, but there is no question that wherever and whenever possible, the very best method of control is natural biological control effected by natural predatory and parasitic insect enemies, and by viruses of the gypsy moth. Throughout the Pinelands, there are at least two such beneficial insects. One is an extremely tiny black wasp that parasitizes the eggs of the gypsy moth. Another is a beautiful, iridescent green, predatory beetle that climbs trees to feed on caterpillars, including those of the gypsy moth. Both are beneficial insects that have been introduced from other areas of the world for the express purpose of trying to control the gypsy moth.

This is not the place to go into the pros and cons of control methods, but this writer believes the best control for individual home owners is the hand picking and destroying of all reachable egg masses as soon as possible after they are laid, even though, obviously, this method is not practical in large, forested areas. One other factor needs to be better understood. Gypsy moth populations, as many other insect populations, tend to be cyclic. This means these populations increase from year to year and build on themselves. Then, suddenly, some natural catastrophe such as a virus will appear and drastically reduce these populations to such low levels they are no longer a destructive force. In summary, the more beneficial parasites, predators, and viruses that can be established as biological controls, the better natural balance will be established, which will result in decreased reliance on chemical pesticides.

Toward the end of April we should begin to see some of the first DRAGONFLIES and DAMSELFLIES of the new season. These are daytime flying insects that inhabit pond and stream edges, swamps, meadows, and other damp places. Of the two, dragonflies are larger, more robust, fly higher and faster, and hold their wings out in a horizontal position from their bodies when at rest. Damselflies are smaller, more fragile, do not fly as strongly, and most species hold their wings upward and back-ward over their abdomens when resting.

Both of these are amphibious insects. Adult dragonflies and dam-selflies lay their eggs in water, and the immature forms (larvae) that hatch from these eggs crawl around in the aquatic vegetation and muck along the bottom of ponds and slow moving streams. Both are entirely aquat-ic, using gills for respiration to obtain their oxygen from the water. At first glance, immature dragonflies look like large, six-legged spiders, but close observation will show these have small wing pads on their backs where their future wings are beginning to develop. On the front and underside of their head, they have a unique lower lip in the form of a mask-like scoop that covers the insect's mouthparts. This lip is folded under and hinged, and can be extended outward well beyond the head to capture soft bodied prey such as small fish, tadpoles, or other insects, and bring this food back and hold it in position up against its mouthparts until it is completely consumed. Mosquito wrigglers (larvae) provide a large per-centage of the food of some immature dragonflies and damselflies.

Following their immature stages, both dragonflies and damselflies emerge from their larval skins, which they leave behind, empty, and transform into winged, air-breathing adults. Dragonflies then begin to fly boldly and aggressively over ponds and streams from mid-spring to early fall, while damselflies tend to hover around the grasses along the edges of ponds and streams. Adult dragonflies have very keen eyesight, each compound eye being made up of thousands of individual lenses. This allows them to capture mosquitoes and other small flying insects while holding their legs together like a basket to catch their prey while in flight. While they use their legs for this and for perching, neither dragonflies nor damselflies have the ability to use their legs for walking.

One of the earliest dragonflies to appear in the spring is the GREEN DARNER, *Anax junius*, which has a bright green body (thorax) and a deep azure blue abdomen, with a wingspan of up to four inches. Two others are the COMMON WHITETAIL SKIMMER, *Libellula lydia*, and the TEN-SPOTTED SKIMMER, *Libellula pulchella*. Both have one to three dark spots on their wings, and fully mature males have an obvious gray-ish-blue or whitish bloom on their abdomens. Among the more com-mon damselflies are several small, bright blue BLUETS *Enallagma* sp., rather feeble flyers which often alight on grasses and other vegetation along the edges of ponds and slow moving streams. Another is the EBONY JEWELWING, *Calopteryx maculata*, which has black, almost opaque, wings on a deep, iridescent, metallic green body, and is most frequently seen flitting about vegetation along the edges of shady, woodland streams. Both dragonflies and damselflies are predators in both their immature and adult stages, and both do a tremendous amount of good in ridding our marshy areas of mosquitoes and other troublesome flies. Both should be regarded as very beneficial insects. Dragonflies are known variously as devil's darning needles, snake doctors, horse stingers, mosquito-hawks, and snake feeders but, in spite of these dangerous sounding names, they neither bite nor sting and are completely harmless to human beings. Dragonflies are among the most ancient of insects and, in times past, were huge creatures compared to today's specimens. The largest dragonfly known, which lived about 250 million years ago and is known only from fossil specimens, had a wing span of two and one-half feet!

18

Shrubs,
Blueberries, and Bees

A few more early flowering Pine Barrens plants usually come into bloom during the last week or ten days of April. A number of these are considered to be either unique or characteristic, or maybe even endemic.

One of the most interesting of all Pine Barrens plants is IPECAC SPURGE, *Euphorbia ipecacuanhae*. This little herb (not a shrub), scarcely more than two to four inches high, is quite common on arid stretches of white sand and along sandy roadsides throughout the Pine Barrens. Its tiny, yellow blossoms begin to appear late in April, even before its foliage. Later, small clusters of slightly fleshy leaves develop, the leaves varying greatly in both size and color. Some leaves are narrow and blade-like, while others are broadly oval. Even more interesting is that the leaves on one plant will be quite green, while on another plant right beside it, all the leaves will be deep maroon. Occasionally, both red and green leaves will be found on the same plant. There seems to be no explanation for these extremes in the shape and color of the leaves of different plants as they grow side by side. This curious plant is a member of the spurge family and, as such, both its stems and leaves are filled with the milky juices so characteristic of spurges.

A very low growing, vine-like sub-shrub is BEARBERRY, *Arctostaphylos uva-ursi*, another member of the heath family. This trailing plant covers its white, sandy habitat with a thick carpet of shining. dark green, evergreen leaves. This is one of the most characteristic plants of the pine plains but it is also quite common along the edges of sandy trails and gravelly roadsides throughout the Pine Barrens. Its tiny, urn-shaped, pink-tipped, whitish, bell-like flowers appear late in April and are very attractive. Later, in August and September, these develop into bright red, berry-like fruits that persist overwinter. These bright red berries are presumably relished by bears, hence the name: *arcto* and *ursus*, Greek and Latin for bear; *staphylos*, Greek for a cluster (of berries), and *uva*, Latin for grape. Thus, we have bear-cluster, the grape of a bear. Bearberry is another northern plant brought down to this area by one of the glaciers.

SAND-MYRTLE, *Leiophyllum buxifolium*, may be one of the truly endemic plants of the Pine Barrens. McCormick, in 1970, listed sand myrtle as one of only two plant species that are known to occur only in the Pine Barrens of New Jersey. The other one is Pickering's morning-glory, which we'll look for in July. Sand myrtle is a low, spreading, evergreen shrub with scraggly stems and branches and with foliage similar to

Sand myrtle

English boxbush. This is another member of the heath family. When in bloom, the branches of this odd little bush are profusely covered with tiny, pinkish-white flowers with conspicuous purplish anthers, and the flowers seem to be particularly attractive to several species of insects, especially beetles and small butterflies.

Although BEACH PLUM, *Prunus maritima*, is a common to abundant shrub all along the coastal dunes and sands of the New Jersey seashore, it also occurs in scattered locations throughout the Pine Barrens. Whether barrens' beach plum shrubs are remnants from ancient times when the oceans covered all of southern New Jersey, including the Pine Barrens, or whether they moved up into the barrens following tidal streams, or whether these have been more recently introduced along former railroad rights of way can not be stated with certainty. Prior to flowering, look for very straggly, branching shrubs from two to four feet high with very rough, blackish bark. The small, five-petaled, white flowers, which burst open late in April, considerably ahead of the leaves, are very showy and sometimes are so densely clustered together that they almost conceal the dark, naked branches on which they are borne. Later, toward the end of August, these flowers will have developed into small, deep purple plums that can be picked and made into delicious jams and jellies. Beach plum, like the earlier shadbush, is another member of the rose and apple family.

Toward the end of April, two other members of this same rose family come into bloom. These are RED CHOKEBERRY, *Pyrus (Aronia) arbutifolia*, and BLACK CHOKEBERRY, *Pyrus (Aronia) melanocarpa*. Both of these are shrubs that grow from three to maybe as much as nine feet in height, although the black form usually ranges from two to only four feet. Both are most likely to be found in low, damp thickets along the edges of swamps and the banks of streams and small ponds, with the black form seeming to be the more common. The red form may begin to blossom a week or so earlier than the black form, so the two may be in bloom at the same time. Thus, in order to tell the difference between them, one should know that the leaves of the red form are woolly-hairy underneath while those of the black form are entirely smooth. Both bear terminal clusters of attractive white flowers with rounded petals that usually are tinged with magenta-pink.

The pruning that blueberry farmers did during the winter months will begin to produce results now, toward the end of April, when their bushes come into bloom. The white or slightly pinkish, bell-shaped, pendant blossoms of the native HIGHBUSH BLUEBERRY, *Vaccinium corymbosum*, make a beautiful sight when masses of them cover every branch of these bushes, whether planted in rows in cultivated blueberry fields or out in the wild in Pine Barrens swamps. The story of the development of the first cultivated blueberries in the world from native, Pine Barrens' stock will be related toward the end of June. For now, the present blossoming of these heath family shrubs is only part of the story. If the blossoms do not produce fruit, there will not be any blueberries to be picked and the commercial season will be a failure. For the season to be successful, cross pollination and resultant fertilization of the flowers must take place and there is only one way this can be accomplished—bees.

Of all the world's bees, the common, golden-brown, HONEY BEE, *Apis mellifera*, is best known, having been domesticated by man for thousands of years. These social insects are probably the most important, single, insect pollinators of fruit and vegetable crops around the world. In addition, these bees produce honey in such quantities from the nectar they gather that man can take some of it without harming the health of the colonies.

These bees are extremely important factors in determining whether Pinelands blueberry and cranberry farmers have good crops. When blueberries come into blossom around the end of April, and cranberries by mid-June, Pine Barrens farmers employ professional beekeepers to bring in hives of bees and place them in strategic locations around their berry fields and bogs to pollinate and fertilize the blossoms. This assures that as many flowers as possible will develop into fruit. When you drive by blueberry fields from mid-April into early May, as you surely will if you are in the Hammonton or Weymouth areas in Atlantic County, or as you pass the many cranberry bogs visible from Route 563 south of Chatsworth in Burlington County during the latter half of June, you will see numbers of small, white (usually) boxes (bee hives) around the edges of the fields or bogs. Then you will know that the bees are doing their thing by visiting the flowers to gather nectar and, at the same time, as they fly from blossom to blossom, they will be cross-fertilizing the flowers so that they will develop into the fruits that will be harvested later in the year. Honey bee colonies, whether in man-made boxes or as smaller, escaped swarms in hollow trees or other shelters, do not die off over winter as most other social bee. wasp, and hornet colonies do, but, instead, maintain themselves on a year round basis, sharing body heat and living on stored honey throughout the winter months.

In addition to the work of the domestic honey bees, wild BUMBLE BEES, *Bombus* sp., are also very important pollinators of both blueberries and huckleberries. The late Phil Marucci, when he was entomologist at the Rutgers Blueberry and Cranberry Research Station on Penn Place Road, south of Chatsworth, used to say that bumble bees were almost as important pollinators of blueberries as were the domestic honey bees. Bumble bees are large, robust, hairy, black and yellow bees that also feed on nectar and the pollen of flowers. Bumble bees nest in small colonies in the ground, often using old, deserted mouse or bird nests. When winter arrives, all workers in bumble bee colonies die and only the newly mated queens survive over winter to start new colonies the following spring. Bumble bees are not to be confused with those very large, all-black bees with bare, shiny abdomens that fly about and seem to hang around old wooden structures. Those are carpenter bees, which we'll learn about in June.

The adage "April showers bring May flowers" may or may not have come true this year, or last year, but in general this is a month in which we hope for somewhat heavier rainfall, but no snowfall. Now and then, however, strange things happen and a light blanket of wet snow may cover the ground in the early morning, as it did on April 23rd, 1986, to remind us that winter has barely passed and may be trying to hang on as long as possible. Also, from now on we should not have any more freezing weather or frosts that might damage this coming summer's blueberry and cranberry crops but, as we will see next month, even these may still occur.

19

May

Spring Wildflowers

During the "merry month of May" natural events in the Pine Barrens will develop so rapidly, so many plants will blossom in such quick succession, and so many more new birds will arrive from the south, that it will be almost impossible to keep up with the rapid succession.

For many people, especially those who keep track of when nature's annual events occur from year to year, there is no more tangible evidence of spring than the appearance of the first wildflowers, those herbaceous plants that must first push their way up out of the ground before they can explode in symphonies of color. It is all well and good to note the first shrubs to blossom and the first birds to arrive, but there is nothing quite like seeing the first green leaf buds of spring wildflowers begin to break through the carpet of brown leaves and dead pine needles on the forest floor. Here is proof positive that spring has fully arrived.

In the Pine Barrens, this development usually begins around the middle of April and by the first of May the woodland wildflower display is nearly at its peak. This won't last long, however, for in another couple of short weeks, by mid-May, the herbaceous flowering season in woodlands and swamps will be largely past. Once the oaks, the dominant broad-leaved trees in the Pine Barrens, along with sassafras, tupelo or sour gum, swamp maple, and sweet bay, finally leaf out fully, the resulting canopy will shut out the sunlight that is essential for the growth and development of small, ground-level, flowering plants. Their beauty enriched the environment while the sun was able to get down to them through bare and leafless trees and while early insects were able to find and pollinate them. But when the trees begin to shade all understory and ground-cover plants and the sun can no longer reach them, plants such as pyxie, trailing arbutus, swamp pink, and lady's slipper will no longer blossom but will simply maintain themselves until another year. Most of the flowering plants that will come into bloom during the remainder of the spring, summer, and fall seasons will be those that can obtain their needed sunlight in areas along the edges of woods and in more open areas such as fields, meadows, savannas, marshes, and open bogs.

As early as the first of May, one of the most beautiful, yet fairly common, spring wildflowers to be found in Pine Barrens woodlands begins to bloom. This is the lovely orchid, the PINK LADY'S-SLIPPER, *Cypripedium acaule*. This has several common names such as moccasin flower, or whip-poor-will's shoe as some old-time natives still call it because it blossoms shortly after the whip-poor-wills arrive from the south and begin to call. Sometimes it is called the stemless lady's-slipper because its flower stalk and two opposite leaves arise together from its underground stem.

Although the blossoms of this exquisite flower are usually pink in color, a few almost pure white blossoms can sometimes be found. The "slippers" of this orchid are the longest worn by any member of this popular group of lady's-slippers. It is through the narrow slit in this slipper that bees and other insect pollinators must force their way inside the baglike slipper in order to obtain nectar and pollinate the flower. Lady's-slippers get their Latin name from the Greek *cypris* for Venus and *pedilon* for buskin or shoe, thus Venus' shoe!

Another attractive wildflower that begins to bloom very early in May is FROSTWEED, *Helianthemum canadense*. The yellow flowers of this small, one- to two-foot plant are so bright that they can not help but call attention to the plant. The first blossoms to appear are large, one to one and one-half inches across, with five wedge-shaped petals. These early blossoms are showy and usually solitary, or paired, but they open only in sunlight and each lasts for only one day. Thoreau referred to these flowers as "a broad, cup-like flower, one of the most delicate yellow flowers, with large, spring-yellow petals." Later in the season, side branches of this plant grow longer and produce small flowers without petals, the flowers clustered at the bases of the leaves. Frostweed gets its name from the fact that ice crystals sometimes form around the cracked bark of the lower stem and root of this plant in late autumn.

As you may wander off almost any Pine Barrens trail, practically anywhere in the Pinelands but perhaps more commonly in moist thickets, you are nearly certain to run into a prickly tangle of vines that make it difficult to continue. Undoubtedly, this is one of five species of greenbriar, the most likely being COMMON GREENBRIAR, *Smilax rotundifolia*. If you run into some of these vines at this particular time of year, early in May, try to take your mind off the problems of fighting the greenbriar long enough to look over the vines for clusters of small, inconspicuous yellowish-green flowers on stems that arise from the leaf axils. By mid-autumn, these flowers will have developed into small clusters of fleshy, blue-black berries that contain six small, hard seeds. One would think these would make good food for birds and other wildlife, but this seems not to be the case for large numbers of these berries, which persist on the vines long after the leaves have fallen, remain on the vines, uneaten, through most of the winter months.

Running into a tangle of greenbriar is far from being one of the more pleasant experiences in the Pine Barrens, for one has to constantly move these vines aside in order to get through, being careful all the while to avoid getting one's flesh torn from the stout thorns which grow all up and down the strong, twisting vines. In places, greenbriar grows in such thick tangles that it is simply impenetrable. In short, from a human point of view, this is a very invasive pest. Yet, it does have value in that its thick tangles provide wonderful abodes and hiding places for several small mammals such as cottontails as well as nesting sites for birds.

During March and April we found several members of a group of Pinelands shrubs in the heath family. These were trailing arbutus, leatherleaf, bearberry, sand-myrtle, and highbush blueberry. Now we are about to look for three more heaths: black huckleberry, stagger-bush, and fetterbush. BLACK HUCKLEBERRY, *Gaylussacia baccata*, is undoubtedly the most abundant, most widespread, and most characteristic heath-type shrub in the Pine Barrens. In fact, it is so common it may even be considered to be ubiquitous, often covering vast areas of both upland and lowland woodlands with its one- to three-foot shrubbery. When in flower early in May, black huckleberry can easily be recognized by its brick-red and yellow, pendant, bell-shaped blossoms, similar in size and shape to those of highbush blueberry. The berry-like fruits that develop later are black. When black huckleberry has neither flowers nor fruits to help identify it, look on the undersides of the leaves for tiny, orange resinous dots, which are best seen with a small pocket or hand lens, for these dots are a good field mark for all members of the huckleberry genus.

Closely related to black huckleberry and blossoming at just about the same time is another heath, STAGGERBUSH, *Lyonia mariana*. This shrub ranges perhaps a foot higher than black huckleberry and has large, snow-white, waxy, bell- or urn-shaped blossoms borne in clusters on the sides of upright, leafless branches, the leaves developing later. This is a very common shrub throughout sandy, Pinelands areas and its dense, white masses of blooms are one of the very attractive features of the Pine Barrens while these are in blossom. According to Witmer Stone back in 1910, "the flowers of this little shrub are the largest and handsomest of any of the urn-shaped blooms so frequent among the huckleberries and ericaceous shrubs." One major difference between staggerbush and blueberries and huckleberries is that, while the latter two produce edible fruits, staggerbush produces only seed-containing capsules without any enveloping pulp as fruit. The name staggerbush is said to have been given to this shrub because it was believed to be poisonous to cattle and sheep and caused these animals to stagger about; but sometimes, when one looks at a branch in full flower, one might imagine the name to come from the fact that the clusters of blooms seem to stagger from side to side as they rise higher on the branch.

A couple of weeks later, another closely related heath comes into bloom. This is FETTERBUSH, *Leucothoe racemosa*, a lowland shrub that grows to heights of two to five feet and is often found mixed in with highbush blueberry and sweet pepperbush. As mentioned earlier when talking about leatherleaf, because of its long, dense, one-sided flower clusters, this shrub also is often referred to as the false teeth bush. Like staggerbush, the bell-shaped flowers of fetterbush produce only dry seed containing capsules without any edible fruit.

Rising up from a thick, basal clump of stiff, grass-like leaves, a spike some two to four feet high bears a dense, foam-like head of beautiful white, six-petaled, star-like flowers. This is TURKEYBEARD, *Xerophylium asphodeloides*, one of the truly characteristic plants of the Pine Barrens. Frequently, clumps of turkeybeard are scattered among dense stands of black huckleberry and the tall, white, flowering heads of the turkeybeard provide an interesting contrast with the lower undergrowth of the

Turkeybeard

huckleberry. In addition to the beauty of its white flowers, this plant is interesting on two accounts. First, this is a southern plant that reaches its northern limit here in the Pine Barrens, having moved up north along the Appalachian Mountains. Second, it is a member of a genus that has only one other species in the United States. If you have ever traveled out west

95

to visit Glacier National Park, you may have seen its near look-alike relative, known there as beargrass.

Another characteristic Pine Barrens plant is GOLDEN or PINE-BARREN HEATHER, *Hudsonia ericoides*, a low shrub commonly found in open, white, sandy, Pine Barrens areas, often in places where little else will grow except ground-level lichens. During blooming season, from about the third week in May into early June, great patches of this small shrub present a massive carpet of bright, golden bloom. Although called heather, the name is misleading for this shrub is not a true heather, like

Golden heather

the heather of Scotland. Thus, this is sometimes called false heather or, more commonly, just hudsonia from its generic name. Hudsonia seldom grows over six to twelve inches high and its foliage is greenish and somewhat bristly. There also is another heather found in a few scattered sites in the Pinelands, sometimes growing side by side with the golden form. This is BEACH or WOOLLY HEATHER, *Hudsonia tomentosa*, which, as its name implies, is far more common on sand dunes along the seashore. One has to wonder about the presence of this basically seashore species, along with the earlier beach plum, in the Pine Barrens. Beach heather is very similar to pine-barren heather except that the leaves of the beach species are scale-like, soft-woolly, and grayish-green. The two species blossom at almost the same time, both with nearly identical yellow flowers. The main differences between the two are in the leaves. Although both of these hudsonias are northern species brought down to the Pinelands by some of the Ice Age glaciers, they did not get their generic name from Hudson's Bay as a possible site of origin, as one might suspect, but from an early English botanist, William Hudson.

20

Warblers, Flycatchers, and a Heronry

Nowhere else in the animal kingdom has sound production become as highly perfected or as widely used as among the birds, and at no other time of the year are bird songs so forcefully brought to our attention as during their annual spring courtship and breeding seasons. Beginning in March and April, when the first red-winged blackbirds arrived from the south, and increasing in volume and intensity ever since, the first light of dawn each day signals an eruption of calls and melodious songs from the throats of birds that is unrivaled in nature.

There is little doubt that the calls and songs of birds have developed as a means of communication, as a declaration of territoriality, and as a way of bringing the sexes together. This is best developed in males and, with few exceptions, is largely confined to them. It is also largely restricted to the establishment of territories by males and to the breeding and nesting seasons. Some birds, like the red-winged blackbirds and warblers, are singing their full songs just as soon as they arrive. Others, like the thrushes, seldom sing until their females arrive on the nesting grounds. Finally, shortly after the breeding season, certainly by the time the young have left the nest, most bird songs are sung much less frequently or have entirely ceased.

The learning and recognition of bird songs in the field is a valuable asset in good field birding. By recognizing and locating a bird's song by ear, one knows what kind of a bird to look for through binoculars and in which direction to look. There are numerous aids available at places like

New Jersey Audubon and other nature centers that can help one learn bird songs. Once you know a bird by both sightings and song, in future field trips the hearing of a bird's song may be sufficient to know what bird is present; but don't pass up opportunities to observe it, for only through constant observations can we continue to learn and experience more about the plumage and habits of birds.

It is during the month of May that the vast majority of our spring and summer birds arrive. Some will be migrants that will simply be passing through as they fly on further north to nest. Many others will stay here all summer to nest and raise their young. Among these are close to a dozen species of warblers, the most colorful and diversified group of small woodland birds and ones having some of the most melodious and distinctive of all bird songs. In addition to the pine and prairie warblers that arrived earlier, another summer resident is the YELLOW WARBLER. This bright and lively bird is easily recognized for it is in shades of yellow all over with light, reddish streakings on its breast (male). No other warbler is so extensively yellow. It has a distinctive song that one should try to learn so as to more easily distinguish other warblers by comparison. Its song is a bright and cheerful, somewhat variable *tsee-tsee-tsee-tsee-ti-ti-wee*.

Another common summer warbler is the YELLOWTHROAT, which arrives from early to mid-May. This bird spends most of its time in low bushes and shrubs along the edges of streams, ponds, and other bodies of water and usually is another bird that is more frequently heard than seen. You may first be aware of a yellowthroat by simply hearing its vibrant, rolling song that sounds something like *witchity-witchity-witchity-witch* repeated over and over. Occasionally the bird may show itself on the upper branches of a low shrub and then it is a delight to observe. The male is more easily recognized because it has a bright yellow throat and breast, with a jet black facial mask bordered with light gray. The female lacks the black mask, but otherwise is similar although more subdued.

With New Jersey's reputation for abundant mosquitoes and with the great numbers of pestiferous gnats, deer flies, and the larger tabanid or horse flies, it is no wonder that insect eating and fly catching birds are common around the Pine Barrens. Some of these birds, for which insects are a main part of their diet, are the whip-poor-wills and nighthawks, the swifts, swallows, martins, many warblers, and the flycatchers. In this latter group are the phoebe, which we heard and saw in March, the eastern wood pewee, the least flycatcher, and two large flycatchers, the great crested flycatcher and the eastern kingbird. These two flycatchers are quite different from each other in their appearance, their calls, and their habitats.

The GREAT CRESTED FLYCATCHER is a bird of open, upland, pine and oak woodlands. It is a large bird, dark olive in color, with a distinctive crest, a grayish-white throat, a lemon-yellow underbelly, and a long, conspicuous, reddish-brown tail. As soon as it arrives from the south around the 10th of May, it calls attention to itself with its slightly discordant, loud *wheep, wheep* call repeated several times as it flies about in the high branches just below the canopy. Like the phoebe and other flycatchers, it will perch on the end of a dead branch and then fly out from it, snap up a passing insect, and return to its perch. One of the more interesting actions of this bird is its habit of finding a castoff snake's skin and carrying it into its nesting site in an old decayed tree cavity.

EASTERN KINGBIRDS arrive around the same time as the great crested flycatchers, but are much more likely to be found near water. Almost every body of water in the pines such as small ponds, and reservoirs for cranberry bogs, will have one or more pairs of kingbirds nesting in its vicinity. Kingbirds are dark gray to black with a slight crest, are almost pure white underneath, and have a conspicuous white band at the tip of the tail. In common with other flycatchers, a kingbird also will perch on dead limbs and other vantage points, fly out to catch passing insects, and then return to its perch to await its next opportunity for food. Kingbirds are apt to be on the aggressive side, and they will constantly chase off other birds that might be a threat to their domain. They are particularly fearless in attacking crows and hawks, and often are observed driving these away from their nest sites. Both kingbirds and great crested flycatchers, along with all other members of this large family of flycatching birds, consume great quantities of insects. Studies of stomach contents have shown that approximately eighty-five percent of the food of these birds consists of insects.

Two more large insect eating birds in the Pine Barrens that arrive from the south around the middle of May are the YELLOW-BILLED and the BLACK-BILLED CUCKOOS. While most of the yellow-billed cuckoos remain here as summer residents, many of the black-billed cuckoos continue to migrate further north into New England and New York state. Cuckoos are rather sinuous appearing birds with brown backs, plain white breasts, and long tails. The yellow-billed cuckoo can be most readily identified by the large white spots on the underside of its tail and by the lower yellow mandible of its slightly curved bill. Both cuckoos are rather quiet, secretive woodland birds that fly stealthfully about in the upper branches of tall trees and seem to slip in and out of trees like ghosts. In fact, cuckoos would rarely be seen were it not for their rather loud, unhurried notes that seem like a series of slow gutteral *ku-ku-ku's* or *kowlp, kowlp, kowlp's*. Both cuckoos are particularly fond of caterpillars, especially hairy ones, and consume these as a major part of their diet. Records indicate that hairy tent caterpillars and fall webworms are preferred prey plus, now, since their introduction, the hairy caterpillars of gypsy moths. Examinations of stomach contents have revealed that caterpillars of various species, particularly hairy ones, constitute forty-eight percent of their diet. So, clearly, these are very valuable members of the Pinelands avifauna.

Early in the morning one day toward the end of May, alongside the Red Lion-Eayrestown Road, just north of the Red Lion Circle, Southampton Township, Burlington County, four GREAT BLUE HERONS were spotted flying north in a rather loose formation. They were flying low, not very far above tree level, on a course that almost paralleled the road, so they were within view for quite some distance. Of course there is no absolute knowledge of where these began their early morning flight, but it is a reasonable assumption that they had just left their Bear Swamp rookery because that site, along Route 206 just south of the Red Lion Circle, is a well known nesting location. Earlier in the spring, around the end of March, considerably before the foliage of the trees had closed them off from sight, a careful count had revealed twenty stacks of sticks and twigs that serve as nest sites for great blue herons. At the time of this count, there were at least twenty-four herons standing or sitting on the tops of their nests or flying about the area. Some herons were still building or at least improving their nests, for one flew in carrying quite a beakful of nesting material. A subsequent count in April, 1997 totaled twenty-four nest sites indicating that, currently, the size of the rookery appears to be stable.

Great blue herons are our largest wading birds. It is their habit to start out early in the morning to forage in ponds, lakes, marshes, and open swamps during the day for their food such as fish, tadpoles, frogs, and other small forms of animal life. In late afternoons and evenings the herons return to their colonial nesting rookeries and remain on their nests all night. Because of its large size, a great blue heron may frequently be seen in a Pinelands pond or other suitable habitat quietly standing in water, waiting for an unsuspecting prey to come within reach of its sharp, spear-like bill. Usually, only one heron will be seen at any one site because these herons tend to be rather solitary while they are foraging for food. It is only at night and during the nesting season that they colonize.

Bear Swamp, on the border between Southampton and Tabernacle Townships, Burlington County, has always been, and still is, a great natural area. Tales about the Red Lion Inn in Carlton Beck's *Forgotten Towns of Southern New Jersey* tell of hunting bear and mountain lions in Bear Swamp, but when you read those stories, allow a little for literary license. It is a fact, though, that today Bear Swamp is an excellent place to observe spring warblers and other migrants. Over recent years, several parcels in the Bear Swamp area, north of Hawkin Road, have been acquired by the Natural Lands Trust of New Jersey for protection and preservation, and efforts are continuing to increase this acreage. It is hoped that, ultimately, the entire Bear Swamp area, including the site of this great blue heron rookery, will be completely and permanently protected and preserved as a natural area for all time to come.

21

The Big Spring Hatch

As we already know, plants are the basic source of food: all other forms of life, both wildlife and human, are, in one way or another, dependent upon them. Just as soon as plants begin to put forth their new green buds in the spring, and these unfold and expand into leaves and reproductive flowers, hordes of immature insects emerge to feed upon them. Many of these insects began their life cycles last summer or fall as eggs laid by adult moths. Now, as these eggs hatch and millions of tiny caterpillars (larvae) emerge to begin their rapid growth, they feed on the tender green leaves and other vegetative parts that plants produce. As they devour the leaves of various plants, they will move from plant to plant in their continuing search for food, for it is only during their larval stages (instars) that insects grow. They grow at no other time in their life cycles. As these hungry larvae move from leaf to leaf and tree to tree, many of them spin a silken thread, drop down to suspend themselves in the air, and let the breezes blow them to a new limb or tree in a process called ballooning. Haven't you ever seen a caterpillar hanging by a thread, swaying in the breeze? Haven't you ever run into one and brushed it away from your face while walking through the woods? This is their way of finding new food and spreading the population. As caterpillars continue to grow and get bigger and fatter, they feed so voraciously and the food they consume passes through their digestive systems so rapidly, that you can sometimes hear the frass (excreted droppings) they produce drop like rain onto the forest floor from the leaves above.

One of the most conspicuous examples of the damage that growing caterpillars can do may be seen soon after the beginning of May almost everywhere throughout the Pinelands. These are the large, whitish, and unsightly clusters of webbing that begin to appear on cherry and some other trees along roadsides and in and around former and existing old village areas. These are being made by and will become the colonial nesting sites of a pest insect, the EASTERN TENT CATERPILLAR, *Malacosoma americana*, the larval stage of a small moth. Sometime during the previous midsummer, female moths laid clusters of two to three hundred eggs in bands or belts around twigs and coated the eggs with a varnish-like covering to protect them against rain and overwinter weathering. Members of the rose family, especially cherry and apple trees, are prime host plants on which adult moths lay their eggs. Then, when the eggs hatch the next spring, about the same time these trees are beginning to produce their new, tender leaves, the tiny young caterpillars will have their favorite foods on which to feed. As these caterpillars begin to grow, they spin webbing in the crotches of the trees and start to build a protective tent-like enclosure around themselves for their nighttime resting. During the daytime, these caterpillars leave their tents and spread out over the branches of their host trees to feed on the foliage. In time, they will completely strip the trees of all vegetation. Usually, many caterpillars will share the same tent and a close look at one of these will reveal considerable frass produced by the caterpillars during the many overnights they spend inside. Finally, when those caterpillars that escaped predation by the cuckoos and others become mature, they will leave their tents, spin cocoons for themselves, and pupate until they emerge as new adult moths to repeat the process. Meanwhile, their empty tents remain in the trees through the rest of the summer as unsightly reminders of their past activity. It is interesting to note that tent caterpillars are far more common in disturbed areas than in still relatively undisturbed, natural areas—a price we apparently must pay as a result of intrusions into the Pine Barrens by human civilization.

Fortunately, not all young caterpillars make it to adulthood. If they did, we, as humans, would be overwhelmed by the zillions and zillions of insects. The timing could not be more perfect. Just as these caterpillars develop through their various larval stages, thousands of them are taken by predators for food and thousands more are fed to hungry fledglings. Some fledglings, however, seem not to always appreciate these morsels, especially if they are the hairy caterpillars of the gypsy moth. Doris once watched one young robin spit out a gypsy moth caterpillar several times before its parent finally stuffed it down its throat. It is the abundance of food that these caterpillars provide that is one of the principal reasons why birds migrate to nest and raise their young. The timing and sequence of nature's annual events are truly impressive. When we take the time to stop and think about it, isn't the natural world wonderfully balanced with producers and consumers, with predators and parasites, and with ecological checks and counter-checks?

Just as we are fortunate that all immature insects don't make it to adulthood, we also are fortunate that some do make it through the gauntlet to escape their predators and parasites and become adults, for some of these provide us with great beauty. Beginning in late April, but mainly throughout May, we may see any of three beautiful swallowtail butterflies flying about in the Pine Barrens. These are our largest butterflies and can be readily identified by their large size and by an elongated tail-like projection from each of their hind wings. The largest of these is the TIGER SWALLOWTAIL, *Papilio glaucus*, which is bright yellow with black, tiger-like stripes. Perhaps the most common of the three is the SPICEBUSH SWALLOWTAIL, *Papilio troilus*, because its larvae also feed on sassafras, which is quite common throughout the Pine Barrens. This can be identified by its blue-green or bluish-iridescent hind wings. At times, it may be difficult to distinguish this from the BLACK SWALLOWTAIL, *Papilio polyxenes*, but this latter butterfly has a conspicuous row of bright yellow dots near the borders of its wings, contrasting sharply with its otherwise black wings.

Two other butterflies commonly seen in the Pine Barrens from late May on are the red-spotted purple and the buckeye. Seen with its wings held wide open in the sunlight, the upper surfaces of the front wings of the RED-SPOTTED PURPLE butterfly, *Limenitis arthemis astyanax*, are bluish-black with slightly reddish tips while the hind wings are bluish-green with the outer part somewhat iridescent. The undersides of its four wings have five basal red-orange spots and a row of reddish-orange spots just inside a blue-banded border. A likely reason why this butterfly is common in the Pine Barrens is that its larvae feed on the abundant black oaks and wild cherry, among other trees and shrubs.

The BUCKEYE butterfly, *Junonia coenia*, is very striking in appearance. On a basic ground color of browns, each of the front wings has a whitish, transverse band at the base of which is situated a very large eyespot. Each of the hind wings has a band of orange near the outer border and two large eyespots just inside the orange band. On the underside, the front wings are similar to the upper sides except they are duller, but the undersides of the hind wings do not have any large eyespots. It is thought that

Red-spotted purple butterfly

the three large eyespots on the upper side of their wings give this butter-fly the appearance of an owl's head with great, staring eyes and that this may serve as a deterrent to scare away possible predators.

Because of their great abundance at this time of year, two insects have had the name of this month applied to their common names. These are mayflies and may beetles. To fishermen, nothing is more synonymous with the month of May than MAYFLIES. These are also sometimes called dayflies because of their very short, adult life span. Although mayflies are not abundant in the Pine Barrens, small numbers may be seen near any body of water. Immature mayflies spend their first few years living as gill-breathing naiads in the ooze and mud at the bottom of streams, ponds, and lakes. Then, from late April into early June, these immatures rise to the water surface in considerable numbers, molt, and change into air-breathing, winged forms known as sub-imagoes or duns and alight on low vegetation. During this time they are easy prey for predators because they are still encased in a thin, gray film that they shed over the course of a day to become glistening white, soft-bodied adults, or spinners, with transparent wings and two or three elongated tails. Mayflies are the only insects that molt after their wings become functional.

Toward evening, these new adults take flight in swarms of dancing mayflies during which mating takes place. Adult mayflies then live for only one or two more days, hence their scientific name, Ephemeroptera, for ephemeral, meaning temporal. The chief importance of both imma-ture and adult mayflies is as food for many freshwater fish and other predacious animals such as spiders, amphibians, and birds. Many of the artificial flies used by fishermen are modeled after adult mayflies.

The other insect that gets its name from this month of May is the MAY BEETLE, *Phyllophaga* sp., sometimes also called a JUNE BUG. May bee-tles are heavy, awkward, scarab beetles that, throughout most of the year, live in the ground as large, white, C-shaped grubs that feed on the roots of plants such as grasses, corn, and strawberries. After they emerge in the spring as adults, they come out after dusk to feed on the leaves of trees and shrubs. One of my earliest introductions to the Pine Barrens of New Jersey was in the spring of 1939 when I used to come over from Philadelphia at night with Mark Robinson to collect may beetles feeding on the blueberry bushes at Whitesbog. May beetles also are attracted to light; so most people are more likely to first notice these large beetles buzzing around porch lights and hitting against window screens.

The Pine Barrens of New Jersey has long been a favorite collecting area for entomologists, especially those from New York City and Philadelphia. In the late 1800s and early 1900s, entomologists from New York and Staten Island would take the old Southern Division trains of the Jersey Central down into the Pine Barrens and get off at stations such as Lakewood, Lakehurst, Whiting, Chatsworth, and Atsion, while

Philadelphia collectors would take shore-bound trains across southern New Jersey and get off at Clementon, Atco, Hammonton, and DaCosta, all to do a day's or a weekend's collecting in the Pine Barrens. In more recent times, and again reminiscing a bit, Mark Robinson and I used to stop at the home of Asa Pittman, also known as "Rattlesnake Ace," beside the former railroad tracks at Upton Station, between Mt. Misery and Whitesbog, to pick up night flying insects that Asa collected for us in his light trap. Few places in North America have been as extensively collected as the Pine Barrens of New Jersey!

The reason for all this collecting interest was the many unexpected yet characteristic species of insects that are found in the pines, some of which are endemic to the region. A few examples are: 1) a species of LEAF-CUT-TING ANT, *Trachymyrmex septentrionalis*, that reaches the northern limit of its distribution here in the Pine Barrens and is the most northern known species of the group of leaf-cutting and fungus-growing ants; 2) eight species of TABANID FLIES that also reach their northern limits here; 3) sixteen species of agile, fast-flying TIGER BEETLES, *Cicindela* sp., for which the hot, sunny sands of the Pine Barrens are a favored habitat; 4) several species of UNDERWING MOTHS, *Catocala* sp., whose forewings are colored like the bark of the trees on which they usually rest and which conceal their brightly colored hind wings; 5) the BUCK MOTH, *Hemileuca maia*, a daytime moth that flies during October and is most commonly observed in pine plains areas; and 6) several small hairstreak, elfin, copper, and duskywing butterflies and skippers.

Some of these small butterflies are so characteristic of Pine Barrens habitats that it was to find and photograph, but not collect, some of these that the North American Butterfly Association held a field trip in the Pine Barrens on May 6-8, 1994. Among the more prized finds were HESSEL'S HAIRSTREAK, *Mitoura hesseli*, found along the fringes of a white cedar swamp, and the OLIVE HAIRSTREAK, *Mitoura grynea*, found in a grove of red cedars. Both adult butterflies are very small, only one to one and a half inches in length, and are generally greenish with white marks on their undersides and tiny tails on their hind wings. In both cases, cedars serve as host food plants for the larvae of these two beautiful hairstreaks. Their future existence, therefore, is completely dependent upon these host trees. Hessel's hairstreak, in particular, is a species of special concern, for if cedar stands continue to be reduced as the result of overcutting or if cedar bogs are destroyed and those habitats lost, the survival of this species may become truly endangered and the natural diversity of these habitats further reduced.

22

Pines, Oaks, and Heaths

A
lthough the whole area we are exploring together is known as the Pine Barrens, or Pinelands, or even just the Pines, there actually are two major groups of trees that create the forest canopy and compete with each other for survival. These are the pines and the oaks, two vastly different kinds of trees. Pines are softwood, evergreen trees while oaks are hardwood, deciduous trees. Although pines are evergreen, this does not mean that their needles (leaves) are evergreen. Instead, needles of pines die and fall to the ground like leaves from other trees. The big difference is that only a few leaves fall off at the same time while the vast majority remain green on the trees, thus making the trees appear to be evergreen.

There are three different kinds of common, native pine trees in the Pine Barrens of New Jersey: pitch pines, Virginia or scrub pines, and short-leaf pines. Of these, PITCH PINE, *Pinus rigida*, is by far the most abundant and characteristic, and is the tree for which the Pine Barrens is most noted. This is a medium-sized, ragged, irregular tree with gnarled branches. Its dark, reddish-brown to dark brown bark is broken into thick, irregular plates which peal off in scales, and is so thick that it makes this tree very resistant to fires. The needles of pitch pines are dark olive-green, coarse, stiff, from two to five inches long, and are produced in bundles of three. Often, pitch pines have dense mats of needles growing from the sides of the trunk and main branches, a distinguishing characteristic, for no other native pines have this feature.

Pine Barrens OAKS, *Quercus* sp., shed all of their leaves in the fall of the year at essentially the same time and, with few exceptions, these trees

111

remain bare of leaves overwinter. There are two main groups of oaks in the Pinelands and when they are in leaf it is easy to identify one from the other. In one group, the white oaks, the leaves have rounded lobes without any bristles at the tips. The bark of these trees is usually light grayish in color and examples of these are white, post, and chestnut oaks. In the other group, the red or black oaks, the leaves usually are deeply cut in on the sides, thus creating sharply elongated lobes, but some, such as blackjack oak, have no lobes at all. However, in both cases the tip ends of the lobes or edges of the leaves have tiny, fine, pointed, almost hair-like bristles. The bark of these trees is usually dark grayish-brown and often is deeply furrowed. Examples of these oaks are black, red, scarlet, blackjack, and scrub or bear oaks.

Early in May, the male flowers on the terminal branches of the pitch and other pines will reach maturity and begin to shed their abundant supplies of pollen grains in order to fertilize the female flowers and reproduce their kind. As all this pollen is simply released into the atmosphere, much of it will fall on the ground in thin layers of bright, yellow dust and will lay on nearly everything, everywhere. To see for yourself, shake a pine branch at this time of year and watch the clouds of yellow pollen drift from the tree. When the pollen grains from the male flowers settle on the female flowers, thus fertilizing them, these develop into the pine cones which will contain the seeds for future pine trees. Meanwhile the male catkins, their task fulfilled, drop to the ground and shrivel up like spent pellets. Pines are ancient trees that existed long before insects appeared on this earth, so they had to develop their own way for their male pollen grains to reach the female receptors. Thus they developed a process of fertilization dependent upon wind. No members of the pine family depend upon insects for the completion of their life cycles.

At almost the same time, the many species of oaks go through a similar process. The long, drooping male catkins (flowers) of the oaks also shed their abundant supplies of pollen grains in order to fertilize their female flowers. Much of their pollen also falls upon the ground, adding to that of the pines. As soon as the female flowers of the oaks become fertilized, they start to develop into acorns and the male catkins shrivel up and drop to the ground.

Male flowers of pine

Oak catkins in flower

In addition to pines and oaks, there are several other important trees that do well in Pinelands habitats. We've already seen and talked about sassafras in upland habitats and about red or swamp maples and Atlantic white cedars in lowland areas. Another characteristic tree in lowland habitats is SWAMP MAGNOLIA or SWEET BAY, *Magnolia virginiana*. This is a small tree, usually not over ten to twenty-five feet in height, whose smooth, green leaves have a distinctive whitish bloom on the undersides. Unlike

Swamp magnolia

most other hardwood trees that shed their leaves each fall, the leaves of swamp magnolia, in our temperate zone, tend to remain on the trees during much of the winter, gradually dropping off by early spring. By late May and into early June, large, showy, creamy-white, cup-like flowers appear, and these give off such a pleasant fragrance that the atmosphere in Pine Barrens swamps may be heavy with their sweet perfume. After flowering, by late August, the resulting seeds turn bright red as they develop in cone-

115

like clusters, and then hang by slender threads until they finally drop. It is said that the leaves of sweet bay provide a nice flavor to roasts and gravy, and that a perfume is made from the very fragrant flowers. One of the best displays of swamp magnolia is found along the edges of the nature trail, especially along the return leg of that trail, at Double Trouble State Park in Berkeley and Lacey Townships, near Forked River, in Ocean County.

There is one other lowland tree that comes into bloom around the middle of May that we need to look for right now. This is BLACK or SOUR GUM, or TUPELO, *Nyssa sylvatica*, a characteristic tree of damp edges of streams, ponds, and swamps. Generally a smallish tree of fifteen to forty feet in height, its lustrous dark olive-green leaves are borne on branches that usually are horizontal or even drooping in position rather than upward. The small greenish flowers, males and females on different trees, occur in small clusters borne on long, slender stems, but they are not very showy. By fall, these will have developed into small, oval, fleshy, bluish-purple fruits borne on long stems, usually in pairs. The reason for calling attention to this tree now, at flowering time, in spite of its inconspicuous flowers, is to alert you to the fact that, come fall, this will be the first tree in the Pine Barrens to take on autumn colors in its foliage. We will talk more about this when we get nearer to that time.

Beginning around the third week in May, two very closely related shrubs come into bloom. These are mountain-laurel and sheep-laurel. Both of these are heaths with evergreen leaves and both have very beautiful flowers that are very similar in structure. The generic name for both of these laurels is in recognition of Peter Kalm, a German botanist and a student of Linnaeus. Kalm visited this country in the middle of the eighteenth century and spent considerable time exploring and botanizing in southern New Jersey.

MOUNTAIN-LAUREL, *Kalmia latifolia*, is a large, sturdy, bushy shrub from three to ten feet in height that often grows in thick clusters, sometimes even forming impenetrable thickets. Older mountain-laurels have irregular, thick, gnarled trunks with ruddy brown bark. Leaves are thick, leathery, smooth, and shiny dark green and have an interesting pattern of curling up very tightly whenever temperatures drop below freezing. Mountain-laurels should not be confused with the larger rhododendrons, which are not native Pine Barrens shrubs and grow in our area only when planted as the result of horticultural introductions.

Flowers of mountain-laurel develop in large, showy, dome-shaped clusters at the tips of branches, often so closely spaced that they touch. Not only are the individual pinkish-white flowers exquisite in color and design, but the male stamens are arranged in a very unique way. Each of them is bent over like a tiny spring and held down in a corner of the flower so that the flower looks something like the inside of an open umbrella showing its ribs. When a bee arrives to gather nectar, its weight releases the springs and they snap up and send a small shower of tiny pollen grains over the insect. Then when that bee visits its next flower, some of that pollen gets rubbed off onto the pistil, thus fertilizing the flower. One can observe this for one's self by touching a stamen of a fresh flower with a pin, then watching the stamen spring out and see the pollen fly off the anther.

Mountain-laurel is also known as CALICO-BUSH, a name that is of particular interest in the history of the Pine Barrens. Back in the early eighteen hundreds, from approximately 1808 to around 1834, there was a small foundry town inhabited by persons who worked at the nearby Martha furnace. This small town was named Calico, apparently because of the great profusion of mountain-laurel that grew and is still abundant in the area. Calico was located on the east side of the Oswego River, a short distance north of Martha, Egg Harbor Township, Burlington County, and is now a part of the Wharton State Forest.

SHEEP-LAUREL *Kalmia angustifolia*, is much smaller, from one to three feet high, and has thin, narrow, drooping, dull olive-green leaves that often are rust-spotted. Beautiful, deep crimson-pink flowers develop on the sides of the upright branches, below the new upright leaves of the season, rather than being terminal. Another common name for sheep-laurel is lambkill, because there is a back-country belief that the foliage of this plant is poisonous, especially to sheep, and this may be true. Sheep-laurel is very abundant in the Pine Barrens, often covering large areas, especially in low, moist ground.

Both of these laurels are additional members of the heath family to which we have previously made several references. Truly, as Witmer Stone wrote in 1910, "The pines seem to be the chosen land of the Ericaceae (heath family) which abound there both in species and individuals" and "by the end of June we may be sure of finding the greatest display of (mountain) laurel that can be found anywhere in the Middle States, even on the mountains themselves which are supposed to be its proper home."

Just as the pines and the oaks dominate the tree canopy of the Pine Barrens, the heaths dominate and are the most characteristic plants in the understory or shrub layers of Pine Barrens vegetation. This is because members of the heath family are able to do very well, better than many other families of plants, in the sandy, acid, nutrient-poor soils of the Pine Barrens. Chief among the heaths are huckleberries, blueberries, and cranberries. Black huckleberry, which we've already seen, is one of the most abundant and characteristic understory shrubs in the Pinelands, particularly in dry to moist thickets and woods. Blueberries and cranberries are both native, wild, Pine Barrens heaths and continue to thrive in the wild but, in addition, both are now cultivated in fields and bogs by Pinelands farmers. We keep referring to heaths at appropriate times throughout this book. In this journey that we are taking together through the Pine Barrens, we have already seen and talked about several other heaths such as trailing arbutus, leatherleaf, bearberry, sand-myrtle, staggerbush, and fetterbush, as well as the two laurels. We will be coming across two more as we continue our explorations in June.

23

Carnivorous Bog Plants

S ome of the both unique and characteristic plants to be found in Pine Barrens bogs are several species of carnivorous plants. Most of these use insects as their usual prey and supplementary source of food but, worldwide, some carnivorous plants supplement their insectivorous diets with small scorpions, amphibians, reptiles, and even small rodents. There is no record yet of any man-eating species!

There are three groups of these very interesting plants in the Pine Barrens: pitcher-plants (one species), sundews (three species), and bladderworts (seven species frequent to common, two or possibly three species quite rare). All are found in acid waters or in nutrient poor, boggy sands that lack the basic ingredients, especially nitrogen, needed for healthy plant growth. Even though all of these can grow and reproduce in their nutrient poor habitats just like other plants do, their ability to obtain nitrogen and other nutritious elements from the bodies of the insects they capture allows them to develop into healthier plants than they otherwise would.

The insect trapping structures used by all carnivorous plants are modified leaves that differ in structure and methods used in each of the three groups. The most easily observable of these methods is the slippery pitfall trap employed by pitcher-plants. Here, tubular or pitcher-shaped leaves, with broad lips at their upper edges, are open to the sky and so become at least partially filled with rain water. The lips of these leaves serve as landing platforms for insects lured by odors from scent glands inside the pitchers. When insects land on these lips and start to search out the source of the scent, they fall in. Because they can not climb back out against inward and downward slanting hairs on the leaf lips and because they can not fly straight up, they can not escape and soon drown. When their bodies decompose, their nutrients, now dissolved in water, are absorbed into the tissues of the plant.

The second method could be called the flypaper or adhesive trap system employed by the sundews. Here, glands secrete tiny beads of sticky liquid on the tips of fine leaf hairs to which small prey are attracted and then become stuck and die. After entrapment, as a part of the digestive process, there follows limited, slow, sticky gland and leaf-folding movement to completely enwrap the prey.

The third and most active method employed by any of the three groups of carnivorous plants may be called the trapdoor system employed by the bladderworts. These plants, which may be either aquatic or terrestrial, grow in quiet, shallow ponds, boggy waters, and the shallow edges of slowly moving waters. Or, they may grow in very damp, sandy, acid soils with the main parts of the plants at or below the water surface or ground level. In both cases, these plants have minute traps as a part of their subsurface leaf systems. Each tiny trap is somewhat bulbous, with a tiny entrance protected by some very sensitive trigger hairs at one end. Any small organism that touches these trigger hairs causes the opening to expand and the victim is sucked in through the entrance, after which the entrance closes and digestion begins. Here again, the plant absorbs into its tissues the nitrogen and other nutrients from the dead organism. In all three methods, digestion is achieved by means of digestive enzymes and acids secreted by the plants.

Because the carnivorous features of these plants are so fascinating, their attractive flowers are often overlooked. Among the three groups of carnivorous plants, the earliest and most conspicuous flowers are produced by the PITCHER-PLANTS, *Sarracenia purpurea*. Beginning as early as the third week in May, large, umbrella-shaped, nodding, reddish-purple blooms arise on one to two foot stems and then bend over to hang like bells above the basal cluster of pitcher-shaped leaves. The odor and raw-meat color of the flowers attract carrion flies that are especially equipped for the cross fertilization of these flowers. After flowering, parts of the flowers dry up but remain standing as brown, tubular seedpods which, locally in the Pine Barrens, are sometimes called "dumbwatches," because these seedpods are thought to resemble open watches without hands and, since there is no ticking sound, these are thought of as being mute or dumb.

Another interesting feature of pitcher-plants is that, in addition to trapping insects, these plants may actually serve as host plants for as many as sixteen species of insects and other creatures that may spend their entire life cycles in and around pitcher-plant leaves without themselves becoming trapped. One example is a harmless species of mosquito in the genus *Wyeomyia* that lays its eggs, and its larvae develop, in the water inside the pitcher-shaped leaves of this plant.

At almost the same time as pitcher-plants are in full bloom, the first three of several species of bladderworts found in the Pine Barrens will begin to blossom. Most of these are much smaller and less conspicuous than the pitcher-plants. In fact, one bladderwort is so small that one may have to get down on hands and knees and use a hand lens to see it well. The capability, as just described, of these plants to trap and digest minute forms of aquatic life is fascinating. Most Pine Barrens bladderworts have yellowish flowers, but there also are two lavender-flowered species. In form, the flowers of bladderworts are usually two-lipped and, superficially, may suggest snapdragon-like flowers.

Of the three early bladderworts that bloom in the Pine Barrens, the PIN-LIKE or ZIGZAG BLADDERWORT, *Utricularia subulata*, named for its extremely fine and slightly zigzaggy stem, is definitely the smallest. In fact, this may be the smallest species of terrestrial plant life to be found in the pines—even smaller than the more widely known curly-grass fern! The flowering stem of this plant rises only one to possibly eight inches and bears from one to seven tiny, bright yellow flowers, one at a time, each hardly larger than the head of a pin.

The other two early bladderworts are both aquatic and, where found, are conspicuous because of their bright yellow flowers that rise up above the surfaces of shallow ponds, edges of still waters, and ditches around cranberry bogs. One of these is FIBROUS BLADDERWORT, *Utricularia fibrosa*, whose four- to twelve-inch stalk may bear as many as seven small but bright, yellowish flowers. The other is SWOLLEN BLADDERWORT, *Utricularia inflata*. The striking characteristic of this plant is its flotation structure midway up the stem of the plant. This consists of from four to ten air-filled bladders, or arms, radiating out some six to ten inches on the surface of the water like the spokes of a rimless wheel. These arms are divided at the ends and often bear traps, and it is these floating arms that support the plant and the flowering stem. The flowering part of the stem is above water while the lower part supports the underwater, vegetative, trap bearing portion of the plant as well as the roots. The bright yellow flowers, which open at the top of the three- to seven-inch stalk, usually number from three to seven but may be as many as a dozen.

The rest of the bladderworts do not bloom until mid-June into early August, so we will defer talking about these until we discuss the sundews which blossom at that same time.

24

Late Spring Amphibians

Shortly after the beginning of May and continuing well into June, a new chorus of frogs is starting to be heard from Pine Barrens ponds, bogs, and wetlands. Two contributors to this new chorus are another treefrog and a toad. The treefrog is the PINE BARRENS TREEFROG, *Hyla andersoni,* one of the best known forms of animal life to be found in the Pinelands. This relatively rare and possibly endangered little treefrog is virtually restricted to cedar bogs in the New Jersey Pinelands and a few smaller colonies in the Carolinas and Georgia. Barely more than an inch and a quarter in length, its body is a light emerald green with a lavender stripe bordered with white along each side. These colors, together with its whitish underparts and yellowish-orange spots under its thighs, make this one of the world's most beautiful frogs.

Starting at twilight and continuing into the evening hours during breeding season, colonies of Pine Barrens treefrogs will chorus their loud, nasal, mating calls of *quonk, quonk, quonk* from the edges of cedar and sphagnum bogs. Because treefrogs, like the earlier spring peepers, have tiny adhesive discs on the tips of their toes, they can climb up on white cedar trees, blueberry bushes, and other shrubs where males expand their throat pouches and produce their deep *quonk, quonk* calls. On any warm evening during this period, put on a pair of waterproof boots and, with a good flashlight, go out to the edge of a cedar bog and listen for the barking chorus of these little treefrogs. When you hear one that seems to be close by, very quietly move up on the sound until you zero in on it. Then use your flashlight to watch one of these little fellows perform

123

its barking call as it tries to attract a mate. Up close, you will realize that the intensity and volume of the sound produced is way out of proportion to the size of this tiny creature. There can be few more thrilling experiences in one's life than to watch one of these little critters pump air from its lungs into its inflated vocal sac under its throat and call its nasal *quonk, quonk* in the early evening darkness. Once again, please don't try to pick one up in your hand for this is a very delicate creature that can easily be hurt, even by the most well-intentioned person.

Although currently an abundant resident of cedar bogs and swamps, the Pine Barrens treefrog is classified as endangered because its future is almost wholly dependent upon our preservation of its habitat. If cedar bogs should become drained or destroyed by human exploitation, this little animal could become extinct.

The calls of the other amphibian that can often be heard on the same warm evenings as the Pine Barrens treefrogs are distinctly different. This is the FOWLER'S TOAD, *Bufo woodhousei fowleri*. At the same time that the treefrogs are climbing cedars and blueberry bushes to call for mates, adult Fowler's toads remain in shallow water. From there, in their efforts to attract mates, they give voice to loud but short nasal sounds that have

Fowler's toad

been likened somewhat to the bleat of a sheep or to a baby crying "waah." Usually, calls of the Fowler's toads will sound more distant than those of treefrogs.

Toads are quite different from the several frogs we have seen so far. In general, frogs have smooth, moist skins. Adult toads have dry, rough, warty skins, are stocky, have short legs, hop rather than jump, and usually are found some distance from water. Fowler's toad is no exception. Adult Fowler's toads look very similar to the better known American toad, but the Fowler's is smaller. Both have a very pronounced white streak down the middle of their backs. Other than size, the best identifying difference between the two is that the Fowler's toad has three or more small warts in each of the dark spots on its back while the American toad has only one or two warts in these spots. After breeding season, these toads usually hide during the day in ground burrows or under some protective covering and emerge at night to catch moving insects with flicks of their long, sticky tongues. Their tongues are unique in that they are hitched at the front instead of the back of their mouths. If you should happen to find one out in the daytime and you pick it up and hold it in your hand, it may make a low grunting noise and you may feel a slight vibration.

25

Black Frosts

E ven late into the growing season, long after one would expect killing frosts, on rare occasions parts of the Pine Barrens may be hit with sudden, extreme drops in temperatures resulting in "black frosts." These are so unusual that, unless you have experienced or seen one, you may not have any idea what a black frost is. One of these occurred on the mornings of May 20 and 21, 1992. In many parts of the Pine Barrens in Atlantic, Burlington, Cumberland, and Ocean Counties, temperatures fell drastically, bringing a surprise frost to low-lying areas. Many blueberry fields and some cranberry bogs, mainly those that were not protected by sprinkler systems, suffered severe damage. Further, some peach orchards, many vegetable crops, and acres and acres of low woodlands were hard hit by the frosts. Farmers sustained substantial crop losses. The damage to some oak woodlands was just incredible. A drive along wooded roadsides revealed mile after mile of blackened and drooping foliage. The new, young leaves of the oaks, particularly the black and red oaks, were so black they looked like they had been hit by a major forest fire. It also was interesting that this blackness was most noticeable on shrubs and low trees and extended from the ground up to heights of only fifteen to twenty feet. Above that, the tops of the trees were frost free.

A full explanation of these black frosts is too technical for this book, so I offer only this simplified version. Both temperature and relative humidity are involved. On Tuesday, May 19 and Wednesday, May 20, afternoon temperatures reached around 80°F. Overnight to Wednesday and Thursday

mornings, temperatures had dropped by 5 a.m. to as low as 24°F in blueberry fields and even down to 13°F in some cranberry bogs. These were
drops of 56° and 67° in just eleven hours! A more significant factor was relative humidity, which reached a low of 5.9 percent on Tuesday at 4 p.m.
At the same time, the weather station in Atlantic City reported a dew point
of about 20°. Because of the extremely low relative humidity, dew points
(temperatures at which water vapors condense to form dew) were
extremely low. Thus dew will not form on vegetation. Instead, water
vapors will condense directly into ice. Normally, when dew points are
above 32°, dew forms on vegetation and then when temperatures drop to
freezing, characteristic white frosts develop as the dew turns to ice. On the
mornings of May 20 and 21, however, because dew points were so far
below 32°, no dew formed to become white frost. Instead, the vegetation
became frozen without the usual protection of ordinary white frost, resulting in what are known as black frosts.

Records maintained over many years by Phil Marucci at the Rutgers
University Blueberry and Cranberry Research Station show that the last
previous time a black frost occurred in New Jersey was thirty-six years
before, on the night of May 24, 1956. These records (as reported by Nick
Vorsa, present director of the Rutgers facility) also show that the 1992
black frost was at least 3° colder than in 1956.

In addition to the damage to vegetation caused by these black frosts,
there was at least one disturbing side effect. Because much of the normal
food on which white-tailed deer feed was killed by the frosts, deer had
to turn to other vegetation for food. One that they turned to and which
most suffered from this additional feeding was young Atlantic white
cedar. Dr. George Zimmerman of Stockton State College, who has been
doing considerable research on cedar regeneration in the Pine Barrens,
says that deer browsing on regenerating white cedars nearly doubled as
a result of the black frosts of 1992. Cedar regeneration is difficult enough
without having to combat the effects of this severe overbrowsing.

26

Orchids and
Other Wildflowers

H ere we are in the first month of summer, but even though we
may already have had a good number of fine, warm days, summer does not arrive, officially, until later this month. June is the
month during which more Pine Barrens plants begin to blossom than in
any other month. In fact, this might be called the orchid month, for as
many as six different orchids could be in blossom at different times during the month. The first of these, the pink lady's slipper, we've already
admired, but these will all be past blooming by mid-June. Taking their
place will be three more beautiful orchids, all bog orchids, that we're
going to look for early this month.

Orchids are considered to be the royal family of the flowering kingdom and many are very beautiful. Together, after the composite family,
orchids comprise the second largest family of flowering plants and, as a
group, they enjoy a mystique that transcends that of any other family of
wildflowers. Unfortunately, some people, in their zeal to find some of
these beautiful and rare orchids, become misguided and seek out locations where they grow for the purpose of transplanting them to their own
private gardens or estates. In most cases, these transplants will quickly
die, for it is almost impossible to duplicate the natural habitat conditions
where they were growing.

Leading the parade of orchids that come into bloom in late May and
early June is arethusa, which began blossoming from mid to late May.
This is closely followed by rose pogonia, and by grass-pink, both of these
coming into bloom by the first week in June. All three are found in Pine

Barrens bogs, savannas, grassy meadows, and other damp, sandy spots, and some, occasionally, even along damp, grassy roadsides.

ARETHUSA, *Arethusa bulbosa*, also known as dragon's-mouth orchid, may be the loveliest of all three. Its magenta-pink blossom has a beautiful lower lip spotted with purple and crested with yellow hairs. This lower lip serves as a landing platform for visiting insects, usually bumble bees. The blossom sits on top of a naked stalk eight inches to a foot in height that grows up from a small bulb. Later, after the flower matures, a single, grass-like leaf arises. This beautiful orchid is named after the nymph, Arethusa, who was one of the attendants of the goddess Diana.

ROSE POGONIA, *Pogonia ophioglossoides*, is a somewhat similar, very delicate little orchid that bears a solitary (usually) rose-pink blossom. Its most interesting feature is its beautiful, yellow-bearded and fringed lip that also serves as a landing platform for visiting insects. A single, oblong leaf clasps the middle of its eight- to twelve-inch stem and a leaf-like bract grows beneath the flower. This is also known as snake-mouth or adder's-mouth orchid for its bearded lip (mouth).

The third of these early bog orchids, GRASS-PINK, *Calopogon pulchellus*, may be the most common and widespread of the three. Its magenta-pink flowers are quite showy, measure about an inch across, and have an erect, yellow-crested lip at the top of the flower. As many as three to nine flowers may open sequentially up a leafless ten- to sixteen-inch stem, beside which there is a single, grass-like leaf. Both the flowering stalk and the leaf arise from a small, round bulb. The generic name for this beautiful orchid comes from the Greek *calos*, for beautiful and *pogon* for its handsome, bearded, uppermost petal (lip).

One of the best places to observe all three of these orchids, as well as other bog plants soon to follow (golden-crest and bog asphodel, and many other interesting bog flora such as golden club, pitcher-plants, all three sundews, and even curly-grass fern), is in the Greenwood Forest State Wildlife Management Area at a site known as the cedar bog alongside the Webb's Mill Branch of Cedar Creek. This bog is in Lacey Township, Ocean County, and the entrance to this site is on Route 539, six and one-quarter miles north of the intersection of Routes 72 and 539. This is an easy, public area to access through a partially burned cedar stand to a circular boardwalk from which all these wonderful flora, and more, can be observed. The boardwalk is maintained by the New Jersey Division of Fish, Game, and Wildlife.

Rose pogonia

Turning to some other Pine Barrens flora, soon after the first of June and continuing well into summer, nearly every body of water in the Pinelands, such as shallow lakes, old mill ponds, cranberry reservoirs, canals, and ditches, in fact nearly every year-round body of water of any

131

size, will be covered with the floating leaves and fragrant, multi-petalled blossoms of the WHITE WATER-LILY, *Nymphaea odora*. Here is an outstanding aquatic flower in form, size, and beauty. Although normally pure white, sometimes the pink color usually present on the undersides of the petals will suffuse the entire flower with a pinkish tinge. Water-lily lore goes way back to very early literature. Pliny the Elder wrote these were considered an antidote for love philters (potions) even in his time!

The closely related YELLOW WATER-LILY or SPATTERDOCK, *Nuphar variegata*, has already been in bloom since mid-May, but this comes from the "other side of the tracks" when compared with white water-lilies. Yellow pond lilies have little fragrance and their blooms are considered just ordinary rather than glamorous. These do have the advantage, however, of thriving in waters too shallow, too muddy, and sometimes too stagnant for the more attractive white water-lilies. Because of their ability to do well in these conditions, these have sometimes been called frog-lilies.

While we are looking at and talking about water-lilies, there is another aquatic flower we should begin to look for toward the middle of June. This is PICKEREL WEED, *Pontederia cordata*, found rather commonly along muddy shores and in shallow waters of ponds and slowly moving streams throughout the Pine Barrens. Look for rather tall, one- to three-foot spikes topped with four- to six-inch dense heads of bright violet-blue flowers, each individual flower marked with a distinct yellow-green spot. Numbers of pickerel weed blooms, massed together, present a spectacular display. Pickerel weed is a very robust plant with large, heavy, heart- or arrow-shaped leaves, the plants sometimes clustered together in great masses of aquatic vegetation. The common name for this plant comes from an old-time belief that its habitat is a favorite area for pickerel to deposit their eggs.

Moving a little away from open water and water edge habitats, but still around wet marshes, bogs, and in and along the edges of cranberry bogs, starting around the middle of June you should begin to see bright, attractive spikes of yellow flowers waving in the breezes. These are SWAMP CANDLES or yellow or swamp loosestrife, *Lysimachia terrestris*, that stand out in any habitat where they occur. Stop and look closely at the five petals of these flowers and you will see they are spotted with numerous reddish dots. Later in the summer, after flowering time, small, elongated bulblets grow out from the axils of the leaves, giving this plant a quite different appearance than during its flowering season, so different, in fact, that Linnaeus mistook this late season plant for a mistletoe! There is an interesting story concerning the common name of loosestrife or a "loosing of strife." It is said that in ancient times yokes of oxen were rendered gentle and submissive when loosestrife plants were attached to the tongue (pulling pole) of a cart or wagon!

Of all the heaths in the Pine Barrens, one of the most showy is SWAMP or CLAMMY AZALEA, *Rhododendron viscosum*, sometimes also called swamp honeysuckle, but this is not in any way a honeysuckle. This beautiful, two- to six-foot tall shrub, with its very fragrant and massed white flowers, begins to bloom early in June and then, because it is so showy, it is seen to be quite common to sometimes abundant in swamps, low thickets, edges of ponds and streams, and along damp roadsides. An interesting feature of its beautiful flowers is that they are covered with sticky hairs, thus "clammy," which may be an adaptation to protect the

Swamp azalea

flowers from crawling insects such as ants. Although most of the flowers on the majority of these shrubs are nearly pure white, sometimes the corollas will show a flush of pink and occasionally most of the flowers will be rather pinkish.

Continuing with other common and attractive Pinelands wildflowers that we should be seeing right now, those brilliant orange balls in low, moist, grassy areas starting around the second week in June and continuing into early fall, are the blossoms of ORANGE MILKWORT, *Polygala lutea*, one of the most showy and distinctively characteristic of all flowering plants in the Pine Barrens. Sometimes even abundant, its brilliant orange colors immediately attract one's attention so that it is easily and quickly observed. There are at least three other milkworts that are rather

Orange milkwort

frequently found in the Pine Barrens but, in general, these are somewhat smaller, their flowers are mostly in shades of pink or purple, and none stand out as prominently as the orange milkwort.

Moving to higher ground in open areas in pine-oak woodlands, a very low-growing, pincushiony and moss-like plant with tiny green leaves is frequent and characteristic of pine needle strewn sands as well as the same bare patches of dry, white sands where pine-barren heather is found. This is PINE-BARREN SANDWORT, *Arenaria caroliniana*, or long-root as it was called by earlier residents because of its long, deep tap root. The slender flower stalks of this interesting plant rise only four to six inches in height and bear small, star-like, whitish flowers with green centers. The flowering stems are rather glandular and sticky so that, sometimes, grains of sand and minute insects are found stuck to them. This is another southern plant for which the Pine Barrens of New Jersey is about as far north as its range extends.

While out on those dry, sandy areas where heathers and sandworts grow, take a moment to look around and see if you can find the only eastern member of the cactus family. This is PRICKLY PEAR, *Opuntia humifusa*, which began blooming around the middle of June and can be found rather frequently in open, sunny places, especially in disturbed areas along the outer fringes of the Pine Barrens. The stems of this interesting plant are composed of large, thick, fleshy joints that are sometimes mistaken for leaves. These joints may grow either erect or nearly prostrate on the ground, often spreading to form large mats. Evenly spaced over the joints may be tufts of small, barbed bristles which, if touched, are easily detached and can become embedded in one's skin, sometimes leading to a painful inflammation. On the other hand, some plants may not have any spines at all. The flowers are large and beautiful, two to three inches across, and are showy and yellow, but each individual blossom lasts for only one single day before starting to turn into a pulpy, sweet, red or reddish-purple fruit that is edible after any possible tiny barbed hairs have been removed.

In dry, open, sandy grounds along the edges of the woods, and in open woodland areas, be on the lookout for a very attractive member of the pea family called GOAT'S RUE, *Tephrosia virginiana*, sometimes called wild sweet pea. This also comes into bloom around the middle of June and, like many others in this family, the flowers of this wild pea are butterfly-like. The terminal flowers of goat's rue are bi-colored with the upper petal (standard) yellow and conspicuous and the wings and keel reddish or purplish. The entire plant is silky-whitish-hairy and, again, as in many pea family members, the leaves are compound and divided into fifteen to twenty-five paired leaflets.

Finally, deeper into the dim-lit fastnesses of the forests, there grows a very different plant in almost all aspects. In the first place, and this is basic, the plant does not have any green chlorophyll in its clammy, wax-like structure—not in its stem, its bracts that pass as leaves, nor in its flowers, so it lacks any ability to manufacture its own food as do other plants. Instead, it is what is known as a parasitic or a saprophytic plant, deriving all its nourishment directly from decaying organic matter in the soil by means of matted, brittle roots. This curious, fungus-like plant is INDIAN PIPE, *Monotropa uniflora.* In its early stages of growth, as its white to slightly pinkish stems and flowers rise up out of the ground, and as it reaches its full growth, the flowers are in a nodding position, but after blossoming, the spent flowers become erect and the whole plant turns black before withering away. This trait of turning black has earned indian pipe other common names such as corpse-plant and ghost-flower. Stone indicated this to be "apparently quite rare in the Pine Barrens," but it really is more common than he thought.

27

Abundance
and
Diversity

D ue to their great diversity, distribution, and abundance, insects
may be the most important group of animals on earth. They far
surpass all other animals in numbers and they occur practically
everywhere. Nearly a million different kinds (species) have already been
described, and it is estimated there are at least as many more still unde-
scribed. Already, there are far more known species of insects than there
are of all the world's other animals and all the plants in the world put
together. Their populations often number well into the millions per acre
and their total biomass is beyond estimation. For sheer survival and pro-
liferation, insects are probably the most successful of all living creatures,
so successful that they just might outlive all other creatures on this earth.

Many insects are extremely valuable to humankind. By means of pollination, bees and other insects make possible much of the food we eat
and many of the materials we use. A few obvious examples are vegeta-
bles, fruits, grains and clovers (food for cattle and sheep and their products of milk, beef, mutton, and wool), cotton, silk, honey and beeswax.
Even though some of these may seem far removed from the Pine Barrens,
we already know how blueberry and cranberry farmers make good use
of industrious bees. Insects also are one of the most important links in
the natural food chain of many forms of wildlife, including other insects
as well as the higher animals. As an example, again, we already know
how and why birds are among the most important consumers of insect
larvae. The food value of insects consumed in food chains is almost
beyond calculation. Although some insects are harmful from man's point
of view, most insects are beneficial in one way or another.

In my second career, I have been an entomologist—one who studies all aspects of insects and insect life: their taxonomy and nomenclature, the characters that separate and identify one species from all others, their morphology and physiology, their roles in natural and man-made ecosystems, and their economic impact. It is natural, therefore, that I have a compelling interest in the insects of the Pine Barrens.

My particular interest has been tiger beetles, and I have studied and worked with these interesting critters for well over fifty years. TIGER BEETLES are small (less than one-half inch to three-quarters of an inch), long-legged, active, often brightly colored beetles that run rapidly along the ground and fly readily when disturbed. These are the little beetles that fly up ahead of you as you hike along any sandy Pine Barrens trail or walk along the dikes around a cranberry bog. All are predacious and carnivorous as their common name of tiger beetles implies, and all actively hunt,

Tiger beetle

capture, and consume any small living creature they can handle. Ants, of which there is an abundance in the Pine Barrens, make up a considerable portion of their diet. Most tiger beetles are found in open, sunny, and sandy locations, so the Pine Barrens is a favored habitat for many species, including at least one that is endemic. Sixteen of the twenty-two species of tiger beetles in the genus *Cicindela* that are known to occur in New Jersey live in the Pine Barrens, and different species may be found at different times from late March through mid-October. Of the truly uncounted thousands of interesting insects in the Pines, I briefly mention three others here because these are among the more noticeable and observable by even the most casual human visitor.

Small cone-shaped pits you see in dry sandy places are the work of tiny doodle-bug larvae of adult lace-winged ANTLIONS, *Myrmeleon immaculatus*. Their pits, barely an inch across and about the same in depth, are most commonly found under some shelter such as a bench or the eaves of buildings where they are protected from rain and other disturbances. They may also be found out in wide open, sandy, sunny areas, in fact almost anywhere in the Pine Barrens throughout the entire year. The tiny doodle-bug larvae are short and stout, from a quarter to three-eights of an inch, and have strong, sickle-like jaws (mandibles). They make their pits by first backing themselves into loose sand. When buried, they use their heads and jaws as shovels to throw out the sand above them and create a small, inverted cone or pit. Then they lie in wait concealed at the bottom of their pits with their jaws open and extended, ready to grab and feed on any creatures such as ants and other small arthropods that may fall into their pits. Adult antlions are more difficult to find because these are flying insects that look somewhat like damselflies and have two pairs of netveined, nearly transparent wings, often with small black or brown spots.

As you cross over almost any small cedar stream or explore a quiet backwater while you canoe down any Pine Barrens stream, you're almost certain to see numbers of small, black or slightly bronzed beetles whirling around very rapidly over the surface of the water. These are WHIRLIGIG BEETLES (Gyrinidae), or "coffee beans" as some old-timers may call them. When picked up and handled, many of these hard-shelled beetles emit a milky white fluid that has a fruity odor, and this has caused these beetles to be called "applebugs." These beetles are often seen in large numbers gyrating ceaselessly on water surfaces, almost throughout the year, each of the individuals whirling round and round without any apparent aim or objective. These very predacious insects are particularly interesting because they have two, not just one, pairs of compound eyes, one pair above, the other pair below the surface of the water. This enables them to see and catch prey that may be either on or under the water surface. One of their principal foods is mosquito larvae and wherever these beetles occur in sufficient numbers, most mosquito larvae will be consumed by these predators.

At the same time, those spidery-looking things that seem to skate over the surfaces of ponds and slowly moving streams are WATER STRIDERS (Gerridae). These insects have very long, hairy, water-repellent legs that make depressions on, but do not break through, the surface film of the water, and so are able to hold their light weight bodies slightly above the water surface. This ability to apparently walk on the water has given rise to one of their common names, "Jesus-bugs." On sunny days, if you look closely, you can see their shadows beneath them, and you may also be able to see the slight depressions in the surface film caused by their legs. Like the whirligig beetles, with which they often keep company, water striders also are predators, and wherever they occur in large enough numbers mosquito larvae are unable to survive.

28

Savannas
of the
Flood Plain

round the middle of June, one year, I spent the best parts of three
days exploring sections of a wonderful peatland savanna along
the flood plain of a Pine Barrens stream. As canoists and kayak-
ers paddled downstream, Doris, Don Kirchhoffer, and Augie Sexauer
accompanied me on different days as we carefully moved around the
boggy streamsides luxuriating in the tremendous diversity of the floral
offerings. Here, as far as we could see, both up and down the expanse
of low vegetation beside the stream, was a wide swath of undisturbed,
pristine peatland—a veritable fairyland of blooms. Here, also, in the quiet
solitude of this beautiful spot, we felt alone with nature and with our-
selves—miles from any civilization, and yet, here, in the very heart of the
Pinelands, we were less than fifty and seventy-five miles respectively
from the great, teeming, metropolitan areas of Philadelphia and New
York City. Only the occasional overhead roar of military aircraft on train-
ing maneuvers brought us back to reality!

We had come to this spot to find and photograph some of the unique
and characteristic flowering plants of Pinelands bogs. The principal
component of this peatland is a soft, spongy mat of varying depths that
lies on top of a characteristically white sand base. It is because of the
varying depths that one has to be careful where to place one's foot, for
one misstep could easily result in a wet, sinking experience! The spongy
mat itself is composed largely of sphagnum mosses, grasses, sedges, and
small hummocks of white cedar lying on top of accumulated layers of
decomposed vegetation, making for very soft, spongy footing. Growing

up out of this morass was a veritable garden of sphagnum and club mosses, lilies, orchids, carnivorous and other flowering herbaceous plants. Among the more conspicuous of these were the pitcher-plants with their reddish, nodding flower heads; bog-asphodel, so abundant that entire sections of the bog were aglow with their waving, yellow candles; and golden-crest, whose tiny yellow stars were just beginning to peek out from their white, downy flower heads. Lower down, in the grasses and sedges and just above the sphagnum mosses, hundreds of rose pogonia and grass-pink orchids and blossoming thread-leaved sundews provided bright spots of contrasting colors. Lower still, and in wetter areas, fibrous, horned, and zigzag bladderworts, all three, supplied bright yellow hues to the symphony of the rainbow that was so wide-

Bog asphodel

spread and so wonderful to experience. It is comforting to know that most of the area we traversed is protected as a part of the Wharton State Forest and part of this has been designated by the state as a natural area to preserve its native plants and animals.

Just as there are many beautiful orchids in the Pinelands, so also are there a number of beautiful members of the lily family. Some lilies, however, may vary a little from the popular conception of a typical lily form. Two of these are the closely related BOG-ASPHODEL, *Narthecium americanum,* and FALSE or VISCID ASPHODEL, *Tofieldia racemosa.* Both are restricted to low, wet, sandy, open and isolated bogs and savannas in the very heart of the pines, and both are quite local in range. Bog asphodel was abundant on these savanna trips and, because it is more frequent and seems to grow in patches, you may be more likely to find a patch of bog asphodel than one of viscid asphodel. The latter seems to be more scarce and more scattered in its growth pattern.

Both asphodels have small, shiny, star-like flowers in a short spike on top of a ten- to eighteen-inch stalk. The most obvious differences between these two plants is that bog asphodel has yellow flowers and the flower stalk is smooth, while the viscid asphodel has white flowers and its flowering stalk is slightly sticky (viscid). If you are fortunate enough to find a nice cluster of bog asphodel, you'll surely be impressed with the golden panorama of the bright yellow flowers standing above their green, grass-like leaves. Sometimes, when their yellow flower heads are standing together, they form a golden sheen over a bog which can be seen for quite a distance. Even later in the fall, bog asphodel makes quite a showing, its seed capsules being a rich reddish-brown. Both asphodels are classified as endangered species and both could face extermination with any damming, flooding, or other disturbances of natural bogs and savannas.

Another great plant found on those savanna trips was GOLDEN-CREST, *Lophiola aurea,* another characteristic Pine Barrens bog plant that was just coming into bloom and will continue in blossom into July. Golden-crest is an unusual and striking plant found only in bogs and savannas in the very heart of the pines, where it grows right out of the watery sands. Its tiny, golden-yellow, star-like flowers, surrounded by dense, white, woolly clusters at the tops of two- to three-foot high white, downy stems, are well worth the effort of searching for this unique and attractive plant. In Witmer Stone's words, "The dense, woolly covering of the flowers recalls the *Eidelweiss* of the Swiss mountains, and from the downy white clusters, the little yellow flowers peep out like tiny stars."

29

More Carnivorous Bog Plants

B ack around the end of May we talked about carnivorous plants and zeroed in on pitcher plants and some early bladderworts. Now that we are in the third week in June, it is time to conclude our discussions of these interesting plants. First, let's quickly highlight the more common and conspicuous of the remaining bladderworts. The HORNED BLADDERWORT, *Utricularia cornuta*, may be the most common and conspicuous bladderwort in Pine Barrens bogs. This is a terrestrial species that may grow up to a height of twelve inches and its conspicuous large, helmet-shaped, yellow flower has an elongated, downward extending spur that may measure from one-third to one-half of an inch in length. A similar but somewhat smaller species is the RUSH BLADDERWORT, *Utricularia juncea*, but this does not begin to blossom until early in August.

Before we finish with bladderworts, one other species needs to be mentioned even though it will not come into bloom until around the middle of July. This is the aquatic PURPLE BLADDERWORT, *Utricularia purpurea*. This plant is not common and is quite localized in acid bogs and slow streams. Its long, brown stems float submerged and from them whorls of branches bear bladder-like traps, all matted together in a mass of fibrous vegetation. The purple flowers that just poke an inch or two above the surface of the water are about an inch long and have a three-lobed lower lip. A single blossom or two is often difficult to find, but occasionally the plants are so clustered together that they may cover the surface of the water with their blooms and then the whole mass becomes rather conspicuous and beautiful.

Round-leaved sundew

As mentioned earlier, the sundews use the flypaper, or adhesive trap, method of capturing their prey and there are three species in the Pinelands: the ROUND-LEAVED SUNDEW, *Drosera rotundifolia*; the SPATULATE-LEAVED SUNDEW, *Drosera intermedia*; and the THREAD-LEAVED SUNDEW, *Drosera filiformis*. All are quite small plants that grow close to the ground. While the leaves of these plants vary in shape, as their names indicate, over the surfaces of all of these leaves are numerous glistening hairs, each tipped with a glob of sweet, sticky, reddish liquid that insects find attractive, possibly because of their color and sparkle. When an insect touches one of the hairs it becomes hopelessly trapped, its feet held by the sticky drops, and as it struggles to free itself, its wings

146

and body also get stuck. The more the insect thrashes around, the more tangled and helpless it becomes, and while this is going on, the leaf hairs slowly bend over to encircle the victim in a death grip. Finally, juices and enzymes exude from the leaf, digestion begins, and the plant supplements its food intake with nutrients from the body of the insect. Sometimes, when looking across a bog containing sundews, particularly the thread-leaved sundews, the sticky drops on their leaf blades glisten in the sunlight like shining dew drops, especially if they are backlit. This is the reason for their common, as well as their generic, name which, in the Greek *droseros* means dewy or glistening in the sun.

Beginning in mid- to late June, the pinkish-magenta flowers of the thread-leaved sundews are the first and most conspicuous of the three sundews to blossom. Appearing near the tops of twelve- to sixteen-inch, thread-like leaves, the blossoms open in early morning sunshine but close by noon or shortly thereafter. Later, in July, the other two sundews produce small, whitish, and inconspicuous flowers on six- to eight-inch stems. It is the insect capturing and digesting capability of these small plants that is of greater interest than their blossoms.

Sandy trail through pitch pines

Swamp-pink

Arethusa

Black swallowtail butterfly

White water-lilies

Narrow-leaved sunflower

Golden-crest

Buckeye butterfly

Turk's-cap lily

Box turtle

Red squirrel

Pine Barrens treefrog

Turkey vulture

Pitcher-plant (cluster of leaves)

Pitcher-plant (closeup of flower)

Drupes (fruits) of sassafras

Dragonfly

Mountain-laurel

Sheep-laurel

Pink lady's-slipper

Great blue heron

Grass-pink

Pine-barren gentian

Nighthawk

Cranberry blossoms *Cranberries (ripe fruit)*

Bearberry blossoms

Bearberry fruit

Leopard frog

Spotted turtle

Prickly pear (cactus)

Thread-leaved sundew

30

Squirrels,
Beavers, and Deer

You may wonder why there has been so little mention of mammals up to this point. This is because people do not see mammals very often in the Pine Barrens for the reason that most mammals remain as much as possible out of the sight of man and several are nocturnal. The two mammals one is most likely to see in the pines are the red squirrel and the white-tailed deer. In addition, abundant evidences of beaver activity can be found in scattered locations throughout the Pine Barrens.

If you will check around on the ground under some pine trees you should be able to spot a small pile of bracts that have been removed from a pine cone. See if you can also find the small stem, or cob, of the former pine cone, all eaten off except for three or four tip-end bracts. You have found a feeding station of a little RED SQUIRREL, for the pile of bracts is the result of a squirrel having stripped them off a pine cone in order to get at and feed on the tiny pine seeds that are hidden deep down between the bases of the bracts of the cone, next to the cob. The red squirrel is an animal of the pine woods and is smaller and more energetic than the familiar backyard gray squirrel. It feeds on the seeds of conifers and other plants, on nuts, buds, mushrooms, some insects, and occasionally on eggs they rob from the nests of birds. A red squirrel can be a noisy little animal, uttering a fairly loud, harsh, scolding or chattering call, apparently aimed at any intruder into its domain.

149

Somewhere on nearly every small cedar stream and flow through swampy areas in the Pine Barrens, one is almost sure to find evidences of BEAVER activity, yet very seldom will one actually see the beavers themselves. As far back as the early 1820s, beavers had been nearly trapped into extinction for their fur. But partly as the result of reintroductions in the late 1800s and partly due to their own abilities, beavers have made a remarkable recovery and today are once again inhabiting the Pinelands. Beavers are medium-sized mammals that grow to two to two and one-half feet in length plus a bare, flat tail of about a foot, and they weigh from thirty pounds up to sixty pounds for large males. Beavers are the largest local members of the rodent family and, like all rodents, they have two large, chisel-like incisor (gnawing) front teeth above and two below. These enable beavers to gnaw large chips out of the trunks of trees until they fell them. Then they gnaw off the bark for food and use the limbs and branches to construct dams and living quarters (lodges).

Beavers are very seldom seen during the daytime, so the best way to see a beaver is to sit very quietly, partially concealed, beside a known beaver site during late afternoon and early evening hours. You then may be fortunate enough to see a beaver swimming about in a pond or other small dammed-up area, possibly carrying a stick or a branch over to its dam or lodge. Beavers build dams across streams in order to raise the water level and make the ponds behind their dams deep enough for their activities. They have been known to build dams as high as fourteen feet (though certainly not in the Pine Barrens) and some of the lodges they build are tremendous structures, always constructed so that there is an underwater entrance that leads up into a high, dry, inside chamber where the beavers live and raise their young.

Beaver dams and the ponds they create become major factors in the ecology of an area. As waters rise upstream of the dam, they flood out all existing trees and vegetation and reduce these to bare skeletons of former life. On the other hand, beaver ponds always provide additional living spaces for more species and a greater abundance of living things than were present before the beavers arrived. Thus beaver ponds become complete new ecosystems of their own. A pond built by beavers is not like any other kind of pond. It develops unique characteristics of its own: the dam, the lodge, the pond itself, and its border of flooded-out dead trees. All this creates new environments and invites new forms of life to enter the pond and its surroundings. Plants and wildlife that had not been present before start to move in. Insects, fish, amphibians, reptiles, birds, and mammals, as well as lower and less frequently seen forms of life such as plankton, fresh water algae, diatoms, protozoans, hydras, and rotifers, all of which are important links in the food chains of the higher animals, become part of the new ecosystem.

There is a very special beaver story right on the edge of the Pine Barrens. This is the story of Hope Sawyer Buyukmihci, her Turkish husband, Cavit, and their experiences in establishing their Unexpected Wildlife Refuge near the border between Atlantic and Gloucester Counties. The stories of their trials and tribulations are too many to retell here, but can be read in a book Hope wrote entitled *Unexpected Treasure*. A highlight of their experiences was Hope's development, over a long period of time and patience, of enough trust by a family of wild beavers that the adult beavers would allow Hope to sit and watch them and their young kits while they fed on bark from a pile of branches right at her feet. One of the kits became so trusting that it climbed right up into her lap. However, Hope was always very careful never to make pets of them and they remained forever wild.

On the other hand, eager beavers sometimes get out of (human) hand. Beavers insist on damming up almost any flow of water and seem to have a particular propensity to build dams right on top of culverts intended to channel water from one to the other side of a road. Beavers plug up the culverts and road crews have to constantly clear away the dam material in order to let the water continue to flow under the road rather than over it. The problem is that the beavers seldom seem to get the message and continually try to rebuild the dam. Sometimes it becomes a constant battle and occasionally beavers have to be live-trapped, removed, and released into areas where they can have more freedom to pursue their lives. There is a story out of *Vermont Life* about a beaver family that caused a lot of trouble where a road crew was trying to lay out a new road. Each night the beavers would build up their dam and flood the area. Each day the work crew would tear it down. It got to be pretty tiresome to the crew and apparently the beavers also got tired of it. One morning the men couldn't believe their eyes. The dam was in place again but there was no water behind it. The crew went over to check things out. They found that the beavers had put a piece of stovepipe right through the dam with a shut-off damper in it. They'd used the water all night and then opened the damper in the morning to let the water out! Some story!

Due to their size, WHITE-TAILED DEER are the most conspicuous animals in the Pine Barrens. Deer may be most frequently seen browsing on vegetation during early morning hours, around sunrise, and in the evening just before dusk. Other sightings may occur as you drive along any Pine Barrens road. Sometimes two or three deer will jump out from the woods on one side of the road and leap across just ahead of you and disappear into the woods on the other side. Other times you may see a deer or two ahead of you standing in the middle of the road watching your vehicle as you approach, until they decide it is time to hightail it into the adjacent woods. Even if you don't actually see any deer, if you are reasonably observant you can see signs of deer all around. Tracks of the white-tailed deer abound everywhere in the Pine Barrens and can be seen on almost every sandy trail or open sandy spot. In addition, there are abundant evidences of deer browsing, and their scats, all through the Pinelands.

The white-tailed deer is now the only large animal to occur in the Pine Barrens, and we will meet up with these again during hunting season. In addition to the red squirrel and the beaver, some other mammals to be found in the pines are opossum, raccoon, cottontail (rabbit), woodchuck, striped skunk, red and gray foxes, muskrat, mink, and river otter. Other than an occasional opossum, raccoon, or cottontail that may come into back yards, or a woodchuck that might dig its burrow near some old forgotten town site, most of these mammals are seldom seen. The smaller mammals are even more difficult to find, for most of them are either shrews or moles that live underground, mice or voles, weasels, or bats and flying squirrels, the latter two nocturnal. The only other mammals likely to be seen are the eastern chipmunk and the gray squirrel, but both of these are more apt to be found around human habitations rather than out in the Pine Barrens.

31

Lizards
and
Rattlers

That little movement you may have seen out of the corner of your eye while you were hiking along the Batona Trail on a warm, sunny day may have been a fence lizard, the only common lizard in the Pine Barrens. Often called pine lizard because of its frequent occurrence in open pine woods, this is a very agile, swift, and secretive little reptile that has strong arboreal tendencies. Like the amphibians (frogs and toads) and the turtles we have already seen, this is another cold-blooded inhabitant of the Pinelands, which is about as far north as it occurs. Fence lizards begin to emerge from hibernation as early as April, but they are much more likely to be seen later in the spring and especially during the hot summer months.

The NORTHERN FENCE LIZARD, *Sceloporus undulatus hyacinthinus*, is a small, gray (female) or brownish (male) lizard with a series of narrow, wavy, darker bands across its back. Males also have blackish-blue patches on each side of their bellies along with some blue under their throats. Moderately large, keeled, and pointed scales give this four- to seven-inch reptile a spiny or bristly appearance. It has long toes with very sharp claws. Its tail is also quite long and tapering, and exceptionally brittle so that it is often broken off. Although these tails do regrow, this takes several weeks and, in the meantime, it is not unusual to see fence lizards with tails in all stages of regrowth.

These small lizards are most frequently seen lying in the bright sun on dead and decaying logs, fence rails, tree limbs, or stumps looking for flies and other insects, or running rapidly along the ground in an effort to find a hiding place so as to escape detection. These are very shy creatures and, when surprised, they will often dash to the backside of the nearest tree, shrub, or other protection and remain motionless. If they are approached while in this hidden position, they will again dodge to the opposite side, keeping out of sight in an expert manner. This process may be repeated several times, thus making these little creatures very difficult to see clearly or to photograph in the wild.

Like the fence lizard we've just seen, snakes are also cold-blooded reptiles. They also are the innocent victims of love-hate relationships with humans. Some people have a deep, though largely unfounded, fear of all snakes, harmless or not. Others have a fascination to collect wild snakes and keep them as pets. This is a practice that should be discouraged, for to take snakes or any other wild creatures out of their natural environment and keep them in confined quarters as pets is wrong. Such activities should be restricted to specimens that have been bred and raised in captivity.

Pinelands snakes generally prefer mixed pine and oak woodlands and keep themselves in protected situations where they can find cover such as downed logs, brush piles, and dense vegetation. They rarely expose themselves out in the open and so are not commonly seen by people who are hiking along Pinelands trails. According to authorities such as Conant and McCormick, there are eighteen species of snakes in the Pine Barrens, but we're going to talk about only three of these because most of the others are seldom seen in the pines by the average person.

The snake probably most commonly seen, especially while it may be sunning itself along the edges of ponds and streams, is the NORTHERN WATER SNAKE, *Natrix sipedon.* Although not poisonous, this Pine Barrens snake is the one most likely to strike if it is cornered. In proportion to its four-foot length, this is a stout, heavy snake with a large, flattish, and roughly triangular head. Older specimens are uniformly dark brown to nearly black, but younger specimens are pale brownish tinged with red, crossed by irregular, dark brown, wavy bands. Undersides are splashed with crimson and black. The general appearance of these snakes, plus their watery environment, lead some people to think these are the deadly water moccasins of the south, but those snakes are not found north of Virginia, so any water snake found in the Pine Barrens is nonpoisonous.

In upland Pine Barrens areas, possibly the best known and most likely snake to be seen is the NORTHERN PINE SNAKE, *Pituophis melanoleucus*, because this reptile is fond of lying in the sun, and specimens are sometimes surprised while basking in the many sandy areas that dot the pines. This is one of our larger snakes, mature specimens averaging around five feet in length. It is a beautiful snake. Its back is grayish-white to white along its sides, with a series of deep black blotches across its back. Its underparts are grayish-white with black markings. When annoyed, pine snakes are noted for their loud hissing, which they do by raising the forepart of their body off the ground, facing their enemy, and expelling their breath with a loud hiss. These snakes are constrictors and feed mainly on rodents, but they also will capture small frogs and birds and take any eggs they can find, so they, like most snakes, play an important role in the natural food chain in the Pine Barrens.

The only poisonous snake in the Pine Barrens is the TIMBER RATTLESNAKE, *Crotalus horridus*. Although its numbers have been greatly reduced over the years due to overcollecting and unnecessary killings, rattlesnakes can still be found in the Pinelands. The most famous of several early collectors was Asa ("Rattlesnake Ace") Pittman of Upton Station who, over a period of twenty-five to thirty years during the early 1900s, regularly captured up to two hundred rattlesnakes a year and sold them to zoos and museums. More recently, within the past twenty years, eighteen timber rattlesnakes were found during just one summer on a twelve-acre piece of previously undeveloped property in the Mount Misery area. But, even though rattlesnakes still exist in the Pinelands, one's chances of coming across one are pretty slim unless, of course, you go out for the express purpose of looking for one!

Many snakes are now considered, or are rapidly becoming, either threatened or endangered species in the Pinelands. This is primarily due to loss of their natural habitat, but many other factors such as suppression of wildfires and illegal collecting are important. In the 1950s, '60s, '70s, and even into the '80s, there was an explosion of housing developments, especially for senior citizens, principally in Ocean and eastern Burlington Counties. These developments resulted in the loss of thousands of acres of natural habitat for these animals and fragmentation of the remaining acreage. Even in the 1990s, the threat of habitat destruction has continued with efforts, though opposed, to extend Ocean County's Mule Road through a prime habitat of threatened Pine Barrens populations of corn and pine snakes and timber rattlesnakes. Fortunately, the Nature Conservancy of New Jersey came to the rescue and put together a package to preserve a major portion of this threatened territory within the

155

Berkeley triangle. In addition, artificial hibernacula have been constructed and placed in operation in strategic locations by Robert Zappalorti and his Herpetological Associates to provide limited refugia for these endangered species, but unless future developments and road building cease or are greatly curtailed, and unless illegal collecting can be controlled, some, or possibly all, of our presently endangered species of snakes may become extirpated in the Pine Barrens.

32

Surprise
in a Cedar Swamp

E
ven after all the years I have spent exploring the Pine Barrens,
there still are many hidden surprises to be discovered. I was asked
to visit a site, previously unknown to me, in the hope I could
identify an unusual formation. The site, a pool or small pond of crystal
clear water, turned out to be one of the most interesting and unique
areas I have ever seen in the Pinelands. Here the water is so clear and
undisturbed that one gets the impression of looking into a spring-fed
pool. Overall, I estimate the pool to be between one-half to one acre in
size. Although entirely surrounded and even invaded by a young cedar
swamp, the water does not contain even the slightest trace of typical reddish-brown tinted Pine Barrens cedar water. Instead, this water is so
clear and clean that, in a glass jar, it is as crystal clear as if it had been
drawn and bottled from a pure underground spring. It has a pH value
of approximately six, which means it is somewhat less acid than typical
Pine Barrens waters.

Another fascinating feature of this site is that everywhere throughout
the pool there are masses of underwater, shelf-like, soft, gelatinous
growths, often clustered so tightly together that they appear to be growing out of each other in tiers or layers, making this a veritable fairyland.
Some of these masses are floating on the surface, but most are attached
to and cover nearly every inch of the many old dead tree trunks and
limbs that have fallen into the water over the years, and that now lay
crisscrossed in every conceivable direction throughout the pool. Unable
to identify these formations myself, I collected samples and sent them to

some scientist friends at the Academy of Natural Sciences in Philadelphia. These turned out to be a blue-green alga, *Fremyella* sp., normally a rare algal form in the Pine Barrens. In fact, as a group, blue-green algae are unusual anywhere in the Pine Barrens.

Still another feature of this beautiful site is that one can look down into what seem to be the great depths of this crystal clear pool and can see everything that lies on the bottom. Standing on the edge of the pool and looking down into it, one senses looking down into great depths even though this is not actually the case. In reality, measurements reveal depths in the pool range only from three to four feet with some spots possibly as deep as six feet. Thus, the sense of great depths is probably due to the clarity of the water.

The entire area surrounding this extraordinary site is a wonderful, young Atlantic white cedar swamp, complete with an almost continuous thick, soft mat of sphagnum mosses. Pitcher-plants abound everywhere, some in large clumps. Leatherleaf and other heaths also are abundant. As in many Pine Barrens cedar bogs that are carpeted with sphagnum mosses, one misstep in the spongy sphagnum can result in losing a leg, or two, up to one's knees, or even deeper, in the shockingly cold water (as I did on a later trip!). This is a warning to always test for solid objects such as roots and fallen trees before placing your weight on your footstep and, above all else, never to go into a sphagnum bog alone!

Wildlife does not seem to be abundant in the area or in the water. On a later trip with Doris and with Don Kirchhoffer, the only animals seen were a small turtle that Doris saw swimming in the pool, and a curious pine warbler that perched on a branch over our heads and sang its trilling song while the three of us lounged on a blanket spread on pine needles above the pool and munched on lunch. It was with reluctance that we finally left the silence and beauty of this great spot.

One has to wonder as to the source of this jewel-like natural phenomenon. Located, as it is, at the bottom of a fifty-foot upland, is it the result of seepage from the slope or is it a natural spring? We don't know. Further research will be needed to answer this question. In the meantime, let's hope this pristine site will be protected as an important and valuable feature of our natural heritage in the Pine Barrens of New Jersey.

SUMMER
SOLSTICE

33

Summer Solstice, Heaths, and Hollies

June 21st! SUMMER SOLSTICE! This is when the sun reaches its most northern point in the sky and will be as close to being directly overhead as it will get. Even though the sun will be at its highest right now, paradoxically, the hottest part of the summer will come later, during the shorter days of July and August, when the earth will be radiating the heat it has been absorbing since spring. June 21st is not necessarily the longest day of the year. In actual fact, all of the days from June 18 through June 25, inclusive, are the same length—fifteen hours and seventeen minutes of sunshine, nearly twice the number of hours we receive at winter solstice! Surely, we can not ask for more. Yet, some say that rather than this being the first day of summer, it is the first day of winter: that from now on everything will go downhill. Days will get shorter, fall will soon be here, and can winter be far behind? Actually, there is some truth in this. Doesn't it seem strange that on the very first day of summer, summer is already on its way out? Each summer day will be getting shorter, moving toward fall. Wouldn't it make more sense for the first day of summer to have been a month earlier, halfway between the first days of spring and summer? Then we'd have a longer summer to enjoy and the longest days of the year would be at the middle rather than the beginning of the summer season.

Oh well, enough of this. For the next three months let's enjoy the summer season to its fullest: ninety-one days of sunshine, humidity, and thundershowers. Although we are following the celestial calendar in this trip through the Pine Barrens, it is interesting to note that in just nine more days, on June 30th, we will be at the mid-point of the Gregorian calendar.

161

Ever since the water was drained off the cranberry bogs in April, cranberry vines have been producing new, green growth that now, from the middle to the end of June, will be in full blossom. Although we tend, today, to think of cranberries as a cultivated crop, actually CRANBERRY, *Vaccinium macrocarpon*, is a native, wild, North American plant that has simply been cultivated by humans.

This is another member of the heath family. Cranberries are low, trailing, bog vines with somewhat woody stems that grow along the surface of the ground and form mats of thickly interwoven vines. From these rise short branches, or uprights, which bear very attractive, pinkish-white flowers with four backward curling petals. It is a truly beautiful sight during the latter part of June to look across a cranberry bog in full bloom: vines covered with thousands of blossoms, a favorable omen for the bright, red fruits that will ripen in late September and October.

Have you ever wondered how the word cranberry came to be the name for this vine and fruit? Since cranberries were unknown to the early colonists before they arrived on these shores, they were introduced to this plant by the Native Americans who already inhabited the area. It is said that when these early settlers first saw the blossoms of this plant, they imagined that the stems and blossoms looked something like the neck, head, and beak of a crane, a European bird, so they called it "craneberry," the words later becoming joined and shortened to the present cranberry.

Soon we will be seeing the familiar boxes of Tru-Blu blueberries for sale in supermarkets, stores, and roadside stands. Tru-Blu is the trade name for blueberries produced by members of the Pinelands farmers' Tru-Blu Cooperative Association based in New Lisbon, Burlington County. New Jersey's blueberries, mainly from Pinelands areas and particularly from around Hammonton in Atlantic County, sometimes called the blueberry capital of the world, are well-known and, during the last couple of weeks in June, the first early varieties of this cultivated fruit become ripe. Some blueberry farmers open up their fields to "pick-your-own" patrons. In commercial operations, hand-picking is the preferred method, but when pickers are unavailable or unaffordable, some of the larger growers use mechanical pickers. From now into July and on into early August, different varieties of blueberries will continue to ripen in succession. Some idea of the extent of the blueberry industry in New Jersey may be gained from the fact that there are (1995) over eight thousand acres under cultivation in one hundred and thirty-five blueberry farms in the state. New Jersey vies with Michigan in leading the nation in the production of blueberries.

Cultivated blueberries that are grown and produced for market are the result of the foresightedness and perseverance of a famous Pine Barrens resident, Miss Elizabeth C. White. Miss White was one of four daughters of Josiah J. White and Mary A. (Fenwick) White. Never married, Miss White worked with her father and helped him conduct the cranberry operations and manage the workers' village at the family farm at Whitesbog. In 1910, Miss White read Bulletin No. 93 entitled "Experiments in Blueberry Culture" by Dr. Frederick V. Coville, a botanist with the Bureau of Plant Industry, United States Department of Agriculture, in which he described his efforts to cultivate the wild HIGH-BUSH BLUEBERRY, *Vaccinium corymbosum.* Miss White and her father invited Dr. Coville to use Whitesbog's facilities to continue and expand his experimental work, and he accepted. Miss White augmented Coville's work by introducing native, wild, "swamp huckleberry" bushes selected for having the largest berries it was possible to find in Pine Barrens swamps and woods. She encouraged her workers to go out and find these and she advertised widely. She even made up special packages with jars, gauges, labels, and typewritten instructions. Although Miss White advertised for "huckleberries," this was simply the common term used by local residents for almost all of the blue to black berries that grew wild out in the swamps and woods.

Upon receiving reports on the locations of spotted bushes, Miss White personally traveled to each site and supervised the digging of the bushes, which then were set out at Whitesbog. Approximately one hundred bushes were found and transplanted by this method. Then, from 1911 to 1916, she worked with Dr. Coville and, by cross-pollinating, hybridizing, grafting, and other breeding combinations of Dr. Coville's experimental varieties with Miss White's native stock, the propagation and cultivation of blueberries became a reality as a successful commercial crop.

Blueberries and huckleberries, both members of the heath family, have several superficial similarities, so many people ask what the differences are between the two. There are two easy ways to tell them apart. HUCK-LEBERRIES, *Gaylussacia* sp., have ten real hard seeds, or nutlets, so hard that they are difficult to crack with your teeth and often get caught between teeth. Most huckleberries are black or blue-black in color. Second, as noted earlier, the undersides of huckleberry leaves have numerous small, orange, resinous dots which glisten in the sunlight and can best be seen with a small pocket or hand lens. BLUEBERRIES, *Vaccinium* sp., have many very small, fine seeds, so indistinguishable when being eaten that they are hardly noticeable. Most blueberries are blue, bluish, or blue-black in color. Second, the undersides of blueberry leaves do not have any of those small, orange, resinous dots that huckleberries have.

In the Pine Barrens, the two most common huckleberries are BLACK HUCKLEBERRY to which we've already referred and DANGLEBERRY, *Gaylussacia frondosa*, whose bluish berries hang in loose clusters. These are more palatable than other huckleberries and often provide tempting bites for Pine Barrens hikers well into August. Two of the more common blueberries are HIGHBUSH BLUEBERRY, which we already know about, and LOW BLUEBERRY, *Vaccinium vacillans*. This low, branching shrub rarely grows higher than a foot to eighteen inches in the Pine Barrens and produces a very sweet, blue fruit.

Most people are well acquainted with the ornamental AMERICAN HOLLY, *Ilex opaca*, and so know this is another of those plants that bear their male and female flowers on different trees. This is why some hollies (females) produce bright red berries in the fall while others (males) do not. Hollies are another of those originally wild plants that man has cultivated for ornamental purposes. The American holly still grows wild, however, and is a rather common tree in low lying, wooded areas throughout the Pinelands, especially along flood plains of river courses.

American holly is included in these discussions for two reasons. First is its connection with Miss Elizabeth White and with Whitesbog. Miss White had particularly strong horticultural interests of which her blueberry experience was only one example. For many years she propagated American hollies as well as English and Japanese hollies, and she established a major nursery at nearby Holly Haven for the sale of these trees. Through her horticultural connections, she obtained specimens of many unusual and rare plants, including the famous and now long lost in the wild FRANKLINIA tree, *Franklinia altamaha*. This tree was discovered on the banks of the

Altamaha River in Georgia in 1765 by John and William Bartram of Philadelphia. On a subsequent trip in 1773, they returned with some young trees and some seeds for propagation. Since another visit in 1790, the tree has never again been seen in the wild. Once Miss White obtained some specimens, she started to propagate them at Whitesbog and for several years she operated a small nursery for the growth and sale of franklinia trees. Today, a few small franklinia shrubs still struggle for survival in the wild on the site of the former nursery.

The other reason for including American holly in these discussions is to introduce another member of the holly family, this one a very characteristic and widespread shrub in moist, sandy habitats throughout the Pine Barrens. This is INKBERRY or SMOOTH HOLLY, *Ilex glabra*. Inkberry is an erect shrub that grows from two to five feet in height and has small, oval, smooth, leathery, evergreen leaves that provide a welcome touch of green throughout the winter. As with American holly, there are separate male and female plants which produce male and female flowers, with the female shrubs producing lustrous black berries, about a quarter of an inch in diameter, which persist over winter.

Like the bearberry we saw in April, another evergreen ground cover and equally characteristic Pine Barrens plant is TEABERRY, CHECKERBERRY or WINTERGREEN, *Gaultheria procumbens*. The tender yellowish-reddish-green shoots and leaves of this low, shrubby heath began to rise from creeping, underground stems early in May, but its small, waxy, white, urn-shaped, nodding blossoms do not develop until late in June. By early fall these will have developed into bright, shiny, red fruits or berries that will persist over winter and provide food for ground birds and mammals. Checkerberry is well known for the spicy, aromatic flavor of its leaves, flowers, and fruits, all of which have a distinct teaberry or wintergreen flavor. This is the active element in oil of wintergreen, which is used as a flavoring in chewing gum, candies, and tea, as a scent for soaps, and a camouflage for bad-tasting medicines. Take a leaf or a berry at any season of the year, chew it a bit, and sample the pleasing flavor of this aromatic member of the heath family.

34

Instinct or Intelligence?

Over the years, from way back to my days as a boy on my family's small New England farm, I have been fascinated with the amazing behavior patterns of insects. Why, for instance, did those small black beetles roll balls of manure from behind the cow barn and carry them down into small holes in the ground? Later, of course, I learned these DUNG BEETLES, or tumble-bugs, members of the scarab family, did this to lay their eggs on the dung balls so that when the eggs hatched into tiny grubs (larvae), they would have a ready supply of food available. As the larvae continued to consume the dung, they developed through stages into adult beetles that would repeat the process. The amazing thing here and elsewhere in the insect world, as we shall see presently, is that the adult beetles did this instinctively. They weren't taught to do this by parents. They simply did it. Just as important, they provided a source of food for their offspring to be. They would never see their offspring, or vice versa, yet they provided for them. Biologists refer to this as "species specific behavior," or instinct, but could this possibly be intelligence?

This has always been a fascinating question concerning insect behavior. This type of behavior may appear purposeful or intelligent, and some people may even wax anthropomorphically about it, but the truth is that, when examined carefully, this behavior is generally found to be automatic. These activities are performed in a characteristic manner by all members of a species. They do not have to be learned and are performed about as well the first time as after practice, and the various individual acts involved are performed in a characteristic sequence. This type of behavior does not involve learning and is generally regarded as instinctive. It has continued all during the course of evolution because of its survival value. Species whose behavior patterns are not beneficial tend to die out, whereas those whose behavior favors survival persist in greater numbers and pass the hereditary elements of this behavior on to their offspring.

Now let's transfer the locale to the Pine Barrens and change the actors from dung beetles (of which there are also great numbers in the Pinelands) to another group of insects that are abundant at this time of year and that also exhibit wonderful examples of instinctive behavior. These are the solitary wasps and bees, which some people may find difficult to distinguish from each other. Both belong to the highest and most advanced order of insects, the Hymenoptera. Most wasps are slightly elongate and thin and have only a few body hairs. Bees are more rounded in shape, usually have a dense coat of feathery hairs on their head and thorax, and have pollen baskets of stiff hairs on their hind legs or body. Further, the young of wasps are provided with paralyzed animal food (spiders, caterpillars, etc.) while the young of bees are fed pollen and honey collected as nectar from flowers. However, as adults, both bees and wasps feed on pollen, nectar, and sweet fruit juices. Most species of both wasps and bees are solitary and nest in burrows in the ground, in the stems of plants, in natural cavities, or construct nests of mud or clay. Paper wasps, yellow jackets, and hornets, as well as bumble bees and honey bees, are social insects that live in well-organized colonies as we shall see in September.

Solitary wasps such as digger wasps, mud-daubers, and potter wasps either dig burrows in sand, gravel, or other soil, or they make their nests of mud. Then they provision their nests with small spiders, grasshoppers, crickets, or other insects that they capture, sting and paralyze, and fly back with or drag to their mud nests or burrows. They next lay their eggs on this captured prey so that when the eggs hatch the newly emerged grubs will have readily available, paralyzed but still live, food. When the grubs finally transform into adult wasps, they fly off to repeat the process. Adult females of both solitary wasps and bees have the ability to sting with their modified ovipositors, but they seldom do so and then only as a last resort. Adult males serve only one purpose: to mate with newly emerged females, after which they die.

So now, let's go looking for some solitary wasps and one solitary bee. Around old open barns, sheds, and porches, look for the nests of mud-daubers that build mud cells under open roofs. The YELLOW-LEGGED MUD-DAUBERS, *Sceliphron caementarium*, use their mandibles to scrape

168

up clayish mud into little balls about the size of peas. Then they carry these pellets between their widespread mandibles and their front feet to their nest sites where they use the pellets in the construction of their tube-like mud structures. Next, they find small spiders, sting and partially paralyze them, bring them back to their cells, lay an egg on each spider in its individual cell, and close up the cells with mud. They repeat this several times until they have constructed a series of cells, each containing an egg and each provisioned with a paralyzed spider. When the grubs finally transform into winged adults, they break out of their cells and start the process all over again.

ORGAN-PIPE MUD-DAUBERS, *Trypoxylon* sp., construct several parallel clay tubes that look something like the parallel tubes of a pipe organ. These daubers partition off the tubes into cells, stock each with a paralyzed spider, lay an egg on it and seal it off. The BLUE-BURGLAR WASPS, *Chalybion* sp., often use water to soften the walls of other mud-dauber nests, break in, toss out the first spiders, restock the cells with spiders they collect, lay their own eggs on the new spiders, and reseal the cells! Here seems to be clear evidence that crime is not confined to intelligent(?) human beings!

POTTER or MASON WASPS, *Eumenes fraternus*, construct clay cells in the form of tiny jugs, complete with necks and flaring mouths, often attached in rows on twigs or branches of shrubs and trees. A female then lays her egg suspended by a thread inside the jug from the lip, provisions the jug with partially paralyzed caterpillars, and seals the neck of her jug with clay.

All these solitary wasps exhibit behaviors that appear very purposeful: building a nest, capturing and stinging but not killing a prey, storing that prey in a cell in its nest, laying an egg on that prey, and sealing off the cell. All these seem to show remarkable foresight, or maybe even intelligence, but much research has shown that all this activity is really only instinctive and hereditary.

So much for solitary wasps, but let's take a moment to look at a large, black, solitary bee that you will often see flying around old wooden structures such as sheds, pavilions, and wooden bridges. This looks like a bumble bee but isn't! It is a male CARPENTER BEE, *Xylocopa virginica*, that is hovering around waiting to mate with newly emerged queens. Many people become quite concerned when they see numbers of these flying nearby and, although at first glance these may look like bumble bees, when you look closely you will see that these are all black and have bare, shiny abdomens. Bumble bees are black and yellow, are completely covered with hairs, and are not at all shiny. In addition, bumble bees do not find anything attractive about old wooden structures because they are nectar and pollen gatherers at flowers, so these two large bees would almost never be seen at the same places.

Mated queens of carpenter bees bore tunnels up to a foot in length into old wood to establish their nests. After their tunnels have been constructed, the queens gather pollen, carry it back to their tunnels, place an egg on it and seal it off like a cell. Each queen will repeat this process several times until she has filled her tunnel with cells containing eggs and pollen. When the eggs hatch, the larvae feed on the pollen, develop into adults, and emerge from their cells and tunnels. As soon as the young queens emerge, they are ready to mate with those males that have been hovering around waiting for them.

So, instinct or intelligence? Our own ability to reason tells us these creatures do not have this same ability and, therefore, their behavior has to be instinct. But it's interesting to think about, isn't it?

Midsummer Wildflowers

C ompared with June, the number of flowering plants that begin to blossom in July start to decrease, and this decline will continue into August and September. But we still have some beautiful wildflowers and shrubs that will come into bloom during the coming months. Leading the parade of July wildflowers is TURK'S-CAP LILY, *Lilium superbum*, one of the showiest of all wild flowers, and *the* lily of southern New Jersey. This lily has everything going for it: color, stature, beauty, and grace. Its large, showy flowers are yellowish-orange to orange-red, with its six individual petals spotted with purple and curled far back exposing rich-brown anthers and the tips of the stamens. It is becoming more and more difficult to find this beautiful plant, so the best you can do is keep a sharp lookout for it in swamps and low grounds almost anywhere in our area. Occasionally one might see it along the edges of cranberry bogs or even along damp roadsides, provided farmers and highway crews have not cut them down with their brush and roadside mowing operations.

Scattered around in most bogs, mixed in with June's stands of bog asphodel and golden-crest, you may have noticed some small, light yellowish flower heads of a bog plant closely related to the lilies. This probably was REDROOT, *Lachnanthes tinctoria*. At that time, this was still in bud stage but now, by mid-July, it is coming into full bloom. Although its small, individual flowers are rather dull looking and inconspicuous, when clustered together in loose flower heads they become more noticeable. Individually, even these flower heads may not be very spectacular, but

171

when they grow in great masses, as they often do, in old and poorly cared for cranberry bogs, these become very conspicuous.

As its name implies, the roots of redroot are quite red, sometimes almost bloodred, in color. If you pull up one of these you can see for yourself the bloodred rootlets at its base. This is a plant that causes all kinds of trouble for cranberry farmers. In the first place, it reproduces so rapidly and becomes so abundant that it gets to be a pernicious weed in cranberry bogs and, unless controlled, it will take over older bogs to such an extent that the bogs may have to be abandoned. Second, the roots of this plant seem to be a preferred food for the tundra swans that over-winter on flooded cranberry bogs. For more on this story, look ahead into November and read all about it!

Another Pine Barrens bog flower you should begin to notice early in July is LANCE-LEAVED SABATIA or CENTAURY, *Sabatia difformis*, a member of the gentian family. Its very attractive, five-petaled flowers that are borne on slender stems are a bright, silky white when in full bloom, but turn yellowish as they fade away after blossoming. This one- to three-foot plant grows in low, wet areas such as swamps, bogs, shallow edges of streams, and cranberry bogs.

Still another early July wildflower in the pines is MEADOW-BEAUTY, *Rhexia virginica*, which can become quite abundant on low, damp, open sands, often where other vegetation is rather sparse. This seems to be one of the first plants to move into an area after damp sands have been dis-turbed for any reason. From now through the balance of summer, its large, showy, pink to deep rose-magenta blossoms, each with eight bril-liant golden stamens, will be quite conspicuous, especially when, as often happens, the plants are so massed together that whole areas appear crim-son. Even after blossoming, the small, round, urn-shaped seed pods of these plants continue to attract the eye, so much so that Thoreau wrote that "the scarlet leaves and stems of the *Rhexia*, sometime out of flower, make almost as bright a patch in the meadows now as the flowers did. Its seed-vessels are perfect little cream-pitchers of graceful form." Occasionally you may find a meadow-beauty that is pale pink rather than magenta-crimson. This will be the closely related MARYLAND MEADOW-BEAUTY, *Rhexia mariana*, which is just as beautiful but nowhere nearly as common in the Pinelands.

More orchids come into bloom in the Pine Barrens during July. Among the more showy and noticeable of these are the WHITE-FRINGED ORCHIDS, *Platanthera (Habenaria) blephariglottis*, which look exactly like their name—a dense head of almost pure white, feathery blossoms with finely fringed lips, atop a one- to three-foot stalk. Fringed orchids are

Meadow-beauty

unique in that each individual blossom usually has a fringed lower lip and a hollow, downward extending spur. These are among the most beautiful of all Pinelands orchids and, although some may still be seen in wet, grassy fields, meadows, bogs and even along damp roadsides, these seem to be disappearing at a rapid rate and are becoming much less common.

Back in April we talked about one of the two plants that, according to Jack McCormick in 1970, are known to occur only in the Pine Barrens of New Jersey. That was sand myrtle. Now, in July, the other of these two plants comes into bloom. PICKERING'S MORNING-GLORY, *Breweria pickeringii* var. *caesariense*, is a unique plant that seems to prefer hot, dry, open, white sandy areas that are devoid of almost all other vegetation. It also is quite rare and has always been so considered. Back in

Pickering's morning-glory

1910, Witmer Stone stated it was "known from probably not more than three or four stations." Today, with more people exploring the Pine Barrens, a few more sites are known, but it is still an uncommon species and one that is clearly endangered. One station is currently being encroached upon to such an extent that it may soon be destroyed. The beautiful, almost pure white, tubular flowers of this unique plant are quite similar in size and shape to those of other morning-glories and bindweeds. Differing from other morning glories, the vine-like stems of Pickering's morning-glory, which lay flat and stretch out along the ground, are so sturdy they are almost shrubby, while the leaves are extremely narrow and grass-like, so much so that they appear almost needle-like.

This brings up the subject of rare, threatened, and endangered species. Ever since living creatures evolved on this earth, species that were unable to adapt and compete in their changing environments have become extinct and have been replaced by species better adapted to survive. These have been extinctions from natural causes. The problem today is that in the past three hundred years, starting with the extinction of the dodo bird on Mauritius Island around 1681, human beings have accelerated the pace of species extinctions through wantom slaughter for food, by introductions of non-native predators, and by direct destruction of their natural habitats.

It is this latter reason that is of greatest concern in regard to the Pine Barrens of New Jersey. This great treasure still provides fine habitats for a number of very special plants and animals. Some of the more notable of these are curly grass and climbing ferns, Knieskern's beaked rush, two twayblades and several other orchids, viscid asphodel, broom crowberry, Pickering's morning-glory, and chaffseed. Animal forms most endangered are the tiger salamander, Pine Barrens treefrog, bog turtle, the pine and corn snakes, and the timber rattlesnake. The Supreme Court of our land has recently ruled, in the case of the spotted owl, that the 1973 Endangered Species Act provides "comprehensive protection" for threatened and endangered species including preservation of the places, their habitats, where they breed, feed, and shelter their young, no matter who owns those lands. Thus it is not enough to protect just curly grass ferns or Pine Barrens treefrogs. Their habitats, in this case cedar swamps and bogs, must also be protected, for if their habitats are destroyed, these and other endangered species will be lost for all time—like the dodo!

Almost the last of the spring and early summer shrubs to blossom are buttonbush and sweet pepperbush. Both grow along edges of swamps. streams, lakes, and other wet areas, but there the similarity ends. BUTTONBUSH, *Cephalanthus occidentalis*, grows in wetter places than sweet pepperbush, sometimes even growing right in the water. Buttonbush also is the earlier bloomer, its spherical balls of small, white flowers coming into bloom shortly after the first of July. It is the flowers of buttonbush that are its most distinctive attraction, for they develop in perfectly round, globe-like clusters, each cluster being made up of scores of tiny, creamy-white blossoms all crowded onto a central

Sweet pepperbush

axis. The individual flowers in each of these clusters are so filled with nectar that they are constantly visited by bees, which is why another name for this plant is honey balls. The leaves of buttonbush are large, three or more inches across, and the entire shrub grows anywhere from three to ten feet in height.

SWEET PEPPERBUSH, *Clethra alnifolia*, begins to bloom as late as the middle to the third week in July, and of all our flowering plants, this is considered to be the most fragrant. Often growing in large patches, this characteristic Pinelands shrub reaches heights of three feet up to eight or ten feet and bears terminal spikes of small, white or pale pink flowers that have a strong, spicy aroma that has been described as "deliciously fragrant." In places, this shrub may be so abundant and its fragrance so strong that its odor fills the entire surrounding atmosphere when it is in bloom. It is alleged that when its blossoms are rubbed together in water, they make a soapy lather so that the shrub is sometimes called soap bush.

Back in April we learned quite a bit about SASSAFRAS trees. Now is the time to start looking at these trees in an effort to find a female tree that is bearing its seed-containing fruits. The female flowers, which were in bloom in the spring, have now developed into deep, slate-blue, oval fruits about three-eighths of an inch long, laying in cup-like ends of thickened, fleshy, crimson-red stems—a brilliant contrast of deep, rich colors. Little can compare with their beauty! Look for these before the birds pick them off for food.

36

Hunters and Those
That Lie in Wait

We are now coming into that time of year, from mid-July into August, when we are most likely to see numbers of fairly large spiders running along the ground. Spiders are not insects because they have only two body parts, a cephalothorax and an abdomen, and have four pairs (eight) of legs. Instead, spiders belong to a different class of arthropods, the arachnids. There are thousands of spiders in the Pine Barrens and they are found everywhere: in burrows in the ground, among dead leaves on the forest floor, in woods, among grasses and weeds, in blueberry fields and in cranberry bogs. Among the most common spiders are the WOLF SPIDERS of the family Lycosidae, the root *lycosa* coming from the Greek for wolf. These are hunting spiders that commonly run over the ground and chase their prey. Most are dark brown and can be recognized by the arrangement of their eyes: four small eyes in a front row, two large ones behind these, and two medium sized ones in a third row.

Wolf spiders are the largest of the common Pine Barrens spiders, their bodies measuring from one-half inch to one and one-quarter inches, and they are powerful hunting creatures. These are not web spinners that spin webs in which to catch their prey. Instead, they simply run along over the ground searching for prey. A few may spin a silk-lined cell as a retreat.

These are the spiders often noticed carrying or dragging a small, round, whitish, silken sac behind them as they move over the ground. This is the female's egg sac, which she has spun in two sections and sewn together after having laid her eggs inside. Female wolf spiders are well known for carrying, protecting, and defending this egg sac, even at the sacrifice of their own lives. When the young inside the sac have developed to the point when they are about to burst out of their crowded quarters, the female bites the sac open at the seam and within a few hours the whole brood of spiderlings has climbed onto her back and remain there in a mass. This cluster may completely cover her abdomen, sometimes two or three layers deep. These will remain there for a week or so until their first molt, and during this entire time the young will cling to their mother while she engages in normal hunting activities. She will run with great speed when pursuing prey or being pursued, or turn to defend herself when cornered, and during all these gyrations the spiderlings continue to cling to her back. Should any get brushed off, they quickly crawl back on if they can catch up with her, if not they just get left behind for the female never stops to retrieve any of them. After their first molt, these spiderlings will leave their mother to take up their own separate lives and begin their own hunting activities.

Another group of very interesting spiders that also are common in the Pinelands are the JUMPING SPIDERS, the Salticidae. These are among the most attractive of all spiders. These also are hunting spiders and capture their prey by leaping or jumping upon them, sometimes jumping distances many times their own body length. When they jump they spin a dragline so that when they capture a prey they can quickly return to their original position by means of the dragline. The eyes of jumping spiders are among the very best in the entire invertebrate world. Like other spiders, they have eight eyes, but the two middle eyes in the front row are very large, almost owl-like, enabling these spiders to recognize prey or predators from four to eight inches distant.

The superficial resemblance of some other spiders to small crabs has given a third group of spiders its common name of CRAB SPIDERS, the Thomisidae. Not only do these spiders look like crabs, they move like crabs, sideways, as well as backward and forward. For the most part these have short, wide, flattened bodies with legs that extend out sideways, the forward two pairs longer and more robust than the others. These spiders have become specialists in ambush and they excel at this by concealing themselves on flowers and waiting until some insect like a bee, a fly, a moth, or a butterfly visits the flower in search of honey or pollen. Then they simply seize the insect with their strong forelegs, inject it with their venom, and proceed to suck out their body nutrients. Usually crab spiders are brightly colored, almost always in cryptic colors matching the flowers on which they await their prey, but some have the ability to change their body color to match the flower on which they lie in ambush.

Crab spiders are not the only predators that lie in concealment on or around the head of a flower waiting to seize a visiting prey. AMBUSH BUGS, or Phymatidae, are small, stout-bodied, predacious, true bugs that act in a similar manner to the crab spiders. When a prey comes within reach, the bug makes a quick strike with its sabre-like front legs, draws the victim within easy reach, and then leisurely sucks it dry. So, look for either one or both of these interesting predators lying hidden within the heads of flowers, especially fall flowers like goldenrods in the composite or aster family, the Compositae.

Two other spiders should be noted, as these are the only poisonous spiders to be found in the Pine Barrens. One is the well-known BLACK WIDOW SPIDER, *Latrodectus mactans*, which is rarely found in open woods, but may be found under boards, in woodpiles, or around stacks of old blueberry or cranberry packing boxes. The female, which often eats the male after mating, thus becoming a "widow," is shiny coal-black, a half-inch long, and bears a conspicuous, red, hourglass-shaped spot on the underside of the body. The male is much smaller with variously shaped red or yellow spots on the abdomen. Although poisonous, black widow spiders are not aggressive and will bite only in self defense. The only other poisonous spider is the dull yellowish-brown BROWN RECLUSE SPIDER, *Loxosceles reclusa*, but this is even less common than the black widow. The brown recluse is a southern species that, in recent years, has slowly moved into this area. It is most likely to be encountered in varied ground litter and around old buildings.

Closely related to spiders and often mistakenly called spiders, HAR-VESTMEN or DADDY-LONG-LEGS, the Phalangiidae, can be recognized by their single, compact, oval body and their eight extremely long, thin legs. These are common on vegetation and often become abundant by late summer and early fall, thus giving rise to their being called har-vestmen. For the most part, these little critters feed on plant juices and dead animal matter.

Spiders, like insects, are not well liked or popular forms of animal life. Far from it. In fact, few creatures cause as many repulsive reactions in humans as do spiders. Yet, spiders are vital in helping to maintain the balance of nature and, in many ways, are actually beneficial to human beings. Spiders are exclusively carnivorous, usually seizing only live animals, and their main source of food is insects. A British acarologist, W.S. Bristowe, in his *The World of Spiders* states that "spiders, together with birds and insectivorous mammals, are the main foes of insects," and "the weight of insects consumed annually (by spiders) in Britain exceeds that of all the human inhabitants." For years, farmers in China and Poland have actually cultivated spiders and released them in their fields to help control insect pests of their agricultural crops. So, in spite of their being disliked by many people, spiders are a vital link in the natural food chain.

One interesting final note about spiders goes all the way back to ancient Greece. A maiden by the name of Arachne had attained such great skills in the art of weaving that she dared to challenge the weaving skills of the goddess Minerva. Minerva then appeared before Arachne and the two had a contest. Minerva wove a scene of her contest with Neptune, ruler of the sea. Arachne wove a scene designed to show the failings and errors of the gods. In anger, Minerva struck the web with her shuttle and rent it to pieces. In shame, Arachne hung herself and Minerva then transformed the rope into a web and Arachne into a spider. Thus the origin of the term arachnids (Arachnida) for a group which includes the spiders!

37

Goldfinches—Again, but Briefly

Back in April we mentioned that the AMERICAN GOLDFINCH is the state bird of New Jersey, and we noticed the changing plumage of male goldfinches from winter's olive-green to summer's bright canary yellow and black. Ever since then, these bouncing balls of gold have been flying about singing their cheerful *per-chic-o-ree* notes as they flash through the air in their typical undulating flight, seemingly without a care in the world.

But now, by mid-July, after many other birds have finished nesting and all others are well underway, goldfinches finally begin to build their nests, mate, and start to raise their young. The likely reason for this tardiness is that goldfinches build their nests of fine grasses and the down gathered from the seeds of thistles and other composite flowers, so they have to wait until these seeds ripen before they can begin their nest building activities. These nests often are so compactly built that they will actually hold water. Goldfinches feed principally on seeds, mainly from the seeds of composite flowers, and use seeds as well as small insects to feed their young. After their young have fledged, sometimes well into September, and the mating season has been completed, male goldfinches again begin to molt and change back to the soft, olive-green plumage of their female mates. Historically, goldfinches have been important in medieval art and appear commonly in illuminated manuscripts from the Middle Ages.

38

Earthstars
and
British Soldiers

The warm, humid days and nights of late July and August are the best times of the year to find and study the many new and different formations that begin to appear in the pines. These seem to spring up out of nowhere and yet everywhere, almost all at the same time, from out of the ground, from around the bases of trees, from the stumps of fallen trees, from the trunks of dead and dying trees, and from old logs lying on the ground. These interesting, fragile, and often beautiful formations are FUNGI, which used to be considered one of the lower and simpler forms of plant life, but now are classified as a separate group of living organisms. Fungi come in a wide variety of shapes and colors, among the better known of which are bacteria, slime molds, mildews, morels, plant rusts and smuts, black (cherry) knots, puffballs, earthstars, stinkhorns, corals, bracket fungi, and mushrooms or toadstools. When we look at any of these fungi, we usually are seeing only their external fruiting bodies, which often are very short lived. Hidden down below, in the ground or inside the decaying tree, is a very extensive network of thread-like strands called hyphae, the whole of which, considered together, is called the mycelium. It is the hyphae, as a part of the mycelium, that are the actual growing and spreading parts of the fungus. It is the mycelium that produces the external fruiting bodies that we see. Along with many other primitive forms of living organisms, fungi reproduce by means of tiny spores which, when mature and released, move freely in the atmosphere until they come to rest and start to grow on some suitable object.

Because fungi have no chlorophyll, they are unable to manufacture any food for themselves, yet they need organic matter on which to live.

185

In order to survive, they must obtain their food from other objects such as mold growing on a piece of stale bread. Thus fungi are either parasitic (living in or on and consuming the tissues of another living organism, its host, and so are destroyers of other objects); or they are saprophytic (consuming dead tissues) and so are scavengers, living on the remains of other living things; or they exist in a symbiotic relationship with the roots of several plants.

Fungi do a great deal of good as decomposers, breaking down and transforming living and dead objects back into the environment. When plants and animals die, fungi, including bacteria, move in and help break down their organic components and return them to the soil and to the atmosphere. Several forms of animal life make good use of fungi as a source of food, and it doesn't seem to make any difference to animals whether or not the fungi are poisonous from a human perspective. Starting with the lowly slug and with snails, both are consumers of any mushrooms they may encounter along their slimy trails. Many insects, especially beetles, use mushrooms as a source of food, and some burrow and tunnel within fungi to use it as a protected habitat. Several species of small scarab beetles, rove beetles, and various fungus beetles are common in mushrooms. One beetle, known as the FORKED FUNGUS BEETLE, *Bolitotherus cornutus*, spends its entire life cycle within and feeding on woody bracket fungi. Among the higher forms of animal life, box turtles regularly feed on mushrooms, but the prime mushroom eaters in the animal world are rodents such as mice, chipmunks, and squirrels, particularly red squirrels.

The next time you do any walking or hiking in wooded Pine Barrens areas, be on the lookout for some of the more common and conspicuous fungi along the trail. One of the first that might draw your attention could be the rough looking BLACK KNOT FUNGUS, *Dibotryon morbasum*, that is common on the twigs, limbs, and trunks of wild black cherry trees. As with many fungi, this fungus usually does not begin to attack until the tree is already in a weakened state from some other cause. Then the black fungus moves in, gradually spreads all over the tree and eventually kills it. The same general process occurs when BRACKET FUNGI, *Fomes applanatum*, start to grow out from the sides of stumps and tree trunks. These eventually develop into large, flat, semicircular, woody fungi, sometimes as large as a foot or more across. Most frequently seen on hardwood trees, especially oaks, this fungus is also known as artist's fungus because the fresh, protected undersides of this shelf-like fungus are so white, smooth, and hard that some people paint pictures on them, shellac or varnish them, and use them as attractive mantel pieces. This

186

practice does not seem to be as common today as it used to be in the 1800s and early 1900s.

Other fungi, such as puffballs and some mushrooms, sprout up right out of the ground. Cultivated mushrooms are a well-known food as are several wild mushrooms, but there also are poisonous wild mushrooms, so one must know the differences between these before attempting to collect and eat any wild mushrooms. One of the most common, and poisonous, mushrooms in the Pinelands is the FLY AGARIC, *Amanita muscaria*, often found under stands of pine and other evergreens. Probably its most conspicuous feature is the numerous small particles, or warts, all over the upper surface of the mushroom, from its earliest small, round, forming or budding stage to its expanded maturity. These small flecks of white or pale yellow particles have sometimes been described as resembling cottage cheese. The fly agaric mushrooms are often brightly colored, ranging from yellow to orange to even reddish. In common with other *Amanita* species, these mushrooms have a skirt-like collar (annulus) on the stem

Fly Agaric mushroom

187

just below the cap. They differ from other *Amanita* in that their bulbous base is never pouch- or sac-like, with an opening out of which the stem rises. Instead, their base is like a tight, solid bulb. So, check any specimens very carefully before collecting any of these as possible dinner fare!

Perhaps the most interesting Pine Barrens fungi are EARTHSTARS, *Geastrum triplex*. When these first appear on Pine Barrens sands they look pretty much like small puffballs, but as each one attains full size and matures, the outer layer of the puffball splits into four to eight sections, like pieces of a pie, and each section curls back to lie flat on the sand like a four- to eight-pointed star. During wet weather these sections may close up again and look like the original puffball, but they will reopen when dry weather returns. Left exposed in the center of the earthstar is a soft, inner sac containing thousands of reproductive spores protected by a thin, paper-like outer skin with a small, central hole. When any outside pressure, even a slight tap of a finger, is applied to the sac, the spores burst out in a tiny, dust-like explosion to float unseen through the air in their search for a suitable site to continue their life cycle.

It is almost impossible to walk anywhere in the Pine Barrens without stepping on some of the many small, low-growing organisms known as LICHENS. Once considered to be one of the lower forms of plant life, lichens now are classified with the fungi because fungi are their major structural components. Lichens are dual organisms that are composed of both algae and fungi growing together in a mutually beneficial (symbiotic) relationship. Sometimes, also, cyanobacteria may be a part of the combined organism. In each individual lichen, the fungus forms the actual body and provides the structural support. It also provides the water and the minerals and is the most conspicuous part of the lichen. The alga or algae, in the form of green cells which contain chlorophyll and thus can manufacture food through photosynthesis, provide the food for the combined organism.

Lichens are pioneer organisms that grow where other organisms can not, and in so doing they break down the surfaces on which they grow and thus they contribute to soil formation. Virtually all terrestrial habitats—sandy soils, decaying woods, old logs and stumps, bases and trunks of trees, and even rocks—contain an abundance of lichens. Extremely sensitive to air pollution, lichens grow best where the air is clean and unpolluted. Thus lichens are good indicators of atmospheric conditions. We should feel good about the great abundance of lichens that thrive in the Pine Barrens—another excellent reason to do all we can to "protect, preserve, and enhance" this treasure we have in New Jersey.

There are so many different kinds of lichens in the Pinelands that it is not possible to do more than generalize about them here. Besides, this is not supposed to be an identification book! Scientifically, there are three major groups of lichens: the fruticose lichens that grow upright in distinctive shapes; the foliose lichens that grow flat on trees and rocks; and the crustose lichens. We're not going to be very scientific here, and are simply going to talk about them in a popular sense. The most conspicuous lichens you see almost everywhere you walk are several different kinds of what broadly are called REINDEER or THORN LICHENS, most of which are in the genus *Cladonia*. Generally, these grow from one to three inches high, are gray-green in color, and are rather branchy

False reindeer lichen

189

looking, something like the branching antlers of reindeer. Under the usual hot, dry, surface conditions in the Pine Barrens, these lichens become quite dry and brittle, and crunch under foot, but when dampened by moisture these become rather soft and pliable. In more northern climates, these lichens grow more luxuriously and are a year-round source of food for caribou and reindeer that in winter will paw away the snow to feed on them. Another group of lichens are some that have very distinctive shapes like pyxie cups, or ladders, or awls. Appropriately, these are called PYXIE-CUP LICHEN, SLENDER LADDER LICHEN, and AWL LICHEN, all, also, in the genus *Cladonia*. These are all low-growing, from one to two inches high, and are gray-green in color.

Perhaps the best known and most readily recognized lichen is the BRITISH SOLDIER LICHEN, *Cladonia cristatella*, whose bright red fruiting tips remind people of the bright red coats worn by British soldiers during the Revolutionary War. (But, be careful, for there is another lichen, sometimes called SWAMP LICHEN, *Cladonia incrassata*, that looks so much like a British soldier lichen that they can be separated only by botanical differences!). A third group of lichens, generally known as SHIELD LICHENS (the foliose lichens mentioned above), look like flat, gray-green rosettes growing on the bark on the sides of trees, especially those of oaks, or on old fence posts and rails.

If you are in a cedar bog or swamp, that bluish-gray-green "bloom" you see up and down the lower trunks of the cedar trees is still another lichen, the SANTEE LICHEN, *Cladonia santensis*. Finally, there is one lichen that may be growing directly under your feet as you walk across bare stretches of sand, but you probably have no idea this is a lichen. In fact, this looks more like some black tar has been poured onto the sands and has hardened. Appropriately, this is known as TAR LICHEN, *Lecidea uliginosa*.

39

Summer's
Insect Chorus

B y late July, the nighttime songs of insects gradually begin to replace the daytime songs of birds, and this will continue well into the fall. Second only to birds, insects such as cicadas, grasshoppers, crickets, and katydids are the world's foremost musicians. Considering their small size, no other creatures can produce such a volume of song. Although their songs may not be as pleasing to many people's ears as the songs of birds, they serve the same general purposes of communication and to attract mates.

On the hottest summer days in July and August, the shrill, rising and falling, pulsating, whirring, buzzing of male DOG-DAY CICADAS, *Tibicen canicularis*, or harvest flies, can be heard from the tops of shrubs, bushes, and trees. More often heard than seen, common cicadas are rather large, robust, blackish insects with broad heads, protruding eyes, and transparent, gauzy, greenish, cross-veined wings held roof-like over their bodies. There are two types of cicadas: common dog-day cicadas that appear every year, which are the ones just described, and the SEVEN-TEEN-YEAR CICADAS, *Magicicada septendecim*, which are somewhat smaller with wing veins outlined in bright red instead of green.

Cicadas, considered to be the noisiest of all insects, produce their songs by vibrating a pair of special membranes or drumming organs, called tymbals, located under the sides of their body and hind wings. Sometimes cicadas are called locusts, but this is a misnomer because cicadas are not even remotely related to locusts. The locust group contains the grasshoppers, katydids, and crickets, all of which have chewing mouthparts.

Cicadas have sucking, tube-like mouthparts which they insert into plant tissues to draw out plant juices, and so are more closely related to aphids, plant lice, leaf hoppers, and the true bugs. Many people seem to fear that cicadas are destructive insects, but actually they do only minimal damage to the tip ends of branches of the trees where they lay their eggs.

Cicadas spend their very short adult lives "singing" in the tops of trees. After mating, females drop down to the lower branches to lay their eggs in slits they make in the bark of twigs, then move up the twigs a bit and girdle them. The twigs then die, break off, and drop to the ground where the eggs hatch. The larvae that emerge then burrow into the ground, attach themselves to the roots of trees, and suck plant juices in order to grow, shedding their outer skin several times during the feeding and growing processes. When fully grown, they burrow up to the surface of the ground, climb any available object, shed their outer skin one last time by splitting it down the middle of the back, emerge as winged adults, and climb or fly to the tops of the trees. Dog-day cicadas complete their underground feeding period within four to seven years, and their broods overlap so that some adults appear every year. There is one species of dog-day cicadas, *Tibicen hieroglyphica*, that is especially characteristic of the Pine Barrens. This is very small, not over one and one-quarter inches, and has an almost transparent abdomen.

The seventeen-year cicadas remain as larvae, feeding on plant juices underground, for seventeen years (thirteen years in the south) before emerging in massed broods in different geographical areas to complete their life cycles. The most recent, major seventeen-year cicada appearance in New Jersey occurred in June 1996 (brood II), so this brood is not scheduled to reappear until June 2013. In the Pinelands, the 1996 occurrence was limited to a few widely scattered localities such as the Atlantic County park at Estell Manor, but there were almost no records from deep within the Pine Barrens, probably due to the lack of suitable host trees.

Another daytime singer is the common black FIELD CRICKET, *Gryllus assimilis*, which is heard almost everywhere, even in houses, especially in the fall of the year when they try to find protection from the coming winter. Male crickets seem to chirp almost incessantly, both day and night. The closely related, straw-colored HOUSE CRICKET, *Gryllus domesticus*, from Europe, has been immortalized in both prose and poetry as, for example, in Charles Dickens' classic, *The Cricket on the Hearth*.

The principal musicians of the evening and early nighttime chorus are the LONG-HORNED GRASSHOPPERS (Tettigoniidae) so named for their long, thread-like antennae, which are as long as and often longer than their bodies. All of these produce their songs by stridulation, that is, they rub a sharp edge at the base of one of their front, or outer, wings along a file-like ridge on the underside of their other front wing. Included in this group are the bush, the angular-winged, and the round-headed katydids, and the coneheaded and meadow grasshoppers. Together, these make up the noisiest family of musicians in the world and, considering their small size, no other living creatures can make as much noise as these insects. Often these will begin their music as early as midafternoon, and then continue well into the evening with short, high-pitched notes or longer, high, piercing, buzzing notes that can be heard for considerable distances. Most of these insects usually stay rather close to the ground in bushy and weedy areas, in high grasses, in meadows, and in blueberry fields and cranberry bogs.

TREE CRICKETS, *Oecanthus* sp., hide under leaves during the day and then come out at dusk to start their fiddling, which they continue well into the night. Tree crickets are small, frail, green insects with gauzy, transparent wings, long, jumping hind legs, and very long, delicate antennae. Although called tree crickets, most are much more common on low shrubs, bushes, and tall weeds. One of the more interesting features of the chorusing of tree crickets is that often hundreds or even thousands of them in the same locality will all chirp in unison. Equally intriguing is that one tree cricket, the small, pale green SNOWY TREE CRICKET, *Oecanthus fultoni*, is also known as the temperature cricket because the number of its chirps in fifteen seconds, plus forty, gives a close approximation of the temperature in degrees Fahrenheit. As the temperature rises, the tempo of the chirps increases and as it falls, the number of chirps become fewer. Listen any evening now to the high-pitched, rhythmic chorusing of these crickets and test this "thermometer" for yourself.

The last member to join this chorus, usually during the first week in August, is the NORTHERN TRUE KATYDID, *Pterophylla camellifolia*, which fiddles from the tops of the tallest trees. These are quite large, all green, grasshopper-like insects with large, convex outer wings and very long antennae. These are called katydids because of the fancied resemblance of their calls to the words *katy-did, katy-didn't, katy-did, katy-didn't*. Males start calling to attract mates shortly after sunset and continue long after darkness falls, and some katydids will continue their calling even into the cool autumn evenings of late October, but by then much more slowly and faintly. Fossil records indicate that insects first appeared on this earth some three hundred and fifty million years ago, while birds arose one hundred and eighty million years ago. Thus, insects were fiddling away in this world millions of years before the first birds evolved to add their songs to the grand chorale.

193

Sedges

in a Savanna

By the fifth of August we have reached the midpoint of the summer season and, if it has been a reasonably average season so far, we've already had a good number of hot, hazy, humid days with the temperatures reaching well into the nineties, coupled with nights when the temperatures refused to go lower than the seventies. Likely there are more to come, especially during the dog days of late August, for this humid weather will stick with us at least toward the middle of next month.

Even in these hot, lazy days, however, there can be some surprises in the Pine Barrens. One year, on the eleventh of August, I flushed a NIGHTHAWK up off the ground in bright sunshine, around 3:30 p.m., along a trail in the old Batsto nature area behind the Pleasant Mills church. Then, on the very next day, I flushed another nighthawk (surely not the same one!) up off the ground around 9:00 to 9:30 a.m. in the pygmy or dwarf forests around the edges of Coyle Field, off Route 72. On still another occasion, on the fifth of June, around 11:45 a.m., while attending some pit-fall traps along the edges of Buffin's meadows in Pemberton Township, with the sun shining out of a clear blue sky and the temperature near ninety degrees, I heard a WHIP-POOR-WILL sing its *whip-poor-will* call in broad daylight. Yes, interesting things do happen in the Pine Barrens!

On another nice, warm, sunshiny day in August, Doris, Don Kirchhoffer, and I headed out to revisit a beautiful savanna Don and I had first visited in January. Don had discovered this site sometime earlier with some members of the South Jersey Outdoor Club. Because life had been pretty dormant over winter, we wanted to see it again now because we were interested in finding out which sedge it was that was so common and widespread all over the savanna. Savannas are grass- and sedge-covered marshes and meadows.

This site is deep in the pines, off Hampton Gate Road in Washington Township, Burlington County. We traveled east over the old Tuckerton Road and crossed the old railroad tracks of the former Southern Division of the Central Railroad of New Jersey at High Crossing. Some distance beyond we turned off onto a side trail and eventually stopped to walk a few hundred yards to the edge of the largest and most beautiful savanna I know in the Pine Barrens. In extent, I estimate it to be between sixteen and twenty acres.

At the time of our January visit, water had covered the entire savanna to depths of several inches but now, in August, the ground was bone dry

A savanna

under an almost complete cover of sedges. The few small areas bare of vegetation were parched dry with deep cracks across the caked surfaces. The three of us tramped all over that savanna, Doris taking pictures of anything of interest that she saw and Don and I gathering samples of the different species of plant life. After we returned home, I did the needed identifications and later had Ted Gordon recheck them for accuracy. By far the most abundant and widespread sedge, covering nearly ninety percent of the savanna, was WALTER'S SEDGE, *Carex striata*. This was not surprising since Stone states this "is the most characteristic and abundant Carex" in Pine Barrens bogs. Other sedges we collected were a BEAK-RUSH, *Rhynchospora inundata*, a TWIG-RUSH, *Cladium mariscoides*, and a SPIKE-RUSH, *Eleocharis olivacea*. In spite of the fact all three contain the word "rush" as a part of their names, all are really sedges (rushes are a different family of plants). One other plant that was widespread all through the central and lower areas of the savanna was the YELLOW-EYED GRASS, *Xyris torta*, which grew in great abundance mingled in with the Walter's sedges.

It is reported that, around 1900, savannas covered several thousand acres in the Pine Barrens, but today most savannas are small and, all together, total no more than a thousand acres. Thickets or spongs of leatherleaf or highbush blueberry, and swamp forests of red maple, black gum, sweet bay, and southern white cedar have replaced most of the former savannas (McCormick 1979). On a U.S. Geological topographical map dated 1956, this particular spot we visited is shown as a body of water, but today the bed of the old lake is a vast sea of sedges completely encircled within a pitch pine forest. Because the former lake has not completely dried up yet, these sedges grow in water from a few inches to as much as a foot in depth. Around the edges of the savanna where the water is more shallow, sphagnum mosses and leatherleaf are beginning to invade the sedges.

This beautiful spot in the pines is a wonderful example of natural succession in action. As the sedges have moved in to cover the former lake bottom they have created land. As this process continues over time the sedges will eventually help form drier and drier land. As the land continues to dry up, bladderworts, sundews, and pitcher-plants, and maybe a few orchids, may move in for a while, but the leatherleaf will continue to move in from the edges. Eventually, the leatherleaf will take over and transform this present savanna into a spong, a lowland area that has become overgrown with a dense intrusion of shrubs, particularly leatherleaf and highbush blueberry. So, though in a constant state of transition, here, presently, is a fine remnant of more extensive savannas of the past.

197

41

Curly-Grass, Club-Mosses, and Orchids

As mentioned back in early March, the Pine Barrens of New Jersey is noted worldwide as a unique botanical treasure, so much so that in 1983 the United Nations designated the region as an International Biosphere Reserve. One of the reasons for this is that the Pine Barrens is a meeting ground for plants from both northern and southern origins that reach the limits of their distributional ranges right here in the Pinelands. In March we observed one northern plant, Conrad's broom-crowberry, that continues to thrive out on the pine plains.

Now is the time to go out and look for another equally well-known northern plant in the Pine Barrens, CURLY-GRASS FERN, *Schizea pusilla.* Like broom-crowberry, this is another disjunct population that is widely separated from the main area where it grows, in this case Nova Scotia, Prince Edward Island, and Newfoundland. Curly-grass fern is a very small plant that is quite unfern-like in appearance. Its nonreproductive leaves or fronds look exactly like its name: tiny evergreen blades of very curly and twisted grass that rise barely an inch in height. The very finely stalked fertile fronds rise from two to four inches and bear one-sided, segmented, fruiting capsules. These contain the reproductive spores which mature and are released about mid-August, probably the best time to try to find and observe this intriguing plant. Its favored growing sites are moist spots in and around the edges of sphagnum and cedar bogs, around hummocks where cedar trees grow, on embedded cedar logs, and around exposed roots and stumps of cedars. To find some of these plants you may have to search hard, probably get down on your hands and knees, and be prepared to end up with damp, if not wet, hands, knees, and shoes!

Curly-grass fern was first known to botanical science when it was discovered in the Pine Barrens back in 1805 near Quaker Bridge by a group of Philadelphia botanists. It seems almost needless to say that this interesting tiny plant is classified as a rare and an endangered species of Pinelands flora.

Other nonflowering, spore-bearing plants also reach their maturity in the Pine Barrens from mid-August into September. These are the club-mosses. In spite of their common name, these are not mosses but, like the curly-grass fern, are vascular plants. Three of these occur rather commonly

Bog club-moss

200

in and around the edges of damp, sandy bogs, savannas, and small ponds throughout the Pine Barrens. These are the BOG, the CAROLINA, and the FOX-TAIL CLUB-MOSSES, all members of the genus *Lycopodium.* All three are small, low-growing, green plants with main stems that creep and root themselves along the ground and send up slender stalks on top of which are enlarged, spore bearing cones. When these become ripe, yellowish-white spores will shake out of these cones at the slightest touch. Like the mosses we talked about in March, club-mosses reproduce by alternation of generations, but club-mosses also propagate themselves by continuing to extend their rooted stems along the surface of the ground.

Club-mosses are among the most ancient of plants and, except for size and abundance, are only slightly changed from when they flourished on this earth some three hundred to two hundred million years ago. During the Pennsylvanian or Carboniferous Period (the Coal Age) in the Paleozoic Era of geologic history, some species of these fern-like plants grew as tall as fifty feet in height and had main trunks as large as five feet in diameter. In addition, these grew in such great abundance that they were the dominant plants in the forests of that period. As masses of those leaves and trees died and dropped to the ground, they became covered with more and more of the same, and as this organic mass built up and became covered with earth, pressure increased from above and these gradually became transformed into coal. One of the best examples of this took place right next door in territory we now call Pennsylvania, which, in modern times, has yielded rich deposits of the coal that was formed from those ancient club-moss forests.

Among the flowering plants that blossom in August are two beautiful orchids, three ladies' tresses, also orchids, and a couple of attractive non-orchid wildflowers. Hidden in the recesses of small savannas along the flood plains of some Pine Barrens streams, deep in the heart of the pines, diligent search may be rewarded with the finding of the SOUTHERN YEL-LOW or YELLOW FRINGELESS ORCHIS, *Platanthera (Habenaria) integra* and/or the CRESTED YELLOW ORCHIS, *Platanthera (Habenaria) cristata.* Both of these bear heads of brilliant, orange-yellow flowers, those of the southern yellow in a dense cluster of fringeless flowers while those of the crested yellow are in smaller heads of flowers with narrow, fringed petals and very deeply fringed lips. The flowers of both species have short spurs of approximately one-quarter of an inch. Both of these are southern species that seem to reach their northern limits in the Pine Barrens and, of course, both are classified as endangered in the Comprehensive Management Plan of the New Jersey Pinelands Commission. The discovery of either of these gems is reward enough for the bushwacking that may be necessary to find them.

While you're at it, also be on the lookout for one or more of the four fairly common species of LADIES' TRESSES, genus *Cernua*, in the Pinelands. The starting times of their flowering periods range from early July to early September, but three of them will be in bloom sometime during August. Superficially, these may all look somewhat similar, so you may find yourself hard-pressed to identify which one you may have found. In most cases, individual flowers are arranged in a row up a single stalk and are small, whitish, and sort of tubular with a forward and downward projecting lower lip. Sometimes the flower arrangement may be in a single row up the side of the flowering stalk, while in other species the flowers are arranged spiral-like around and up the stalk. The braided appearance of the flower bracts on the spikes of some species could account for the popular name of ladies' tresses, but it also is reported that the plant's English name used to be "ladies' traces" from a fancied resemblance between its twisted bracts and the lacings which used to be such an important part of the feminine toilet.

The differences between the species are largely botanical, such as whether the flowers do or do not spiral up the flowering stalk or whether the basal leaves are present or not at flowering time, or whether the root is tubular. Even the larger forms, the ones that grow to heights of three or four feet, have rather small flowers. The different flowering times of the individual species are also important. In most cases, it may be necessary to check their identification in your favorite field guide to determine which species you have found, but don't be surprised if you still have difficulty, for hybrids do occur. Although small, ladies' tresses are quite attractive and, as a group, are among the last of the orchids to bloom.

Getting away from orchids for a moment, one of the non-orchid plants that come into flower in August is WATER WILLOW, *Decodon verticillatus*, also known as swamp loosestrife, the same common name that is applied to the swamp candles we saw in June (see page 132). Water

Ladies' tresses

willow is a very interesting plant but you may have to get your feet wet to find it because it grows along the very edge of water, or right in shallow water itself, around ponds and in swampy areas. Although this is a herbaceous perennial, it is rather shrubby with tall, reclining, or recurved angular stems that are somewhat woody below. These stems sometimes grow so tall (or long), up to ten feet, and they curve over to such an extent, that their tips will often take root when they bend down enough to reach muddy soil. Thus, in places, this plant may form veritable thickets of shrubbery. Growing out from the axils of the uppermost leaves on these curving stems are clusters of small but very attractive, bell-shaped, magenta flowers.

42

Forest Fires
and Regeneration

The Pine Barrens is a region of fires, one of the most important factors in shaping its vegetation. Forest fires are frequent occurrences in the Pinelands, and over recent centuries there have been many major fires. The period between mid-March and mid-May is particularly prone to forest fires because trees are still dry from winter dormancy and the ground is littered with last fall's and overwinter's leaves and broken branches, called duff. Not until spring rains begin, sap starts to flow, and trees "green-up" does the threat of forest fires subside.

From an ecological point of view, and as far back in time as we have knowledge, fires have played a major role in maintaining the New Jersey Pine Barrens in the condition the early colonists found them. The highly flammable vegetation burns readily, providing tinder for frequent and often widely spreading fires. These fires, fueled by the resins of the pitch pines and the dried out but still-resinous leaves of the various huckleberries, repeatedly burn off all the aboveground vegetation as well as the duff on the dry forest floor, but few plants are actually killed. Many plants, especially the dominant pitch pine with its thick bark, are quite fire resistant and soon either resprout from the roots or produce new growth from the trunks and larger limbs of the trees.

Over a period of years without fires, the present Pine Barrens could become an oak forest. Pine seeds are extremely small and light and are hidden deep down between the bracts of pine cones. When the cones open, the winged seeds are released and, wind blown, fall upon the ground. If the ground is covered with a thick layer of dead leaves, pine needles, twigs, and broken branches, these light seeds can not work their way down through this duff to the ground to take root and send up new pine trees. On the other hand, the seeds of the several species of oaks, the other major trees in the Pine Barrens, are, of course, acorns. When these fall to the ground in the fall of the year, they are heavy enough to work their way down through the duff to reach the earth on the forest floor and take root. Next spring, new oak trees will grow up through the duff. Given enough time, there could be a gradual transition from pine woods to oak-dominated woodlands and there might not be a New Jersey Pine Barrens any longer.

Fire is a leading factor in this story. Fires contribute to the ecology of the Pine Barrens in several ways. First, fires burn the duff off the ground to leave the earth exposed; second, the heat of the fire opens up the pine cones so that the winged seeds are released and fall to the ground. Now these pine seeds can take root and sprout new pine seedlings. At the same time, because the bark of oak trees is not thick enough to protect the growing layers of these trees, all the oak trees are killed in a forest fire. The bark of the pitch pines, the most common pines in the Pine Barrens, is so thick that the growing layers of the tree under the bark survive the fire and, in a short while, begin to produce new shoots from the trunks and main branches of the pines. Thus, as a result of wildfires, pines are able to maintain their natural balance in the Pine Barrens through both reseeding and regrowth.

It is estimated that, on average, wildfires need to burn over an area at least once every forty years in order to maintain a pine subclimax and, consequently, the Pine Barrens. In short, from an ecological point of view, fires are essential to the future of New Jersey's *Pine* Barrens. On the other hand, from a human, non-ecological point of view, wildfires in the Pinelands can be very destructive.

One of the worst and most memorable fire storms in the Pine Barrens occurred during the period of April 20 to 24, 1963, when a whole series of wildfires burned over one hundred and ninety thousand acres, caused eight and one-half million dollars worth of damage to property, and resulted in the deaths of seven persons.

Much more recently, on April 4 and 5, 1995, a major forest fire swept across a large section of the Pine Barrens. This one apparently started somewhere east of Pasadena, moved eastward through parts of Manchester, Lacey, Barnegat, and Ocean townships in Ocean County and was finally stopped by backfires set along Route 532 and the Garden State Parkway. A total of nearly twenty-five thousand acres of forest were burned. In some areas the fire burned so fiercely and was so hot that everything in its path was completely consumed. Surely, nothing could survive such devastation.

This burn presented an opportunity to do some limited, informal research on how rapidly these woodlands might regenerate and begin to return to something approaching normal conditions. Starting two weeks after the fire and continuing at intervals throughout the summer, I monitored three hard-hit sites along Route 539: a pine-oak woodland in Manchester Township and two sites in Lacey Township, one a lowland cedar stand, the other a second pine-oak upland. The results were very interesting. At the end of the first two weeks after the fire there was absolutely no visual evidence of any regeneration anywhere. Instead, there were only burned, charred, and dead trees and a dry, blackened and burned layer of leaf litter all over the ground. In some places, the fire had been so hot that even the leaf litter layer had been totally consumed leaving exposed areas of dry white sands. There was, however, one sign of new life to come, because scattered all over the ground everywhere were thousands upon thousands of fresh, new, winged pine seeds that had fallen out from the pine cones that had been opened by the heat of the fire.

By the third week following the fire, tiny, one-half to one-inch high, very reddish sprouts were just beginning to appear around the bases of the former oaks. Here and there in open areas were a few scattered blades of grass, scorched on top, that had grown three to four inches since the fire. There were no other signs of any new life developing from any other type of vegetation. One week later, at the end of the fourth week following the fire, the new reddish shoots of the oaks had grown to an average of one to two and one-half inches, but their occurrences were still few in number and quite scattered. At this same time, the very first huckleberry and blueberry shoots were starting to show about an inch up out of the ground and fronds of bracken fern were beginning to show their fiddleheads just breaking through the ground to, in a few cases, as much as eight inches high.

It was not until after five weeks following the fire that the first evidence of pine regeneration began to be seen in the form of tiny green shoots, only about one-half inch high, at the bases of some of the burned trees. In comparison, by this time the new shoots of the oaks were beginning to turn greenish, were up some six or seven inches, and were becoming quite widespread. The huckleberry and blueberry shoots were now up two to three inches and the fronds of the bracken ferns ten to fifteen inches. It was during this fifth week visitation that the first bird life was observed: a couple of pine warblers and a towhee passed through the area.

Two weeks later, seven weeks after the fire, the first new shoots began to appear out from the sides of the burned trunks and branches of the pines. This was the first aboveground regeneration. Up to this time all of the regeneration had been from the bases, or stumps, or roots of the oaks and the pines and from the roots of the huckleberries, blueberries, bracken ferns, and grasses. Here was the first real evidence of the protection afforded by the thick bark of the pitch pines and of the continuing life beneath that bark even after it had been well burned on the outside. This was the evidence I had been waiting to find, and it is this type of regeneration, along with the regeneration from the forest floor that, in time, will create a new forest to replace that which had been burned.

The first reddish teaberry or checkerberry leaves began to appear out of the ground after the eighth week, and by this time the base shoots of the pines were up four to five inches, the trunk and branch shoots three to four inches. At the same time, oak shoots were up eighteen inches, huckleberry shoots six to eight inches, and bracken fern fronds were practically up to their full height of two to two and one-half feet.

One month later, or three months after the fire, the very first, tiny, new pine seedlings began to appear up out of the ground, the result of those pine seeds that had fallen all over the ground from the opened pine cones immediately after the fire.

Although my monitoring program continued all summer long, I will cut short my story of it here and begin to summarize. At the end of four months following the fire, or by the second of August (the reason for including this as an August topic), the base shoots of the pines had grown as much as eighteen inches to two feet and the trunk and main branch shoots some twelve to fifteen inches. The oak shoots were now up three and one-half to four feet and were clearly the dominant ground level vegetation, although the huckleberry shoots were up fourteen to eighteen inches and staggerbush (now identifiable) nearly two feet. All were abundant and widespread as were the teaberries and bracken ferns.

A random count of pine and oak regeneration at this four-month interval revealed that, at one site, more than fifty percent of the pines had regenerated from their bases, but less than fifty percent had regenerated from their trunks and branches. At the other upland site, approximately eighty-five percent of the pines had regenerated either from their bases or from their trunks or, in most cases, from both. At both sites, nearly one hundred percent of the oaks (now identified as mostly blackjack oaks) had regenerated from their roots. However, in spite of the clear head start the oaks had over the pines, in the long run the pines will win out because of their trunk and main branch regeneration capability, whereas the former oak trees and shrubs, because of their thin bark, were so completely burned that their former trunks and branches will never regenerate. These must depend entirely upon their root systems to rebuild new, aboveground tree and shrub trunks.

So far, this story has been based entirely upon observations and measurements taken at the two upland pine-oak and oak-pine woodland sites. The story becomes rather different when we look at the results in the one lowland-cedar bog site as of this same second of August date. First of all, here the ground was neither hard nor sandy as in the upland areas, but was very spongy and consisted mainly of a carpet of dead, dried sphagnum mosses that ordinarily would have been saturated with surface water but now were practically bone dry due to that summer's (1995) drought. Every step taken made deep impressions in this dry, spongy mat. The dominant trees, the Atlantic white cedars, were all dead. None showed any evidence of regeneration. This is because the bark of the cedar trees is so thin and nonresistant to fire that all the internal growth layers of the trees were killed. Scattered among the dead cedars were a few pine trees, most of which showed new growth from both their bases and their trunks and branches.

In contrast to the stark reality of the dead cedars, the ground was heavily covered with such a new growth of shrubs that there were only a few small areas of bare, dead sphagnum. Most prominent among the regenerated shrubs were stands of inkberry that ranged around two feet in height. Old, burned, dead stalks of highbush blueberry were common, but new growths taking their place were already up two to two and one-half feet. There also were scattered patches of sheep-laurel and black huckleberry and even a few scattered cranberry vines. Even though all the cedar trees had been killed, regeneration of other vegetative forms was thriving, and in a few short years the floor of the old cedar stand will be heavily revegetated. It remains to be seen in years to come how much, if any, cedar regeneration may develop from seeds that could blow in from adjacent unburned cedar stands.

To conclude, fires are important to the preservation and continuation of the Pine Barrens as we now know them. Although fires consume, they also cause new growth and help maintain the ecological balance between the pines and oaks. On the other hand, fires destroy human resources, property, and even lives, but as long as humans insist on building homes within and near the pines, protection of these will be an increasing threat to the future of the Pine Barrens in which they are built. A balance must be struck for, although we must preserve our personal possessions and our lives, we also have a responsibility to preserve the natural world in which we live—the Pine Barrens of New Jersey.

43

Mosquitoes, Flies, and Ticks

Allll through August, the insect chorus continues both day and night, slowing down only on chilly evenings and in early morning hours. But at the same time these choristers are enriching our lives with their musical renditions, other insects seem to take every opportunity to be as pestiferous and annoying as possible as we travel over sandy Pine Barrens trails and canoe along its streams. One can hardly go through a summer in New Jersey without meeting up with some of our well-known and infamous New Jersey mosquitoes. MOSQUITOES, having only one pair of wings, are, in reality, flies (family Culicidae) that have slender, delicate bodies, long slender legs, and long slender beaks which female mosquitoes use to suck blood and thus bite. Females do this in order to obtain the nourishment they need for the development of their eggs. Males do not bite. Instead, male mosquitoes feed on nectar and other plant juices. Also, female mosquitoes are the only ones that sing or whine, which they do by vibrating certain body parts. Adult mosquitoes usually are most active during twilight hours and at night, and spend most of their daytime hours resting in hollow trees, under culverts and in similar hiding places.

Female mosquitoes lay from one to four hundred eggs, singly or in small clusters called "rafts," on the surfaces of stagnant, fresh, or brackish water in small ponds, puddles, and water-filled depressions, or any place where water is just standing like the fluid-filled leaves of pitcherplants. The larvae which develop are known as wrigglers from their method of traveling through the water. Most mosquito larvae have a short breathing tube near one end of their bodies, and the larvae make frequent trips to the surface to breathe. In contrast to the sucking mouthparts of adults, the mouthparts of the larvae are of the chewing type and they feed on microscopic animal and plant life. In a short while, these larvae develop into pupae, called tumblers, and soon after they develop into adult mosquitoes. The entire life cycle of summer generations of mosquitoes may require only two to three weeks.

In addition to being pestiferous, mosquitoes are very important from the standpoint of human welfare because worldwide, especially in the tropics, several species are carriers of very important diseases such as malaria, yellow fever, and encephalitis. Ecologically, adult mosquitoes form a large part of the diet of dragonflies and damselflies, and of birds like swallows, swifts, nighthawks, and flycatchers, as well as those night-flying mammals, the bats. Larvae and pupae are devoured in great quantities by small fishes and aquatic insects such as water striders and whirligig beetles, and especially the aquatic nymphs of dragonflies and damselflies. Adult mosquitoes also are models for the dry flies which fishermen call spinners.

Mosquitoes are common in aquatic habitats throughout the barrens, as well as in pine and oak woodlands and in open areas. The most common species in the Pine Barrens is the BANDED-LEG SALT MARSH MOSQUITO, *Aedes sollicitans*, which flies in from nearby salt marshes where it breeds. This is the famous "New Jersey mosquito" but, although abundant and a major pest, it is not known to carry any disease organisms. Other common species are the swamp and the house mosquitoes.

Mosquitoes are not the only offenders to our peaceful existence as we travel around in the Pine Barrens. DEER FLIES, *Chrysops* sp., are small, yellowish-brown, biting flies that are slightly larger than house flies. These have short, broad heads, large bright green and gold eyes, and smoky patches or darker designs on their single pair of wings. Female deer flies are most annoying as they persistently buzz around your head and hair while you are hiking in the woods, and they often alight to bite with their piercing mouthparts. These are most likely to be encountered near streams and marshes where they breed.

Mosquitoes and deer flies, as well as the small black flies, the large biting and bloodsucking horse flies, and the greenhead flies of the salt marshes and the seashore, all of which we encounter during the summer months, are all abominations on this earth. Humans and other creatures could certainly do without their aggravating annoyances and their

212

capacity to transmit diseases, but we also need to recognize they play an important role in the overall balance of life.

While we are dealing with nuisance insects, a word is surely in order about ticks, which are common throughout the Pine Barrens almost the entire year, except during the coldest, midwinter months. First of all, ticks are not insects but belong to a closely related group of arthropods. Ticks have eight legs, not six, and their two body parts are so tightly fused together they appear to have only one unsegmented body. There are two common ticks in the Pine Barrens: the larger DOG TICK, *Dermacentor variabilis*, and the much smaller DEER TICK, *Ixodes dammini*. Both are small, oval, hard-bodied, and reddish-brown with a very small protruding head and mouthparts. The dog tick may be as large as a small watermelon seed and usually has one or two whitish spots on its back. The very tiny, hardly larger than a pin-head, deer tick usually does not have any whitish body markings.

Ticks are pests for reptiles, birds, and mammals, including humans. People walking through Pine Barrens vegetation may find one or more ticks on their clothes or body. These should be removed as soon as possible because a small percentage of ticks may transmit a bacterial disease. Dog ticks may transmit Rocky Mountain spotted fever and tularemia. Deer ticks may transmit Lyme disease. Anyone who has been bitten by a deer tick and is concerned about Lyme disease should watch for a diagnostic pink ring around the bite, but this does not always develop. If it does, one should see a physician to begin antibiotic treatments. If a ring does not develop, one should see a physician to get a blood test. The best protection against ticks is to wear long clothing to cover both arms and legs, and a head covering. Leg clothing should be tucked into socks and closed boots, and shirts into pants/jeans. Apply insect repellent on clothing but not on exposed skin unless you know it is harmless. Finally, upon return home, be sure to check yourself over carefully before you shower.

44

Wild Fruits
of the Pines

N
ow that midsummer has passed, we begin to see lots of signs pointing toward the completion of nature's cycle for this year. In other words, fall is coming. Although there still will be a number of late season and early fall wildflowers that will come into bloom, the general trend will be toward fall and preparations for next year. This year's new pine cones that were created in last spring's windblown fertilizations are now developing rapidly, but, depending upon species, it may be several years before they reach full maturity. This year's acorns on the oak trees are also developing rapidly. Some of these will mature this fall and some next fall to sprout the following spring, and to provide overwinter food for squirrels and other wildlife. Plant seeds are ripening everywhere and seed pods are breaking open to release their seeds for next year's growth. Seed containing fruits are also becoming ripe and getting ready to be picked. And so we move toward the end of August and the approaching fall season in the Pine Barrens.

The Pine Barrens are not really barren. They are, in fact, quite productive and, as we move toward the end of August and into the early fall months, we see evidences of this everywhere. It is often stated, and generally assumed, that the pine *barrens* received this name from the early colonists and settlers who, having brought traditional crops with them to raise in this new land, found that the droughty, nutrient poor, and acid, sandy soils of the area were not conducive to raising these crops. So, perhaps with a few epithets, they called these areas the barrens. Instead of planting crops, they timbered the forests, used the area as range land for

215

cattle, and helped bring about the extinction of the heath hen by shooting "grouse" (heath hens) out on the pine plains.

Today, we know better. The Pine Barrens *are* productive. Throughout this series of discussions we have learned about many forms of native plant life in the barrens that produce edible foods for human beings as well as for wildlife. The Pine Barrens are *not* barren. It's just that the plants that grow and produce here are the ones that have adapted to the limited resources of this environment (sandy, acid, nutrient-poor soils, repeated fires, etc.) and can survive in spite of these limitations.

Even though we've talked about most of the fruit producing Pine Barrens plants from time to time throughout this book, at the risk of being repetitious this is the place to pull these all together so we have a complete but brief review of the total story about fruits of the Pinelands. We already know how important cultivated blueberries are but, although now cultivated, these were actually developed from the native, wild, Pine Barrens HIGHBUSH BLUEBERRY that still grows wild in Pine Barrens swamps and other lowland areas. This is only one of many native Pinelands fruits. There are other native wild blueberries out there, such as the LOW BLUEBERRY, that produce very palatable fruit from the end of June into early August. There also are at least two huckleberries, BLACK HUCKLEBERRY and DANGLEBERRY, which produce edible fruit from July well into August. The blue fruits of dangleberry are particularly tasteful for people hiking along Pinelands trails, but the fruits of the abundant black huckleberry have so many hard seeds they are less desirable. All the fruits of these important members of the heath family are a valuable source of food for birds, mammals, and other wildlife.

Before moving further into August, let's not forget the bright blue fruits of SASSAFRAS that we mentioned in July which, when ripe and set out on the ends of their brilliant red stalks, provide birds with a valuable source of food.

In August, several fruits become ripe, including those of two very low growing shrubs or sub-shrubs in the heath family, BEARBERRY and TEABERRY or CHECKERBERRY. We spoke about bearberry in April and teaberry in May. Both of these evergreen, ground level plants produce good-sized, roundish, bright red fruits or berries, those of teaberry perhaps slightly the larger. Bearberry fruits turn red from early to mid-August, while those of teaberry do so toward the end of August. In both cases, the berries, or fruits, persist well into the winter months and become excellent foods for many forms of wildlife.

216

Two trees first mentioned when they were in flower in May are now, in August, producing their fruits: the SWAMP MAGNOLIA early in August and the TUPELO toward the end of the month. Both produce small, fleshy-covered seeds called drupes, those of swamp magnolia in bright red, cone-like seed heads, and those of tupelo in paired, long-stemmed, dark bluish-black drupes.

Back in April, we talked about BEACH PLUMS that occur in the Pine Barrens as well as along the shore. Now, in late August, is the time that country folk get out to wherever they know beach plums grow and pick the bluish-black plums of this shrub, which make delicious jellies and jams.

The most widely known fruit of the Pinelands is the AMERICAN CRAN-BERRY, which we've already mentioned several times and whose harvesting we will get out to watch in late September and October.

Rivaling cranberries in food value and volume of production are the abundant acorns of the many species of oaks in the Pine Barrens. While not strictly a fruit in the sense of having relatively soft, edible, pulpy material surrounding internal seeds or a drupe, in a much larger sense acorns also are very important fruits of the Pine Barrens, as we shall see in October.

Late in the year, the fleshy fruits of two members of the holly family that were mentioned in June begin to turn color and ripen: the black berries of INKBERRY in late September, and the red berries of AMERICAN HOLLY in November and December.

So, in spite of its name, the Pine Barrens is a very productive resource for both humans and wildlife.

45

Galls and
Their Makers

M ost people, at one time or another, have noticed one or more small, round, unnatural looking growths on the leaves, stems, or other parts of plants and have wondered what they were and how they got there. Undoubtedly, these were galls. GALLS are special structures that plants produce in response to an outside stimulus such as when an insect lays one of its eggs on some part of a plant, but it is not known what is the exact nature of that stimulus. It may be a chemical the insect injects into the plant at the time it lays its egg; it may be the result of mechanical irritation caused by the insect or the larva that hatched from its egg; it may be the result of saliva secreted by the insect or its larva; or it may be the waste material from the insect's body that is responsible. In any event, the plant produces a growth that encloses the egg and the new larva and continues to grow around the grub until the gall reaches its full size. The larva then feeds on the tissues of the plant inside the gall until it is mature and is ready to pupate. Just before it pupates, it eats its way almost out of the gall, leaving just a very thin wall between itself and the outside world. Then it pupates, after which it bores through the outside wall of the gall and flies out. Thus the plant has provided both shelter and food for the developing insect, but the plant has neither gained nor lost anything from the association.

Plant galls come in almost every conceivable form and color, ranging from spheres to tubes, and from those with smooth surfaces to those with spines. Galls range in size from very minute to some that are as large as two inches in diameter. Most galls are caused by insects, mainly wasps, but some are caused by mites, nematodes (microscopic worms), bacteria, fungi, and viruses. Almost every insect group has gall-producing members, but most galls are produced by gall wasps or by gall gnats or midges.

It is remarkable that each kind of gall forming organism produces its own special kind of gall on just one type of host plant, even on just one particular part of that host plant. It is equally remarkable that the gall that forms around the egg and the larva is always the same size and shape. Thus, because gall makers are host specific and because their galls have a characteristic size and shape, the identification of galls can assist in both plant and insect identification.

Certain plant groups are more attractive to gall producers than others. Oak trees, which abound in the Pine Barrens, are heavily favored by a large variety of gall producing insects, over eight hundred in fact, while herbs and the lower plants are less frequently infested. In the Pine Barrens, a few of the more noticeable galls on oaks are the OAK APPLE GALL, *Amphibolips confluenta*, round and up to two inches across, the WOOL SOWER GALL, *Callirhytes seminator*, covered with a white or pinkish wool, and the OAK BULLET GALLS, *Disholcaspis omnivora*, small, round, hard galls that develop in pairs or small clusters on oak twigs. All three of these are produced by gall wasps. There also are two differently shaped round swellings on the stems of goldenrods: the GOLDENROD SPHERICAL GALL, *Eurosta solidagnis*, produced by a fly, and the GOLDENROD SPINDLE GALL, *Gnorimoschema gallaesolidaginis*, produced by a moth. It is not possible here to mention others, but keep your eyes open and whenever you find a gall or galls, cut one in half with a knife and see for yourself the tiny grub that will be inside feeding on the tissues provided by the plant.

46

Early Signs of Fall

Sometimes with great suddenness, fields and woods, savannas and spongs, and those roadsides that have not been mowed become alive with a blaze of fall colors. Chief among these are such fall flowering plants as asters and golden asters, blazing-stars, bonesets, goldenrods, gerardia and fern-leaved false foxglove, all of which contribute beauty to our fall scenery. The various asters range in color from bright yellows to pale blues and pale to deep lavenders. Bonesets generally are whitish, nearly all goldenrods come in shades of yellow, and geradias are a lovely shade of magenta-pink. Together, these several groups of fall flowering plants produce a symphony of beauty that can be rivaled only by the developing red, yellow, and orange hues of the leaves on the deciduous trees, the two complementing each other perfectly.

Most of these fall flowers are members of the largest family of plants, the Compositae or Asteraceae, the common characteristic of which is a massing together of innumerable individual florets into a single head of flowers. If you will closely examine any of these you will discover that their centers are really clusters of tiny flowers tightly grouped together, and thus are composite flower heads. Many of these, notably asters, goldenrods, and sunflowers, also have outer rows of ray flowers that look like colored petals. Sometimes these are of the same colors as the center flowers, while sometimes they are in contrasting colors. In many flower heads, the outer ray flowers serve as colorful attractants and landing platforms for visiting insects while the inner, center flowers produce the pollen and the seeds. Both asters and goldenrods are fine examples of these flowers, and their abundant supplies of pollen and nectar are outstanding attractions for a myriad of insects including bees, wasps, flies, beetles, and butterflies. Because so many insects visit the flowers of goldenrod, these also are favorite hiding places for ambush bugs and crab spiders to lie in wait, ready to seize an unsuspecting victim for their next meal.

This parade of fall composites actually began late in June with the trailside and roadside flowering of two species of WHITE-TOPPED ASTERS, *Sericocarpus (Aster)* sp., but because both of these summer asters are white and are not particularly spectacular they perhaps did not catch your eye. The real parade of fall flowering composites began in July with the blossoming of the GOLDEN ASTERS of which there are two species in the Pine Barrens. One, the MARYLAND GOLDEN ASTER, *Chrysopsis mariana*, is so abundant, especially along roadsides, and lasts so long, well into September, that it is one of the dominant fall flowering composites. In places, great masses of these bright golden-yellow flowers that are nearly an inch across are so abundant and conspicuous that they almost illuminate the roadsides. The other golden aster, however, is not at all common or conspicuous. In fact, it is quite rare and is classified as an endangered species. This is the SICKLE-LEAVED GOLDEN ASTER, *Chrysopsis falcata*, the unique features of which are its woolly stems, its small, linear, curved or sickle-shaped gray-green leaves, and its light golden-yellow flowers. A major difference between the two golden asters is that the common golden aster grows up to heights of one to two feet while the sickle-leaved form only grows from six up to fifteen inches. Look for the sickle-leaved form in the same type of bare, sandy areas where you would expect to find hudsonia and pine-barren sandwort.

There are so many aster species, nearly a dozen, in the Pine Barrens that it is not possible to do more here than talk about them in general terms. ASTERS make up a large group of composite family members. All have compound heads composed of central, tubular flowers and outer ray flowers which, in most cases, are bluish, lilac, purple, pinkish, or white. Many species are quite variable and some hybridize, so identifications can be difficult. Most asters start coming into bloom late in July. Among the more common species are the SHOWY ASTER, *Aster spectabilis*, with deep blue-violet rays, the most showy aster in the Pine Barrens; the LATE PURPLE ASTER, *Aster patens*, with heartshaped leaves that clasp the stem and with blue-violet to purple rays; the BUSHY ASTER, *Aster dumosus*, with small, pale lilac flowers on long, wiry branches with tiny leaves; and the BOG ASTER, *Aster nemoralis*, that is found mainly in cedar and other bogs. Among the less common asters is the SILVERY ASTER, *Aster concolor*, with silvery-hairy leaves and lilac or blue-violet ray flowers, that is classified as an endangered species.

As with the asters, BONESETS, or THOROUGHWORTS are so numerous, with at least eight species in the Pine Barrens, that we can only generalize. Bonesets are tall, erect herbs with numerous flowering branches near the tops of the plants that, as a group, begin to blossom by the middle of August. All have white, tubular flowers which, individually, are not very impressive, but massed in flat-topped clusters, they make a presentable appearance. One of the best ways to identify individual species is in the shape and arrangement of their leaves. Most species are found in dry to moist, open, sandy fields, peats, and roadsides, but one species, the PINE-BARREN BONESET, *Eupatorium resinosum*, is a rare and endangered species that is restricted to wet bogs in the heart of the Pine Barrens.

A third major group of fall flowering composites is the GOLDENRODS, which should not need much in the way of an introduction to readers of this work. As with the asters and the bonesets, this is a large, diverse group of composites. All have compound flower heads composed of tiny, tubular flowers on a central disk, surrounded by a few to several small ray flowers which, in all cases but one, are in shades of yellow. Most begin to blossom from the middle to the end of August and many continue to bloom into early October. To help in identifications, goldenrods are arbitrarily grouped according to the shape of their flowering heads into wand-like, plume-like, or flat-topped species. Two of the more common species worthy of mention are the FRAGRANT GOLDENROD, *Solidago odora*, the first Pinelands goldenrod to bloom, and the FIELD GOLDENROD, *Solidago nemoralis*, which, more than any other goldenrod, tends to become a weed in old fields and along roadsides. Both have flowering heads in the plume-type arrangement. Two goldenrods of particular interest are the WAND-LIKE GOLDENROD, *Solidago stricta*, and SILVERROD, *Solidago bicolor*. The flowering heads of both of these species are in tall, slender, cylindrical, wand-like spikes. The bright yellow wand-like goldenrod is an endangered species, while the silverrod is the only white flowering goldenrod in the Pine Barrens.

Sunflowers, another group of composites, are represented in the Pine Barrens by two species, only one of which is widely distributed. This is the NARROW-LEAVED SUNFLOWER, *Helianthus angustifolius*, whose bright yellow flowers, with contrasting purplish-black central disks, add to the beauty of damp roadsides and boggy areas, sometimes even growing in shallow water.

One composite deserves special attention because it is one of the truly characteristic fall flowering plants in the Pine Barrens. This is HAIRY BLAZING-STAR, *Liatris graminifolia*, whose tall, wand-like spikes of

Blazing-star

attractive, lavender to pale violet blossoms may be seen rather commonly among the asters and goldenrods in dry, sandy grounds in late summer and early autumn. One of the unusual features of this interesting flower is that, contrary to the more common pattern, the first flowers to open are at the top of its stalk and later flowers open progressively down the stalk. This plant is most often called blazing-star, but some locals prefer to call it gayfeathers. A check of all available references found only one, Edgar Wherry's *Wild Flower Guide* of 1948, that used gayfeather as *the* name for this plant. A couple of others show gayfeather as an alternate name. Not only does Wherry call this plant gayfeather, but he does not even include blazing-star as an alternate name. Instead, he goes so far as to state that "these plants are inaptly termed in some books as BLAZING-STAR, although there is nothing fiery or starry about them." Dr. Wherry was a professor of botany at the University of Pennsylvania and an outstanding local botanist, so it is possible that gayfeather is a local, eastern Pennsylvania and southern New Jersey colloquial name. Witmer Stone, in 1910, called this same plant hairy button snakeroot, a name that is still given as an alternate in several references.

So much for the validity of common names, even though many of them may be aptly descriptive. All this points up the need to learn and use correct, scientific (Latin) names when identifying plants (as well as all other forms of life), because there can be only one of these for each plant (or animal) and these are the only ones that are universally accepted and used worldwide.

In addition to the many composites, don't miss out on three other attractive and conspicuous fall flowers, all of which belong in the gerardia family. The middle of August is the time to start looking for the FERN-LEAVED FALSE FOXGLOVE, *Aureolaria pedicularia*. This is a handsome, bushy-looking plant with slightly sticky, fine-hairy stems and light green, somewhat fern-like leaves that are deeply cut into many toothed lobes. The large, showy, bell-shaped flowers have five broad, spreading, and rounded lobes and are almost pure lemon-yellow in color. When you find one or more of these shrubby looking plants in bloom, watch it for a while and observe all the bumble bee activity, for bumble bees are the main pollinators of these flowers. Like many other gerardias, the fern-leaved false foxglove seems to be more or less parasitic, and draws at least some of its nourishment from the roots of other plants.

The other gerardias you should not miss toward the end of August are the PINE-BARREN GERARDIA, *Agalinis racemulosa*, and the BRISTLE-LEAVED GERARDIA, *Agalinis setacea*. Both bear beautiful, funnel-shaped, deep pink to rose-magenta flowers with five wide, flaring lobes,

225

but the flowers of the pine-barren gerardia are almost twice as large (up to one and one-quarter inches) as those of the bristle-leaved gerardia (up to three-quarters of an inch). The pine-barren gerardia is one of the truly characteristic Pine Barrens flowering plants and is distinctive in being wiry-branched, almost wand-like, in having very narrow, thread-like leaves, and in its larger, tubular flowers. Whether you find the pine-barren gerardia along the edges of dampish, sandy trails or bogs, or the bristle-leaved gerardia on drier sands or along dry roadsides, you are sure to be rewarded with their beautiful bright colors.

Now, just a word about where to find some of these beautiful fall flowering plants. For sheer numbers and ease in finding them, many Pine Barrens roadsides offer the best viewing, provided they have not been mowed by roadside crews or cranberry farmers. One of the very best of these roadsides is Route 563 in Burlington County, from Route 72 in the north all the way south to Route 542. In the fall of 1996, as a result of efforts by the Burlington County Natural Sciences Club, and with the cooperation of county highway personnel, much of Route 563, as well as prime sites on several other county roads, were not mowed until after the end of the season. As a result, these roadsides, with their outstanding displays of autumnal colors, offered beauty and pleasure to passers-by as well as naturalists. Similar successful results were achieved by a small group of private citizens working with county personnel in protecting a choice roadside site in Ocean County.

As August comes to a close, there are more clear signs of the approaching fall season. Tinges of color begin to show in the foliage of some of the trees. First of these to show color is the sour gum or tupelo, a clear early sign of the coming season. The first of the fall broods of tiger beetles will soon be emerging and flying ahead as you walk along sandy Pine Barrens trails. Overhead, two of the more noticeable signs will be the honking flights of the Canada geese and the lining up of large flocks of tree swallows on dead tree branches and on utility wires. And, in September, the Pine Barrens gentians will come into bloom!

Jointweed
and
Gentian

As we move into September, far fewer flowering plants will begin to bloom, for this will be the last month of the spring-summer-fall seasons when there will be any flowering plants just starting to blossom. The reason for this is clear. As the temperatures get colder and winter approaches, the growing seasons have passed and there is precious little time left for plants to blossom, those blossoms to get fertilized by insects, and the seeds to develop, ripen, and scatter for next year's replacement plants.

In addition to the abundance of asters, golden asters, bonesets, and goldenrods that are continuing to bloom all this month, there are two newly flowering plants that deserve your attention. One of these, JOINT-WEED, *Polygonella articulata*, is common to abundant in well drained, sterile, sandy soils, especially along the edges of sand roads and along dikes around cranberry bogs. This small, very slender much branched annual with jointed stems and the tiniest of leaves is a striking autumnal plant. Its numerous, tiny flowers are mostly white when they first come into bloom, but they tend to turn pink or even reddish as the season progresses, especially, it seems, after the first good frosts. Thoreau, under a September 26 date, wrote that this plant reminded him "both by its form and its colors, of a peach orchard in blossom, especially when the sunlight falls on it."

Because of its beauty and its rarity, the other newly blossoming plant this month is a delight to find. This is the well-known but not easy to find PINE-BARREN GENTIAN, *Gentiana autumnalis*, which is classified

Jointweed

as an endangered plant in the New Jersey Pinelands. The gentian family contains many well-known very beautiful flowers, among them the fringed gentian and the lance-leaved sabatia. Gentians received their name from King Gentius of Illyria who, according to the Roman naturalist, Pliny the Elder, discovered the medicinal quality of its roots as an emetic, cathartic, and tonic. The gentian of the Pine Barrens is probably the least well-known of the family, but it compares very well in beauty with other gentians. The pine-barren gentian is an erect, slender, perennial herb, six inches to one and one-half feet high, that flowers from September into October in open, damp, sandy areas. It also has a tendency to inhabit low, grassy, roadside areas and several of the better stands are so located. Witmer Stone wrote that "its flaring mouth, the delicate markings within, and the intensity of the blue make it one of the choicest blooms of the region." Although this plant was apparently first discovered by William Bartram of Philadelphia prior to 1758, undoubtedly from the New Jersey Pine Barrens, it was not properly described and named until 1791 from specimens found in pine barrens areas of South Carolina.

48

Fall Migrations

It is in September that a good many summer resident birds start to migrate south again. Some examples of these are whip-poor-wills, nighthawks, kingbirds, crested flycatchers, barn and tree swallows, and purple martins. TREE SWALLOWS, particularly, become quite conspicuous during the early fall as hundreds of them gather on dead tree limbs and branches, especially in the vicinity of ponds and other small bodies of water, and hundreds more begin to line up along roadside utility wires preparatory to starting their migrations south. On a day early in September, Augie Sexauer, Ralph Wilen, and I were scouting around Whitesbog doing some birding and botanizing when, on the side of a dike between two old, abandoned cranberry bogs, over one hundred tree swallows settled on the dead branches of a maple almost overhead. Settled may not be the right word, however, for they were constantly preening and twittering, and flying off and coming back, almost in perpetual motion.

Many other birds are also starting to migrate south. Some of them nested both here and further north and now some of those more northern nesters are moving down through our area. Among these are several WARBLERS, such as the black and white, parula, black-throated green, and chestnut-sided, and the American redstart, also a warbler. Some others had simply passed through last spring without stopping to nest, and had nested further north. Now, these are beginning to pass through here on their southward migration. Two of the best examples of these are the yellow-rumped and the blackpoll warblers. The yellow-rumps, formerly known as myrtle warblers, are among the more noticeable of the

231

migratory warblers, for groups of these can often be seen flitting around in both tree tops and bushes feeding on insects and bayberries during both their spring and fall migrations through the Pinelands.

Where are all these birds going in the fall? Actually, they're going home, for further south is where they spend most of their year. Even though we may tend to think of these as our birds, in reality they are southern birds that spend most of their time in their home ranges and only come north for a relatively short period of time to breed, nest, and raise their young, after which they return home again. When we finally realize this, we may be better able to understand why there is so much concern about the current pace of deforestation going on in tropical and subtropical areas, not only in our Western Hemisphere but around the world. As the pace of this deforestation continues, habitats with their sources of food for resident and migratory birds, as well as for countless insects and other arboreal wildlife, are being destroyed. The results are already becoming clear in greatly reduced numbers of migratory birds arriving in and passing through more northern areas each year.

In addition to the migration of birds, many other forms of wildlife migrate. Caribou migrate annually across the sub-arctic; wildebeast migrate across the plains of the Serengeti; even some butterflies have been known to migrate over great distances. Some of these migrations, in the form of great masses of butterflies all flying in the same direction, have been observed miles out at sea. So it is not surprising that some local butterflies, notably the monarch, are migratory. MONARCH BUT-TERFLIES, *Danaus plexippus*, begin to fly south along the Atlantic flyway starting in August and continue all through September. A few of these will travel far enough inland for us to see some of them on goldenrods and other fall flowers in the Pine Barrens.

How do these butterflies migrate two to three thousand miles to a winter refuge they have never seen, the same refuge their great, great grandparents left the prior spring? The answer: "It's amazing!" Apparently, this is something that is genetically programmed into these butterflies. The life cycle of the monarch butterfly is classic and consists—like all butterflies, beetles, and higher insects—of four stages: egg, caterpillar (larva), chrysalis (pupa), and adult. Male and female monarchs are very similar in appearance, the distinguishing feature being a slightly enlarged dark area (scent gland) on the third vein of the male's hind wing. The entire life cycle of the monarch from egg to adult can be completed in as few as twenty days or take up to a month depending on weather. The average monarch lives only a few weeks, so it takes several generations to complete the annual migration cycle. Thus, their individual life cycles are repeated over and over as these butterflies migrate south each fall and north again in the spring. In sharp contrast to birds which migrate mainly at night, monarch butterflies migrate almost entirely by day.

The story of monarch migration is well worth retelling. The monarch butterflies that fly south through our area and beyond us in the fall over-winter in Mexico—well, that's almost true. What really happens is that progeny of the monarchs that pass through here are the ones that over-winter in Mexico. The monarch butterflies that summered in the north, say, in the Maritimes and New England, start flying south early in August. These travel some distance, stop off to mate, and females then lay single, whitish

Monarch butterfly

eggs on the undersides of the leaves of milkweed plants, *Asclepias* sp. Soon thereafter, both males and females die. Given warmth from the sun and sheltered from the weather by the leaves, the eggs hatch into tiny caterpillars in a week to ten days. After first eating its own egg shell, each young caterpillar feeds on the leaves of the milkweed, grows larger, sheds its outer skin and continues to grow, repeating this several times as it consumes milkweed foliage. In two to three weeks it grows to its full two- to three-inch size and now appears as a smooth, bright green caterpillar with alternating cross bands of white, yellow, and black.

This mature caterpillar spins a silken thread and attaches itself by its tail to the underside of a leaf. Then it begins to shrivel up and cast off its skin to reveal a beautiful, pale green chrysalis that has formed inside the caterpillar and taken its place. After resting a few days, orange wings of the newly developing butterfly can be seen through the transparent outer skin of the chrysalis. Within a week to ten days the chrysalis splits open and a new mature monarch emerges. At first, its wings will be moist and crumpled up, but with the butterfly hanging in an upside down position the wings are able to unfold, fully expand, and dry. This new butterfly, now able to fly, soon takes wing and joins others and together they continue a further distance south on the migration route of their kin.

Along the way, some may mass together to form nightly gatherings of several hundreds of butterflies hanging from tree branches in much the same manner as they will eventually hibernate overwinter. There are several favored and well-known locations where these overnight gatherings occur each fall, and some of these are in the Cape May area. So, in this manner, monarch butterflies continue to migrate by a succession of generations until, finally, adults of the last surviving generation fly across the Gulf of Mexico to reach their winter hibernating sites in small, isolated areas high in the mountains of central Mexico, places they had never seen but had to find. In the spring, this process is repeated but in reverse, however, not in such unison, so that the annual spring migration north is more scattered and does not attract as much attention.

49

Social Insects

In contrast to the solitary wasps and the one solitary bee we saw in June, there are several social insects in the Pinelands. The two most important of these are the honey bees and the bumble bees, but we observed and talked about both of these back in April in connection with pollinating and fertilizing blueberry and cranberry crops. Now let's take a look at some social wasps, hornets, ants, and termites.

All social insects live in highly organized colonies that sometimes consist of thousands of individuals. A distinctive feature of insect societies is the differentiation of members into castes, with the members of each caste performing different tasks. Bees and paper wasps, including yellowjackets and hornets, have three castes: a queen, drones (males), and workers (infertile females). The same is true in ants, only here the workers are further differentiated into soldiers, food foragers, and brood tenders. In termites, there are four castes: the reproductives (kings and queens), supplementary reproductives, workers, and soldiers. In all insect societies, though composed of many individuals, the society operates as a unit in which the society itself, not the individuals in it, is all-important. This is why worker bees and wasps will not hesitate to use their stingers (modified ovipositors) as a defense mechanism, and sacrifice their own lives in so doing, if they sense the safety of their colony may be threatened.

Among the social wasps, two are so common and so obvious at this time of year that they can not help but be encountered by people. These are the yellowjackets and the baldfaced hornets. Both of these are aggres-

235

sive wasps that live in nests of paper they manufacture by scraping fibers from the bark of weathered trees, dead limbs, and old fence posts, and masticating this into a paper of excellent quality. Anyone who has ever been on an outdoor picnic in the pines in late summer and early fall, and had jelly sandwiches and sodas as part of the menu, has surely experienced numbers of pestiferous yellow and black YELLOWJACKETS, *Vespula* sp., trying to lap up some of the juices from those sweet foods. These are more bothersome at this time of the year because they are particularly fond of ripe and decaying fruit and fruit juices, and because foods are beginning to get scarce as the season draws to a close. Yellowjackets live in small colonies in paper nests they construct in the ground, often making use of old mouse nests. They may also build under any projecting surface or even in the low branches of shrubs.

The other common social wasps in Pinelands areas may be the most spectacular of all paper making wasps. These are the black and white BALDFACED HORNETS, *Vespula maculata*, which build nests consisting of tiers of hexagonal cells enclosed within large, globular, paper nests that often are right out in the open attached to the branches of a tree. Usually these nests measure only one to two feet in diameter and serve as homes for several hundred wasps, but there are records of much larger nests containing thousands of individuals. Like the yellowjackets, these wasps feed their larvae small insects which they have softened up by chewing them into hamburger-like food pellets. Adults of both yellowjackets and baldaced hornets, however, feed only on liquid food because their throats are too small to admit solid particles. By late fall, all activity ceases in the nests of both yellowjackets and baldfaced hornets, and all the wasps die except the newly hatched and mated queens, which hibernate overwinter in protected locations. When they awaken the following spring they lay their eggs, build new colonies, and continue the chain of hornet and wasp life from summer to summer.

Ants are the most common, most abundant, and most successful of all insects, and occur practically everywhere in all terrestrial habitats. Indeed, ants are so abundant that, in terms of number of individuals, they make up the dominant family of insects, the Formicidae. Ants are easily recognized and should be well-known to everyone. The most distinctive structural feature of every ant is that its hind end (abdomen) is attached to its forepart (thorax) by means of a very constricted, almost thread-like part of the abdomen known as the pedicel, and the identification of many ants is determined by the shape and number of upright lobes on this pedicel. In addition, the antennae of ants are usually elbowed off from a very long basal segment.

All ants are social and live in colonies that vary in size from a few dozen to many thousands of individuals, and they nest in all sorts of places—sand or soil, under debris, in plant tissues including insect galls, in dead and dying trees, and in buildings. In the Pine Barrens there may be more than fifty species of ants ranging in size from a tiny black ant less than one-tenth of an inch in size to the large, common carpenter ants that nest in old stumps and logs and in dead trees, but do not actually feed on the wood as do termites.

The most unusual ants in the Pine Barrens belong to a species of leaf-cutting ants and are a particularly interesting part of Pine Barrens fauna. Leaf-cutting or fungus-growing ants are a large group of nearly one hundred species that are confined almost exclusively to tropical and subtropical America. So it was an item of unusual entomological interest when a Rev. George K. Morris discovered a species of these ants in New Jersey while he was vacationing at a camp meeting ground at Island Heights in July of 1880. This proved to be a species new to science, the NORTHERN LEAF-CUTTING ANT, *Atta (Trachymyrmex) septentrionalis*, now known to extend as far north as Long Island. As adult ants, these look like any other very small, barely one-eighth of an inch long, leaf-brown ants that can most easily be identified by two distinctive characteristics. First, their tiny mounds of sand outside their burrows are crescent-shaped, not circular. Second, when found, these ants may be seen traveling in two lines. In one line, each ant will be carrying a tiny piece of fine pine needle toward its nest site. In a parallel line, ants will be returning empty to cut, pick up, and carry another small piece of pine needle. Observations have shown that these ants also cut up and carry small pieces of both the foliage and flowers of cow-wheat, a common Pinelands plant. The ants carry these down into their nest chambers and use the vegetation as a culture medium for the fungi on which they feed. So, be on the lookout for these unique little ants anywhere in sandy areas throughout the Pine Barrens from late April into early October.

The other common social insects in the Pine Barrens are termites. All Pinelands termites are the EASTERN SUBTERRANEAN TERMITE, *Reticulitermes flavipes*. These are so common they can probably be found in just about every old dead stump, dead tree, or fallen log. Just kick over a stump or turn over a log, break it open and look for those very small, pale white, grub-like worker termites. When some people first see these, they call them white ants. Not so, because a termite has such a broad and close connection between its abdomen and mid-section (thorax), there hardly seems to be any separation at all. In addition, the antennae of termites are never elbowed. Termites establish their nests in the ground and,

237

even as they invade aboveground wood, they must always maintain a connection with the ground in order to obtain needed moisture. Thus, termites constantly move between their nests in the ground and the wood they are consuming, but in doing so, they always remain hidden inside their nests, their tunnels, or the woods in which they are working, and so never expose themselves to the outside world. From a human point of view termites are very destructive if they enter our homes and buildings, but from an ecological point of view termites are very beneficial in wooded areas such as the Pine Barrens because they help to convert dead trees and other plant products back into organic matter to become the basis of new plant life.

AUTUMNAL
EQUINOX

50

Autumnal Equinox
and
Cranberry Harvesting

T he midpoint between summer and the coming winter takes place right now, on September 21 or 22. Just as during the spring equinox in March, for a few days the number of hours between sunrise and sunset will be just about the same as the number of hours between the preceding sunset and sunrise. Day and night will again be nearly equal in length, each just about twelve hours. The big difference from spring to fall is that from now on each succeeding day will be getting shorter and each succeeding night longer. These conditions will continue until the winter solstice on December 21 or 22, when we will have come full cycle on our seasonal journeys through the Pine Barrens.

The advent of the fall equinox and the almost simultaneous start of harvesting cranberries in the Pine Barrens is sure proof that fall is upon us. Of all our native Pine Barrens fruits which we've already reviewed, without question the best known and most important is the AMERICAN CRANBERRY, *Vaccinium macrocarpon*, another member of the heath family. When these fruits begin to ripen about now, cranberry farmers get into high gear to harvest this very valuable agricultural product of the pines, and this becomes the most colorful time in the cranberry cycle.

241

The harvesting of cranberries has undergone many changes over the years. From the time that cranberries were first grown under cultivation as early as the 1830s, ripe cranberries were picked by hand. Men, women, and even children picked cranberries by getting down on their knees and either picking or stripping the cranberries off the vines and putting them into baskets or peck-sized boxes. Many of these early pickers in New Jersey were Italian immigrants who, as late as 1913 at one farm, worked an average of eight and one-half hours a day, picked an average of 2.74 bushels a day, and were paid at an average rate of forty cents a bushel. Hand picking of cranberries continued until the early 1930s when pickers

Cranberry harvesting

began to use cranberry scoops, which today are scarce antique items. Pickers still had to be on their knees to use the scoops, but these saved wear and tear on their hands and only one-third as many workers were needed to pick the crop. This method continued until the 1950s when a Pine Barrens cranberry farmer, Thomas B. Darlington, a grandson of J.J. White, invented the first successful dry harvesting machine. Superficially, this looks something like a motorized, old fashioned (today), reel-type lawn mower with a bag on the side into which are blown the cranberries (not grass clippings!). This method is still used today and is known as dry harvesting. Finally, the now much more commonly used wet harvesting method was introduced between 1963 and 1965 by William S. Haines on his extensive cranberry bogs south of Chatsworth.

Much is written and many photographs shown in the public press and on television at this time of year about cranberry harvesting in the Pine Barrens. Almost all of this publicity revolves around the wet harvesting method, because it is so colorful and photogenic. Most farmers use the wet method to harvest their berries, because they gather a much higher percentage—from ninety to ninety-five percent—of their crop. Wet harvesting begins with the flooding of the bogs. Because cranberries are buoyant, when bogs are flooded the buoyancy of the ripe berries lifts the vines a bit off the ground. This allows the mechanical picking machines, called beaters or knockers, that are guided or driven by workers to strip the cranberries from the vines and the bright red berries pop up to the surface of the water. Here they are gathered together and corralled by booms, guided onto loading conveyors, dropped into trucks, and driven to processing plants for cleaning and shipment to market.

Upon their arrival at food processing plants, all wet-harvested cranberries are first quick-frozen and then later, throughout the year, turned into processed foods such as juices, sauces, and preserves. Dry-harvested cranberries are the only ones that are sold in food markets as fresh fruit to be used by housewives and cooks who wish to make their own relishes and sauces. The reason for the different uses of wet- and dry-harvested berries is that, because wet-harvested berries are in water from several hours to a day or so, water can get into the berries, especially where they were separated from their stems. This causes a breakdown in their cellular structure so that wet-harvested berries do not keep as well, even under refrigeration. Dry harvested berries, on the other hand, can be kept refrigerated for long periods of time and almost indefinitely if frozen so there is a continuing demand for dry harvested cranberries.

Currently (1996), there are forty-five cranberry farmers in the New Jersey Pine Barrens, five of whom dry-harvest their berries. All together, these farmers have more than three thousand acres under cultivation. Most, but not all, cranberry farmers in the pines are members of the Ocean Spray Cooperative, which takes and processes their fruit. Cranberry production in New Jersey averages a little better than one hundred 100-lb. barrels of cranberries per acre and, in total production, New Jersey ranks third to Massachusetts and Wisconsin.*

*One word of caution needs to be added. Because the wet method of harvesting cranberries is so colorful and photogenic, many people want to see it happening first hand. However, cranberry bogs are farms and, as such, are privately owned property. The word of caution is that whenever you see ongoing harvesting operations and you would like to observe it a bit and possibly photograph some of it, please stay on the public highway and its shoulders. Please do not enter upon private property unless you have permission from the land owner. This is for your own safety as well as the farmer's protection. You could get in the way of the workers or their machinery, an accident could occur, and insurance problems could result. So, please, observe and photograph from the public highway, not on the farmer's private land.

51

October

Autumnal Colors
and Acorns

For different people the seasons have different meanings and bring different joys. For the sports minded, nothing can surpass the winter months for skiing and skating, and the summer months for swimming and boating. For naturalists, spring and fall seasons are highlight periods for different reasons: the renewal of plant and animal life all through the spring and the brilliant displays of autumnal colors as plants shut down for the year in the fall. During both of these seasons, much of the excitement comes from the rapidly changing, temporal nature of the season. Each day brings changes and in the course of a week or a month these put new faces on the rapidly changing landscape.

While spring is almost universally recognized as a reawakening or a renewal of life, fall may be interpreted by some as the passing of life and its dormancy over the long, cold winter ahead. Others revel in the glorious beauties of the autumnal foliage. Starting back as early as late August, the first trees that showed color were the SOUR GUMS or TUPELOS, *Nyssa sylvatica*, whose leaves were even then beginning to show tinges of light red. As the fall season progresses, tupelos often seem to be on fire in varying shades of rich, deep red, soon to be followed by the yellows and oranges of SASSAFRAS, *Sassafras albidum*. Often the tupelos turn to their crimson colors so early that their leaves are already starting to fall by the time the RED MAPLES, *Acer rubrum*, change to their palette of reds, oranges, and yellows, and, though not as spectacular, GRAY BIRCHES, *Betula populifolia*, add their touch of golden colors to the scene.

Last to show their fall colors are the most important and most abundant deciduous trees in the Pine Barrens, the many species of OAKS, *Quercus* sp. Most of these begin to change to their fall colors in October and continue the process throughout the month and well into November as they take on rather subdued hues of yellows, oranges, and bronzes that dominate over their few remaining green leaves. Oaks are the last of the deciduous trees to finally shed their leaves. Most beautiful of all fall oaks are the SCARLET OAKS, *Quercus coccinea*, whose leaves nearly all turn to a scarlet red until they too drop to the ground and quickly fade to brown on the forest floor.

Two basic processes are involved here. First to occur is the change in colors that has just been mentioned. Second is the separation of the leaves from their trees and their dropping to the ground. Many factors are involved in both processes. As the number of hours of sunlight decreases and as temperatures get cooler in the fall of the year, chlorophyll, that green substance that is essential in photosynthesis, is no longer manufactured by the leaves, and what remains in the leaves begins to break down and disappear. As this takes place, other pigments, the oranges, reds, and yellows, that have been in the leaves all along but have been overshadowed by the green chlorophyll, begin to replace the chlorophyll and, together, present a spectacular and colorful display of fall foliage.

Following this, trees begin to shut down their supplies of water to their leaves in order to reduce their normal loss of water (transpiration) into the atmosphere. At the same time, trees grow a very thin, protective layer of cells (scar tissue) where the stem of each leaf is attached to a branch of the tree so that the tree will be protected when all the leaves fall to the ground. Thus, this entire process of fall foliage colors and leaf separation is really a case of self-protection by the tree from the approaching winter weather. To grow, trees use great amounts of water, but water is not as available to them in the winter. Therefore, leaves, users of water, must be discarded in order to insure the future of the trees.

Toward the end of October it becomes more and more evident that autumn has truly arrived. The weather has changed. Trees and shrubs stand like silent sentinels waiting for winter. Ground level herbs have become dead organic matter that will decay over winter and help enrich the sandy soils for future seasons of growth. This is the season when the many species of oaks begin to shed their acorns that have been developing all summer. Back early in May we observed the windblown pollination and fertilization of the oaks. Now we see the results of that earlier process. Although in a popular sense acorns are classified as nuts rather than fruits, these are, nevertheless, the fruits of oak trees. Of all the fruits of the year that we have seen, none is more valuable to wildlife than the acorns of oaks.

As noted back in May, there are two different groups of oaks: the white oaks and the black or red oaks. Applying what we learned then to their fruits, acorns of the white oak group are generally larger, sweeter, and more palatable than those of the black oak group, which tend to be smaller, more bitter, and somewhat astringent. Acorns of the white oak group mature in just one season while those of the black oak group need two seasons to mature.

Acorns are rich in both fats and carbohydrates and so, throughout the history of civilization, acorns have been an important source of food for human beings, and they still are for a number of native people. Acorns were a major source of food for the Native Americans. They gathered large quantities of acorns and ground them into a sort of flour which, mixed with other ingredients, was baked into a type of biscuit or bread. In the mountains of Mexico and Central America, native people still use acorns in this manner. Other native people roast acorns, grind them, and use the product as a substitute for coffee. Although bitter and somewhat astringent when raw, acorns lose these properties when leached, and they become a nutritious, nutty, and thoroughly palatable meat, rich in oils and starches.

Today, the primary value of acorns in the Pine Barrens is as food for several forms of wildlife, even including insects. For instance, there is a whole group of beetles known as acorn weevils that have long, slender snouts which they use to bore holes in acorns in order to lay their eggs inside. Then each larva that hatches feeds and develops on the rich, nutty meat of the acorn. Birds such as wild turkey and grouse are major feeders on acorns, and a portion of the food of white-tailed deer consists of acorns that have fallen to the ground. Probably the animal best known for feeding on acorns is the familiar gray squirrel. These common animals of oak woodlands and backyards rely heavily on a good supply of acorns for food, and their habit of burying acorns as storage for their future food supplies is well known. What may not be as well-known is how these squirrels know where their acorns are buried so that they can dig them up and feed on them during the winter. Recent research has shown that they rely principally on a keen sense of smell. Of course, they probably never find all the acorns they bury, so the following spring some will germinate to produce new oak trees for future generations.

52

Day-Flying Moths
and
Lady Beetles

Back in February and March, we were thrilled to see two of the very earliest butterflies, the mourning cloaks and the spring azures, begin to fly in the spring Pinelands. Now, in October, when there is a slight nip in the air even on the most pleasant of days, is the best time to get out into pine plains areas to watch for the erratic flights of small, attractive day flying buck moths.

Some people ask what are the differences between butterflies and moths. There are several. Usually, but not always, butterflies hold their wings erect (vertically) over their bodies when at rest whereas moths hold their wings either straight out from their sides or fold them roof-like over their bodies. Bodies of moths usually are larger, heavier, and more plump and hairy than those of butterflies. Further, the antennae of butterflies are club-like, ending in a swollen tip or knob (butterflies) or the tips are turned back in sort of a hook (skippers). The antennae of moths are seldom club-like and often, especially in males, are quite feathery. Finally, as a rule, butterflies are daytime flyers whereas most moths fly at night.

Contrary to this, BUCK MOTHS, *Hemileuca maia*, are daytime flying moths which usually reach the peak of their flight activity between 11 a.m. and 3 p.m. on warm, sunny, fall days in scrub and blackjack oak forests. Adult buck moths are very attractive. Both their front and hind wings are semi-translucent black, with a narrow white vertical band across the middle of each wing. A black-bordered spot on the front wing touches the basal black patch. Wing spans range from one and one-half to almost three inches. The tips of their abdomens are red in males and black in females,

249

and their antennae are feathery, doubly so in males. The common name of buck moths is said to have been given to these insects because they fly during the season when deer stalking and hunting is in progress.

As with all newly emerged adult insects, as soon as buck moths emerge from their pupal stage to become adult moths, their very first activity is to mate. Females will fly to nearby oak branches and passively cling to them while they emit strong scents called pheromones to attract the smaller males. After mating, females lay their eggs in small clusters of up to one hundred eggs, encircling twigs of scrub and blackjack oaks. These become the overwintering or hibernating stage of their life cycle. The eggs hatch in late April or early May as tiny caterpillars which soon develop brushy, branching spines tipped with nettling hairs in rows along their bodies. Gregariously at first, then individually later, these larvae feed on the leaves of scrub and blackjack oaks and undergo five growth and molt cycles until, as fully developed caterpillars, they burrow into the surface of the ground to pupate. Then in early to mid-October, they emerge as the winged adults we see in rapid, erratic flights just above the oaks of the pine plains.

A few years back, around the middle to the end of October, a couple from New York City, Ed and Lana Mills, used to drive down to spend a day looking for buck moths in the West Plains section of the pine plains. Though our contacts never went beyond phone conversations and correspondence, I helped them a bit with directions, maps, and other information and each year they would graciously write me a letter with a report of their sighting results. Their base data are interesting enough to be included here for the record.

On October 20, 1986, from 11 a.m. until 3:20 p.m., they sighted eighteen buck moths flying while they patrolled the Red Road (Stephenson's Road) from about one-half mile south from Route 72 to about one and one-quarter miles. The weather was clear and bright with light breezes from the south. The temperature was in the sixties. They returned the next day, October 21, and between 10:45 a.m. and 1:40 p.m. they sighted forty-nine buck moths flying in approximately the same area. The temperature was slightly warmer with lighter breezes. Next year, the Mills returned to the same area on October 17 and reported sighting twenty-eight buck moths in flight. They also reported one buck moth they found clinging to a sprig of hudsonia. From 11:40 a.m. until 1:25 p.m. they watched and recorded detailed observations of its movements on the hudsonia, from as close as six inches away, until the moth finally took flight.

In 1989, the Mills reported on another trip. On October of that year they sighted twenty-two moths from 10:30 a.m. to 1:00 p.m. (Almost coincidentally, three days earlier, on October 25, Don Kirchhoffer, Doris, and I had walked the diagonal sand road— Stevenson Road on some maps—from Route 72, starting just east of Coyle Field, across the West Plains over to the Red Road about one-half mile south of Route 72, and on this walk we sighted twenty-one buck moths. The day was clear, sunny, and relatively calm with only a slight breeze. The temperature was in the low seventies).

The last report from the Mills was of their trip to the same area on October 21, 1990, when they sighted fourteen buck moths in a little over two hours. From these reports, it is clear that a trip to the West Plains area of the pine plains (undoubtedly also the East and other pine plains areas) on any good, clear, sunny, relatively mild and calm day from mid-October to the end of the month (probably earlier and possibly somewhat later) should be a rich and rewarding experience, for it truly is a thrill to watch these small day-flying moths in their rapid and erratic flight just above the low coppice of stunted blackjack oaks and pines.

One other moth seen rather frequently in the fall is the woolly-bear caterpillar of the small orange-yellow to yellow-brown ISABELLA TIGER MOTH, *Pyrrarctia isabella*. Nearly everyone is familiar with these hairy caterpillars, which are often seen traveling along the ground and that have the interesting habit of rolling up into a small ball when disturbed. Though called woolly-bears, their hairs are not really woolly to the touch but, instead, are rather short, stiff, and bristly and cover their bodies very thickly. Sometimes these are called black-banded caterpillars because their hairs, which are quite reddish-brown in the middle of their bodies, are quite black at both ends. There is an old saying that the relative intensity and length of the black bands in the fall are an indication of how severe the coming winter will be. Actually, the length of their bands and the intensity of color change as these caterpillars molt and grow from stage to stage in their development, the black end bands becoming shorter and less black and the middle reddish-brown band becoming longer and more intensely reddish-brown as they age. Thus differences in color and length of their bands are merely indications of their stage of development as they prepare to overwinter rather than being a reliable indicator of the severity of the coming winter.

When winter does arrive, these caterpillars find protected hiding places in holes, under loose bark, or in old sheds, and then roll up and hibernate over winter. Often, they will actually freeze solid and yet, when

251

it becomes warmer next spring, they will thaw out, pupate for a short while, and emerge as small, attractive moths that will take flight, mate, and lay eggs which will hatch into that year's new caterpillars, and so the cycle will continue.

   In the late fall of the year, for people who live in and around the Pine Barrens and other country places, there are two insects that sometimes occur in such great numbers that they may become pests around peoples' homes. These are the boxelder bugs and a newly arrived species of lady beetles. BOXELDER BUGS, *Leptocoris trivittata*, are small, elongate-oval, flattened bugs that are dark brownish-black with narrow, brick-red stripes on their sides and on the margins of their wings. These bugs feed principally on the boxelder or ash-leaved maple, *Acer negundo*. In the spring when the buds of the boxelder begin to open, these bugs will emerge from hibernation to lay their eggs in crevices in the bark of these trees. The young larvae that emerge will feed by sucking plant juices from the buds and other tender growth. The first adults appear by midsummer, and by fall they begin to congregate up and down the trunks and branches of the trees. When the leaves drop, they fly off in search of winter hibernating quarters. This is when most people are apt to become aware of these insects, for sometimes great numbers of them will congregate on the sides of houses and other buildings. They especially seek hiding places around window frames and even inside houses where, of course, they become nuisance pests. Other than being a nuisance, however, they do no damage.

   From mid-October on, the other insect that may become a nuisance is known as the ASIAN or HALLOWEEN LADY BEETLE, *Harmonia axyridis*, a relatively recent immigrant into the United States. On the third of November, 1995, while I was doing some photographing around the bog at Webb's Mill on Route 539, Lacey Township, Ocean County, hundreds upon hundreds, maybe even thousands of these beetles were flying all around, landing on me, on my equipment, flying off and landing again and again, and were all over my car when I returned to it. At a meeting of The American Entomological Society a few weeks later, Mark Darlington reported similar aggregations of these beetles around his place along the edge of the J.J. White Cranberry Company bogs in Pemberton Township, Burlington County.

There are many species of lady beetles, often incorrectly called lady-bugs (incorrectly because these are not true bugs at all, but beetles). The name ladybug dates back to the Middle Ages when some of these beetles rid grape-vines of insect pests, and so were dedicated by grateful friars to Our Lady, the Virgin Mary. Most lady beetles are small, approximately pea-sized, and occur in combinations of orange and black, many orange with black dots, some black with orange dots. Most are very beneficial insects because both their immature larvae and the adults are voracious feeders on aphids, plant lice, and scale insects, all of which are harmful suckers of plant juices from a wide variety of trees, especially fruit trees. In the fall of the year, lady beetles seek hiding places where they can hibernate over winter. The great majority hibernate outdoors beneath leaf litter, under loose bark of trees, or in clumps of grass, but some seek hiding places around peoples' homes and this is when most persons will find them as they seek safe sites around window frames, in insulated attics, and other protected spots. In spite of their being nuisance insects in the fall and over winter, they are not at all harmful: they neither bite nor sting; they are not poisonous; they carry no diseases; and their benefits in consuming thousands upon thousands of plant sucking insects far outweigh their nuisance factor.

Just before we leave October we have one last duty to perform. This is the annual ritual of turning our clocks back one hour to standard time. According to the adage spring ahead, fall behind, ever since the first weekend in April we have enjoyed and appreciated an extra hour of evening sunlight. Now we will lose that extra hour and darkness will come upon us much more quickly, jolting us to the full realization that our days are truly getting shorter as we approach winter's solstice.

53
November

Tundra Swans

E arly this month or, in some years late in October, TUNDRA
SWANS, formerly known as whistling swans, begin to appear on
shallow ponds, lakes, and flooded cranberry bogs throughout
the Pine Barrens. These beautiful, large white birds can only be confused with the slightly larger mute swans. Tundra swans have black
bills, often with a small yellow spot at the base of the bill in front of
the eye, while mute swans have orange bills. Immatures of both swans
are dingy grayish-white with flesh-colored bills. Whereas mute swans
are year-round residents, tundra swans are migratory and spend their
spring, summer, and fall on their northern breeding grounds in the sub-
arctic, north of Hudson's Bay, to where they will return beginning in
late February and early March.

Why do so many of these birds come here to spend the winter? This
is due somewhat to our warmer climate, but the principal reason is the
availability of food, the same reason song birds migrate north in the
spring. Tundra swans, as all swans, feed by submerging their heads and
long necks under water to dig up and feed upon the roots and stalks of
aquatic and semiaquatic vegetation. They also feed on various forms of
small animal life. One of the plants upon which they feed is REDROOT,
Lachnanthes tinctoria, which we observed in flower early in July. As we
learned then, redroot is a pernicious weed in cranberry bogs, so when
cranberry farmers flood their bogs for the winter, the birds use these
bogs as feeding areas. One might think that cranberry farmers would be
happy about these birds feeding on their weed plants—not so, because,

255

in the process of digging up the roots of redroot, the birds also disturb and partially dig up the shallow roots of the cranberry vines. Therefore, farmers do everything they can to discourage these birds from feeding on their bogs, including patrolling the bogs and using loud noise machines to scare them away—everything short of shooting the birds, which would be illegal because they are protected by the Federal Migratory Bird Treaty Act of 1918.

Two good places to view flocks of these magnificent birds are the old and now-abandoned cranberry bogs (but not the recently rebuilt, new bogs) at Whitesbog in Lebanon State Forest, off Route 530, east of Browns Mills, Pemberton Township, and the Forsythe (Brigantine) National Wildlife Refuge at Oceanville in Atlantic County. Both are public property (state and federal) and therefore are available and accessible for public entrance and viewing. Other good places to look for tundra swans are small shallow ponds and old, abandoned, and isolated cranberry bogs that remain flooded over winter. If you should happen to spot any tundra swans on newer, modern bogs, please remember these will undoubtedly be on private property and it is important that permission be obtained before entering upon any of these properties.

54

Wild Turkeys

Wild turkeys are back! Now, on occasion, small flocks of wild turkeys may be seen crossing or running along sandy, Pine Barrens roads. The wild turkey is a large, spectacular native American bird that is unmatched as a game bird. It should not, however, be confused with the domesticated turkey of Thanksgiving. That domesticated bird is the descendent of turkeys that the early Spanish explorers took from Mexico and brought back to Spain, were then domesticated all over western Europe, and then brought back to America from the barnyards of Europe.

The fact that WILD TURKEYS, *Megeagris gallopavo*, were common to possibly abundant in New Jersey is well documented. Witmer Stone, in his *Bird Studies at Old Cape May*, 1937, reports several previously recorded accounts. One such is Samuel Smith's *History of the Colony of Nova Caesarea or New Jersey*, 1765, in which he states that "there are a great plenty of Wild Turkey." Even earlier, in 1648, Beauchamp Plantagenet mentioned a flock of five hundred turkeys "got by nets." However, by the early nineteenth century, wild turkeys had been hunted to near extirpation almost everywhere in New Jersey and throughout the northeastern states.

Today's wild turkeys are birds that have been introduced back into the Pine Barrens, as well as into other areas of the state, but these are not descendants of the original wild turkeys from this area. Instead, it is likely the breeding stock for today's wild turkeys in the Pinelands came from southern or Gulf States birds. At the present time, according to Boyle, 1986, the wild turkey has been "successfully reintroduced" throughout the state, is now "fairly common," and its numbers are "rapidly increasing." In fact, there now are brief, restricted hunting seasons for turkey in limited areas in the state.

Wild turkeys travel in flocks both before and after breeding season. They are polygamous, a strong gobbler often having two or three hens under his care. Following mating in the spring, hens lay large sets of speckled eggs in secluded nests on the ground and rear the young poults without any assistance from the dominating gobblers. The young are able to run about and leave the nest soon after hatching. At night, the chicks snuggle under the body, wings, and tail of the female, on the ground, until they are about four weeks of age.

Turkeys feed on seeds, fruits, and acorns, and they are always ready to raid an isolated corn field. They also feed on insects, principally grasshoppers, other small invertebrates, and even small vertebrates. Wild turkeys are extremely wary and shrewd; at night they seek roosting places in trees, preferably in impassible, deciduous swamps. Although they spend little time on the wing, they are strong fliers.

It is a thrilling sight to see birds that once were seriously proposed as our national emblem, and then were hunted to near extirpation, again inhabiting the Pinelands. Hopefully, recent introductions will continue to be successful and wild turkeys will once again take their rightful place, now under controlled conditions, as a valuable game bird in the Pine Barrens.

55

Winter Snows

As we move into December, the first day of winter is just three short weeks away and a new winter season is fast approaching. This will begin when the WINTER SOLSTICE takes place, and then we will have come full cycle from the time when we started together on this odyssey a year ago. It is interesting what a few days' difference can make, for there is an almost abrupt change in the atmosphere, or upon our outlook on it, between November and December. Now there is a distinctly new winter quality in the gusts of wind that sweep across the bare tops of the trees and rustle the leaves on the forest floor.

During these last few weeks of traveling through the Pine Barrens, there may not be as many new and exciting events as on our earlier travels. Most forms of plant life will remain dormant throughout the winter and many animal forms will be at reduced levels of activity. Many of the smaller forms of animal life, such as insects, amphibians, and reptiles, will be totally inactive. Only warm-blooded animals will remain active, and even some of these will either hibernate or function at reduced levels of activity. This pretty much leaves birds as the most active form of life to be found in the Pine Barrens from now through the coming winter, but since we talked about most of these back in February, we will not repeat here.

Anytime from now on, the strongest indication of the coming winter will be the first significant snowfall. In spite of the hardships that snow brings to everyday life, snow is really a very beautiful substance. Each single snowflake is actually an accumulation of many individual snow

259

crystals all massed and frozen together. Snow, of course, is white, but snow is water frozen in the shape of crystals. Since water is not white, one might wonder why snow is white. The answer is that as individual crystals of snow become massed together they trap particles of air between them, and it is the refraction of light through this air that causes the snow to appear white.

As snowflakes fall upon the earth, they slowly build upon each other in layers to become soft, fluffy blankets of snow that cover everything and provide protection to the earth and the forms of life within it. The earth has heat inside it. The temperature of the atmosphere often become much colder than that of the earth, causing the surface of the ground to freeze, sometimes to depths of several feet. A good blanket of snow helps maintain the warmer temperatures of the earth, the ground is not frozen as deeply, and the soil around the roots of plants is kept warmer so that plants and small animals living in the soil have a better chance of surviving the winter. Another major benefit of a good blanket of snow is that much of the melt from the snow soaks down into the soil to help maintain the high water table needed for renewed plant growth in the coming spring. So, even though some people may not care for snow because of the hardships it brings, it is an important and valuable natural resource, and it does add beauty to the landscape.

56

White-Tailed Deer

ecember. Traditionally, this is the month for which hunters and sportsmen have waited all year. In southern New Jersey and the Pine Barrens, many belong to hunting and sportsmen's clubs and at this time of year they come out to spend a week hunting for WHITE-TAILED DEER. So, a word about these deer and hunting for them seems appropriate.

Historically, white-tailed deer were abundant in New Jersey, but by 1903, due to unrestricted hunting, they became virtually extinct in the northern part of the state and in the next year, 1904, they were considered extinct in southern New Jersey, including, of course, the Pine Barrens. Then, according to Witmer Stone in 1908, the "southern counties were restocked with deer from elsewhere," including over one hundred from the Worthington estate near the Delaware Water Gap and from Michigan. From these transplantations and other introductions, plus a temporary ban on hunting deer, the deer population increased to the point where today the white-tailed deer is the most conspicuous and only remaining large mammal in the Pine Barrens.

White-tailed deer are reddish in summer and grayish in winter, and the undersides of their short tails are white. One of the more characteristic sightings of white-tailed deer is to see them bounding away through the woods with their tails raised high, waving from side to side like white flags. White-tailed deer in the Pine Barrens are not large, standing only three to three and one-half feet high at the shoulder. Adult male deer begin to grow antlers in April. As these develop over the summer they are relatively soft and covered with velvet. After the antlers harden in early fall, male deer, or bucks, rub their antlers on saplings and small trees to scrape off the velvet and prepare for the rut. This is when they will be in prime breeding condition and will compete with other bucks for the right to mate with the does. This preparation usually takes place from around mid-November into early December. Shortly after mating, usually from late December into early February, male deer shed their antlers, which fall to the ground and become valuable nutrients for rodents and other small mammals, and for bone-feeding insects, as we noted in February.

Fawns are born in late May or early June and remain spotted as long as they continue to nurse. Deer feed on woody browse such as shrubs, saplings, and low branches of trees, on acorns, and on herbaceous plants including grasses.

Now to touch briefly on the controversial subject of hunting vs. non-hunting of deer and other game animals. To many, hunting of any type is an ancient right and sport that they have inherited from their ancestors. Apparently, many of these people fail to realize, or are unwilling

White-tailed deer

to acknowledge, that we are living in a different world today than existed a few to several hundred years ago. The proportion of human beings to wildlife has increased dramatically, and while humans continue to multiply and increase their population, the numbers of wildlife are being drastically reduced, primarily due to loss of habitat. Many people cite this as a strong argument to preserve what remains of wildlife and to ban the hunting and killing of game and other animals. To many of these people, the hunting and killing of any wildlife is despicable and ought to be outlawed.

As in most controversies of this type, neither extreme is one hundred percent right, and it is unlikely that either side can win outright. The facts are that 1) throughout southern New Jersey, including the Pine Barrens, man has eliminated, both by killing and by loss of habitat, the natural predators of the white-tailed deer, like the panther, the bear, and wolves, and that 2) humans have in the past and presently continue to extend housing and industrial developments further and further into natural areas. Because habitats for wildlife are continually being encroached upon and reduced, it would appear that a limited amount of harvesting of the game animal crop may be necessary in order to keep its numbers within manageable limits, compatible with the amount of available habitat, to maintain healthy animal populations.

Epilogue

Now that we have completed this series of explorations through the Pine Barrens of New Jersey, I hope you have enjoyed your experiences. Further, I hope you have not been just an armchair participant, but have actually gone out into the Pinelands to look for and see some of the things we have discussed and explore some of the places we have mentioned. Only then will you appreciate the beauties and the values of this great area.

More than that, I hope you now have a better understanding of why this area is so valuable and why it is worth preserving. Unfortunately, in spite of the protection currently afforded by both federal and state legislation, there are many who still want to construct more new housing developments, shopping malls, industrial parks, and roads in the name of progress, but at the sacrifice of losing more and more of this wilderness area.

This is not just a local or regional matter. The Pine Barrens belongs to all the citizens of New Jersey and, in a larger sense, to all the citizens of our United States. Everyone needs to become involved. So I hope you are now stimulated to do all within your power to help those who are already involved, in the words of the Pinelands Protection Act of 1978, to "protect, preserve, and enhance the significant values of the land and water resources" of the Pine Barrens of New Jersey.

Bibliography

Beck, H.C., 1936. *Forgotten Towns of Southern New Jersey.* Reprint 1961. Rutgers University Press, New Brunswick, NJ.

Boyd, H.P., 1991. *Field Guide to the Pine Barrens of New Jersey.* Plexus Publishing, Medford, NJ.

Boyle, W.J., Jr., 1986. *Guide to Bird Finding in New Jersey.* Rutgers University Press, New Brunswick, NJ.

Bristowe, W.S., 1958. *The World of Spiders.* Collins Clear-Type Press, London.

Buyukmihci, H.S., 1968. *Unexpected Treasure.* M. Evans & Co. and J.B. Lippincott Co.

Candy, R. 1967. Fur-coated Landscaper in *Vermont Life Book of Nature.*

Carson, R., 1962. *Silent Spring.* Houghton Mifflin Co., Boston, MA.

Carter, A., 1979. *Bits of a Batsto Year.* Published 1986. Batsto Citizens Committee, Batsto, NJ.

Conant, R., 1958. *Field Guide to Reptiles and Amphibians.* Houghton Mifflin Co., Boston, MA.

Coville, F. V., 1910. "Experiments in Blueberry Culture." USDA, Washington, DC.

Heinold, G., 1960. The Love Life of a Shy Bird in *The Saturday Evening Post.*

McCormick, J., 1970. *The Pine Barrens: A Preliminary Inventory.* New Jersey State Museum, Trenton, NJ.

McCormick, J., 1979. "The Vegetation of the New Jersey Pine Barrens," in Forman, R.T.T., ed., *Pine Barrens Ecosystem and Landscape.* Academic Press, NY.

New Jersey Pinelands Commission, 1980. *New Jersey Pinelands Comprehensive Management Plan (CMP).* N.J. Pinelands Commission, New Lisbon, NJ.

Smith, S. 1765. *History of the Colony of Nova Caesaria or New Jersey*

Stone, W., 1911. *The Plants of Southern New Jersey.* Originally published as Part 11 of the Annual Report of the New Jersey State Museum for 1910. Reprint 1973. Quarterman Publications, Boston, MA.

Stone, W., 1937. *Bird Studies at Old Cape May.* Reprint 1965. Dover Publications, NY.

Teale, E.W., 1951. *North with the Spring.* Dodd, Mead & Co., NY.

Wherry, E.T., 1948. *Wild Flower Guide.* Doubleday & Co., NY.

Index

271

Other Titles of Interest about New Jersey

A Field Guide to the Pine Barrens of New Jersey

By Howard P. Boyd

This book is a 423-page volume containing descriptions and illustrations of over 700 species of flora and fauna that inhabit the area of New Jersey known as the Pine Barrens. Throughout the book the author reviews how the Pine Barrens was developed and used by man for such things as agriculture, lumbering, iron mining, and glass manufacturing. The majority of the book focuses on the species descriptions, along with illustrations. Descriptions are thorough and precise without being overly technical, so the book can be used by scientists and nonscientists alike.

1991/420 pages/hardbound/ISBN 0-937548-18-9/$32.95

1991/420 pages/softbound/ISBN 0-937548-19-7/$22.95

Natural Pathways of New Jersey

By Millard C. Davis

Natural Pathways of New Jersey describes in eloquent detail over 100 natural places in New Jersey. Not only does the author give beautiful descriptions of each of these areas, he provides directions on how to find each of these amazing natural places for your own enjoyment and experiences. *Natural Pathways of New Jersey* is divided into sections by county, making it very readable and easy for anyone to find the areas. The book includes over 100 original watercolor illustrations, by artist Valerie Smith-Pope, to display landscapes and creatures native to New Jersey.

1997/262 pages/softbound/ISBN 0-937548-35-9/$19.95

Old and Historic Churches of New Jersey Vol.2

By Ellis L. Derry

This inspirational book of history tells the stories of how our forefathers established their religious communities and houses of worship, often with great hardship and sacrifice. To be included in this moving history, a church had to have been built by the time of the Civil War and still be in use as a church today. In all, 23 churches are described in an enjoyable and very readable fashion. Striking photographs bring each church alive, enabling the reader to visualize the exciting history as it unfolds. This is a book not only for those interested in New Jersey history, but also for those interested in church history as well as the history of our country.

1994/372 pages/hardbound/ISBN 0-937548-25-1/$29.95

1994/372 pages/softbound/ISBN 0-937548-26-X/$19.95

Pinelands

By Robert Bateman

This novel is set in the New Jersey Pine Barrens, a unique natural area located in the midst of some of the most densely populated urban areas in the country. In this novel, the integrity of the Pine Barrens has collided with what some would call progress. In a compelling blend of history and fiction, *Pinelands* examines the seductive legacies of the past and how they are used by many to resist the abrasive realities of modern life.

1994/248 pages/hardbound/ISBN 0-937548-27-8/$21.95

1994/248 pages/softbound/ISBN 0-937548-28-6/$12.95

Whitman's Tomb: Stories from the Pines

By Robert Bateman

This book is a compilation of 13 fictional short stories, set in the unique area known as the "Pine Barrens" in Southern New Jersey, which examine the mysteries of everyday life and the chaotic world we all live in. Bateman uses a variety of different characters to examine the personal struggles we go through on a daily basis and the previously untold truths that we discover throughout our lives.

1997/215 pages/hardbound/ISBN 0-937548-32-4/$21.95

To order directly from the publisher, include $3.00 postage and handling for each book ordered.

Plexus Publishing, Inc., 143 Old Marlton Pike
Medford, NJ 08055 (609) 654-6500

NOTES